TELLING TALES
FROM TURKEY

The three co-authors of this book are British women who have lived in Turkey for many years, arriving there at different times and for very different reasons.

Tina came as a scientist to a teaching post at a private high school; Celia travelled out as a 'bride to be', whilst Ros arrived to set up a choreology department for a Conservatoire. Their paths crossed many years later, and they became firm friends.

All three fell in love with the people and fascinating culture of the country, and all three have married into it.

Tina Caba was born in London and graduated in Physics from Edinburgh University. She received a Certificate in Education from Cambridge and taught for three years at St Paul's Girls' School before moving to Turkey in 1970.

From then on she had a varied career, teaching Science and Maths in secondary schools, English in universities and language schools, and giving private lessons.

Altogether, she has been hired six times, fired twice, and married once to a Turkish architect. She also lived as a suburban housewife for fourteen years, bringing up two children. Now retired from these activities, she travels, grows cacti, reads, daydreams and writes reminiscences.

Ros Elliott-Özlek came to Turkey in 1987 to open a choreology department for a State University's Conservatoire.

Whilst building this new curriculum she was asked to add tap dance to the department's expanding modern dance programme. Since almost everyone she met wanted to improve their English, she retrained as an English Language teacher as a side line job; this proved useful when events in 1994 forced her to become a fulltime TESOL teacher. Moving to Izmir in 1995, she added yoga to her teaching repertoire, and settled down, becoming Ros Elliott-Özlek in 2004 and finding the 'dream house by the sea'. Since then she has been teaching English, yoga, and piano to all sorts and all ages. Ros recently retrained yet again – this time as a Bowen therapist.

Celia Gaşgil, a History graduate from Southampton University, first came to Turkey on holiday in 1976 where she fell in love, first with her future husband and secondly with the land itself. 1977 saw her back in Turkey, getting married and taking her first faltering steps in the English teaching profession.

She returned to the UK with her husband in 1978 'for a year or so'. Fourteen years and two children later, she once again set up home in Izmir. She started her teaching career in earnest in September 1993 and has survived to tell the tale. She has worked in 3 private schools, become an examiner for international exams and has worked as a teacher trainer for the British Council. She has also worked for a publisher as an adviser and editor of new teaching materials.

Now a widow and with her children working far away, she enjoys classical music and reading, swimming and yoga, and the company of many friends. As a dual national, she makes regular visits to see family and friends and tries to keep up with developments in her beloved mother tongue.

Tina Caba
Ros Elliott-Özlek
Celia Gaşgil

TELLING TALES FROM
TURKEY

AUSTIN MACAULEY
PUBLISHERS LTD.

Dedication

To all the people in Turkey, who have enriched our lives
and given us so much to write about.

Acknowledgments

We wish to thank all those who kindly helped with proofreading, especially Simon Mumford and Barbara Towes. Many Thanks also to Funda Işcioglu and Gülay Kaya for their skilful artwork in drawing our flower symbols, to Levent Gaşgil for technical assistance, and to Şerif Baykal for information on carpet symbols. Last but not least, we would like to thank all of the friends who encouraged us to write this book.

INTRODUCTION

The three authors of this book have an enormous amount in common: all British, all long-time residents of Turkey, all currently or previously married to Turkish men. However, each of these women has lived and worked in this large and diverse country in very different circumstances. Tina came first as a science teacher. Then Celia arrived to get married. Last but not least came Ros to take up a post as a teacher of choreology. Their paths crossed in Izmir many years later and they are now firm friends.

The book was first conceived as a guide for prospective teachers of English as a foreign language. Lots of practical information has therefore been included: health care, pensions and negotiating contracts, to name but a few. Also included are less happy tales of jobs being lost. These sections are written in an anecdotal form to amuse and entertain as well as inform.

Besides this there are many tales of teaching people of all ages and abilities. Between them the authors have taught students from aged three to eighty-three, in schools, universities and other institutions as well as giving lessons to individuals in their own homes.

The book is not just about teaching. It contains a vivid portrait of daily life, of high days and holidays and a picture of the country itself. You can read about earthquakes and forest fires. More mundane issues, such as shopping and cleaning ladies, present a challenge in a foreign language and are here described in a lively fashion.

Whether you are planning to visit Turkey or prefer armchair travelling, there are many stories here that give a feel for the people and the country at the heart of this book. It will take you into a world that the authors have lived in for more than three decades.

These three women have distinctive styles, born of their varied experiences but their shared love of Turkey, the meeting place of East and West, shines through all their writing.

Ros Elliott-Özlek

Tina Caba

Celia Gaşgil

CONTENTS

Scorpion

This motif invokes protection against the poisonous animal it depicts and wards off the power of the Evil Eye. Here it symbolises forces that can work for or against one when seeking and keeping employment.

1 - Being Hired and Fired

Becoming an English Teacher

My dwindling government salary meant I had to look elsewhere for some much needed pocket money, as I was sending most of my pay packet – after changing it into sterling – to the UK to cover my steadily-rising mortgage installments. It was the end of the 1980s and I had been given the mortgage because of my prospective new job with its high Turkish salary. However, inflation had halved the original amount within the first year, and the second contract did not attempt to make up the shortfall. Moreover, it was evident that my hefty salary (in Turkish terms) had attracted a lot of jealous attention from other teachers -Turks and foreigners alike – school employees, administrative staff, and even the director himself.

Salaries and most personal information is not considered a private matter in Turkey, and taxi drivers will commonly ask how much one earns, after the requisite barrage of questions: *"where are you from, how old are you, are you married and how many children do you have?"* The other foreign teachers were now demanding a similar salary to mine.

In those days it was not the norm for teachers of dance and dance-related subjects to have university degrees as most of their training would be practical over many years with some teaching exams taken both practically and orally. I had been encouraged by my far-sighted mother to follow an Open University degree in my 'spare time' after qualifying as a choreologist. This had stood me in good stead as the Turkish Conservatoire was under the auspices of a university, meaning that my degree and all the dance and music teaching exams together with the Benesh choreology studies earned me many more points up the salary scale – higher even than the director himself.

When I had arrived at the Conservatoire the director was a top professional musician with a lot of international experience and a sympathetic ear for this upstart choreologist who felt her Turkish salary should match her UK budget needs. The fact that he didn't speak English did not deter said upstart who marched into his office several weeks after arriving in Turkey and demanded to be told when her first pay check was going to appear. Director A was kind and listened, and also spoke French, which meant that I could understand most of what he said but was unable to do more than start my sentences as my school French had mysteriously disappeared. Fortunately Director A was also telepathic – it must be in the music training, I feel. Every sentence I began in faltering French was finished perfectly correctly by him. *Voila!* We understood each other and parted on good terms, although he had no idea when the salary would arrive. I didn't mind. We'd got on well.

By the start of the autumn term Director A had been replaced by Director B. Changes may happen instantaneously in Turkey, and seemingly out of the blue, although they may have been simmering underground for years, so one forgets about the possibility of something happening until one day it has suddenly occurred. Director A had gone to direct a bigger and better option (a private university Conservatoire) on the outskirts of town. Director B was a well-known actor of the old school, and highly respected as such, well past normal retirement age and with no English or French. None in evidence, that is, as in fact many Turks have learnt English but are afraid to speak it for fear of making mistakes and thus losing face. (Beware of intimate conversations in public places, assuming nobody can understand you. I have been caught out more than once.)

However, Director B ruled with a rod of iron – no cosy chats, no access without an appointment made several days in advance, no guarantees he would be there when one arrived for said appointment. An interpreter was always necessary and I was never given the chance to speak directly to him. My interpreter did all the correct bowing and scraping and rarely said what I'd instructed her to. She had to obey their code of conduct and offered Director B the highest respect, which meant just listening to him and nodding. He only addressed her and would not even meet my eyes.

Disaster! My marvellous salary now halved while my mortgage was rocketing upwards in the UK. What was I going to do? My colleagues were sympathetic but it was obvious that Director B was not. I would have to make other arrangements. More serious moonlighting now seemed the only choice.

Looking back, my first attempts at teaching English were abysmal, or at the very least it is embarrassing to recall how ill-prepared I was. As a 'Native Speaker' I assumed I knew enough to follow a textbook and impart the knowledge in a mainly 'teacher centred' way rather than the required 'learner centred' approach which was being promoted at the time in the UK and elsewhere, and which I was to learn a few years later when I embarked on some proper ELT training.

I started this phase of moonlighting with evening classes at an English Language School downtown which someone had mentioned to me. The director was kind and patient and indicated she would help me earn the necessary qualification to become a professional teacher of EFL – though I had no idea what the acronym meant at that time. She offered me a class of adult professionals including a couple of doctors nearing the end of their training as neurosurgeons. They always seemed half asleep, poor souls, as their work demanded night shifts and they frequently did double shifts too. I admired their discipline in taking the course and attending these poorly taught classes of mine.

The course was halfway through when I took it on from some other overworked teacher, and when it ended after the second month I took a few weeks break in the UK as the Conservatoire was also on semester break. On returning to Turkey I was shocked to find there was no work for me at the language school and immediately assumed I had really been a bad teacher for them. With hindsight and experience I think that what the secretary had actually said was that there were no surplus classes running at that time and therefore they did not need an extra part-timer. They probably expected me to keep checking back with them to prove my reliability and interest. When enough students signed up for a course, then it would open, and I would probably have been re-hired. This seems to be the norm in Turkey with this kind of work, if one is not on a contract. Even with a contract one's security of tenure is not certain – one can be 'terminated' abruptly, leaving one high and dry with only recourse to the legal system – a long and rocky road, especially as a foreigner. One may have every right to sue for compensation and early termination, but the results of a lengthy lawsuit may still not turn out in one's favour.

My second effort at teaching English came as a result of my learning Turkish at another language school downtown – this one under the control of another university. The father of one of my choreology 'degree' students was connected to this language school through his work for its university governing body. His position gave him the right to a free language course for each of his daughters, and he decided to give one of these 'rights' to me to learn Turkish. Again with hindsight I wonder if I was expected to reciprocate this 'help' with his daughter (my student) rather more than I was able to. In my first two years at the Conservatoire I had already secured British Council Scholarships for my assistant and one other student to study at the Benesh Institute of Choreology in London. Perhaps a third one was expected, but I was rather naive in those days with regard to back-scratching and Turkish ethics.

The Turkish course had gone well for me and when it ended one of my teachers suggested I keep up my Turkish practice by giving an hour's conversation to their groups learning English in exchange for attending one of their Turkish conversation classes. I jumped at the chance, especially as no expense was involved on my part, and began my second embarrassing attempt at 'teaching' English.

However, I had no idea of the level of the students, or even their number. The first hour of the morning's four hours was assigned to me and I later realised it was the 'dead' hour, as students arrived one by one during that 9.00–9.50 a.m. slot. They also arrived half asleep and not ready for their English grammar lessons which would follow chatting to me.

'My' students, unfortunately, were nowhere near ready for 'conversation' as I knew it. I think 'Speaking Practice' would have been a better term, and speaking short sentences or 'drilling' them, rather than attempting an on-going dialogue. I did my best at the time, and they were very polite, friendly and receptive. I think they genuinely enjoyed my being there even if our conversations were stilted and awkward. I had tried taking very short (one paragraph) newscuttings for them to read and discuss but they didn't have enough vocabulary to understand even the headlines, and newspaper language is somewhat different from general chit chat – a whole new genre in fact.

Possibly the best success I had with them was playing the card game Happy Families. This got them practising '*Have you got....?*' and '*Can I have.... please?*' – both very useful sentences, although I felt a complete fraud as a teacher, since I was only 'playing a game' with them.

The teacher I was covering for was also unsympathetic and we soon crossed swords. She did not appreciate my giving up my time 'for nothing' and was possibly looking for a regular slot with her teaching day starting a little later. I was unable to do three mornings a week and preferred to stick to a 'floating morning' as my own time-table varied with extra commitments and rehearsals. I can understand how this would infuriate her, but with a little patience and kindness we could have organised something. In those days there were no cell phones and the language school switchboard was unreliable as well as difficult to navigate, so I could not easily reach the person I wished to speak to and I was regularly cut off in mid-request. I could not have left her a message as she probably wouldn't get it, so I had to find her in the staff room after my hour and tell her when I could come the following week. Sometimes she was not in the staff room and I would have to leave a message, with my former Turkish teacher, Neşe, as the go-between. Funnily enough I could always find Neşe as she was always in the staff room in the breaks and always available for students and teachers to consult her.

Thus my second attempt at teaching English fizzled out and I never did get to those Turkish Conversation classes we'd bartered for. A few further tries at teaching students privately showed me I really was on the wrong track with what the students wanted as opposed to what they needed. It was time to study for this properly, so I took a correspondence course to get the necessary piece of paper.

It was fortuitous that I did so, as my Conservatoire contract was suddenly terminated mid-year and I was forced to change career. Again.

Finding Jobs

I've lived here for forty years and held about twelve different regular jobs, some of them part-time. After all that, the only generalisation I can make about the acquisition process is that each one is completely different and you never know what to expect. I will tell you about the most interesting ones.

In the late spring of 1975 I came back to Turkey after a three-year absence. Before that I had been single and employed; now I possessed a husband but had no job. What to do? Not far from our flat was a well-known establishment called the Turkish-American Association. Among other activities, they taught English.

So I tidied myself up nicely one day and walked into the secretary's office.

"Good morning," I said. "I'm British and I'm looking for a job."

"I not know," she responded. "You talk Ahmet Bey. He come two o'clock." So I said thank you politely and left. When I reappeared a few hours later, Ahmet Bey was in his office. He was friendly, but brief.

"Do you have a residence permit?" I had. "Any teaching experience?" I had that too; I told him truthfully I was a Physics teacher.

"Fine. You can start on Thursday. Half past two."

"Er, is there a book?" I asked. I had never taught anyone English before, and hoped for some guidance.

"The girl will give you a book. See you." So I left. On the way out I asked the secretary for a book, and she said,

"No book today. When you start? Thursday? OK. I give then."

Fast-forward to the next one. I was then mother of two, and wanted, for various complicated reasons, to give my twelve-year-old son a year of private education for one year. For this I had to earn some money. I had been a housewife for fourteen years, and I was terrified. With shaking knees, I sat down by the phone and called in turn the big private schools which employed foreign science teachers. I talked to endless secretaries, in both English and Turkish. The person I needed was always in a meeting, could I call back later? And then, when I did, he or she had gone to lunch, or left for the day. But eventually I got a voice which said, "Come and see me."

So I went to see Zuhal Hanım. Her office was on the fifth floor of a tall building surrounded by other concrete towers, with grey basketball courts in between. The room featured an enormous expanse of shiny desk, a huge coffee table with heavy cut-glass ashtrays, and black leather visitors' armchairs so vast that three people of my dimensions could have fitted into one of them. (Does one sit in the middle to look larger, or on the side nearer the interviewer, to look more enthusiastic?) It was an office designed to impress, if not to intimidate. Zuhal Hanım behind the desk was a large, fierce-looking lady, but she spoke pleasantly in excellent English, and as the interview progressed I began to relax. At the end she said, "Come on

Monday and sign a contract. Bring your CV and your diploma."

I went on Monday but there was no contract, nor the next day when I went again. I had to meet a succession of dreary grey men in grey suits. Such are the highest authorities in most Turkish institutions. They would look at me doubtfully and then ask Zuhal,

Türkçe biliyor mu? "Does she speak any Turkish?" Then I would interrupt in what I hoped was an eager, confident tone:

EVET, Türkçe biliyorum. "YES, I speak Turkish."

I wondered if they had seen my CV, or if the fact that it was in English had put them off even looking at it. The problem was that Zuhal Hanım was Head of English, which I had no qualification to teach. My expertise included maths, and, although much of that was taught in English, they had never had a foreigner before and the Head of Department didn't speak a word. After much shilly-shallying they said they would employ me as a maths teacher, which they did. The contract took several months to appear, and my husband and I had to make expensive trips to an official translator and a notary before my documents were accepted.

Fast-forward again, this time for five years. Remembering my good times at the Turkish-American Association all those years before, I trained as an English teacher and I applied for a job at the University of the Aegean, where all students had to study English for one year before starting their main subjects. It was called a "prep" year, and they needed a lot of English teachers. One phone call led to an interview, and I set out, documents in hand, on a long rattling bus-ride to the university.

The Foreign Languages department was plain and functional, with stone tiled floors and notice boards on the walls. A secretary showed me to a cluttered office with an iron desk and cheerful posters, where I was cordially received and offered a glass of tea. Izmir's oldest state university did not need any ostentatious decor to impress people and I felt comfortable there at once. There were several jobs available, starting in September. They said they would let me know.

It was then July. After a fortnight I rang up and asked about my prospects. They said the boss had gone on holiday and I should ring again in September. Disgruntled, I went on holiday too; I went to Britain for six weeks. When I got back I rang them again.

"Ah," said a secretary, "I not know. Mustafa Bey not here now. Meeting for teachers Monday. Ten o'clock."

I rang again on the Friday before the meeting and got another secretary, this one in Turkish, very polite.

"I really can't say anything definite. Unfortunately Mustafa Bey isn't here today, you see. If you want to work here, perhaps you had better come to the meeting on Monday."

So I went. Fate was kind; I had a friend who had also applied there and we went in her car. There were crowds of people milling around everywhere when we arrived. They were greeting and chattering and embracing each other; it was clearly a great social occasion. My friend and I wriggled our way through the crush to the secretary's office. "Do you by any chance know," I asked in my best Turkish accent, "if there are jobs for us?". She answered,

Sizi çalıştırırız. "We'll put you to work." And they did.

For eight months there was no official confirmation. We were paid with envelopes of grubby banknotes each month, usually on time. Then, in April, the contract at last appeared.

One day five years later I found myself sitting in a smart office with a stunning view of Izmir Bay. "Are you thinking of applying for a job here?" asked the Head of Foreign Languages at the private university. I had been offered a choice of at least six different kinds of tea, and we had been cheerfully discussing theories of English teaching for over half an hour. Applying for a job had not been on my agenda. I had come for a casual visit because I had been invited by someone I knew. I had not expected to meet the Head of Department, much less have tea in her office. But it is always my policy to keep options open, so I said brightly,

"Well, I might be."

When I found out that I would halve my travelling time and almost triple my salary, I applied. The procedure was complicated; I had to make five separate trips to the university. It was by then vacation time so I was not working, but it was demoralizing and inconvenient. They would phone me a day or a few hours before, and I had never the slightest idea when the next summons would be. On several visits I had to wait for hours, though I spent the time chatting to other candidates, which was interesting. At other times I was just asked by a secretary to sign something, or to supply some obscure piece of information. At one interview I had to sit at the end of a huge, long table of very academic-looking people who were all looking at me. That was the scariest bit. Some of them asked me about my views on different aspects of English teaching, and I tried hard to sound intelligent. Then, on another day, I had to see three grey men who didn't speak any English. They didn't ask anything really, but just wanted to have a look, as if I were a new piece of furniture. That turned out to be the last interview, because they were the highest authorities of all. Somehow or other, I was accepted.

Now for my last job, which was the most surprising of all. It was a weekly conversation class at a language school. I made no application, had no interview and signed no documents. The lady in charge had heard of me from my children, who had both worked there. So she just rang up one day and asked if I could do it. I could, and it turned out to be a real pleasure.

Teaching in Turkey can be great fun, and it can be hell. There are a lot of jobs out there, and you never know what you are in for until you start. Good luck to all who aspire to give it a try.

Losing One's Job

To lose one's job is perhaps to lose one's face professionally – certainly it may seem like that when it happens. One may feel like a failure, as if one has performed badly at work or somehow done something very wrong.

In my personal experience, having lost my job in Turkey at least three times, I can now say that the most important cause seems to be cultural differences in behaviour and thinking, and nothing to do with 'failing in one's duty' at all. In fact, paradoxically one's measure of success may be found in the loss of one's job, having been deemed a 'threat' to other local and more insecure colleagues.

I will start with the second time I was fired, which was the shortest and least emotionally charged. I had been teaching English for a large company in Turkey while I was employed as part of an English Language School. When my year's contract with the Language School ended I was not planning to continue with them as I had successfully applied to another establishment. However, the company's twenty-odd students asked to continue with me as their teacher, having 'bonded' well together during the two months or so of lessons. They had classes with me two nights a week and Saturday mornings, for three lesson hours each time – a lesson hour lasting about forty-five minutes with a ten minute break every hour. An arrangement was made to pay me on a monthly-in-arrears basis. The proposed hourly rate was acceptable to start with that autumn, but I made it clear to the manager who signed me on that I would expect an increase in the New Year, since prices generally and petrol costs in particular were rising alarmingly. On leaving his office I understood that we would discuss it again in January.

My first mistake: How dare I try to take control of the proceedings?

When New Year arrived and the lessons had been going reasonably well, I approached this manager and asked to talk about a possible increase. He indicated that it was unlikely and that the lady teaching them German had no such presumptions for more money. The rate would stay unchanged until next autumn. I decided to leave it a week and try again.

My second mistake: Fools rush in where angels fear to tread.

The following week I tried to gain admittance to the manager's office, but was repeatedly told he was in a meeting. I said I would wait, and sat down outside prepared for a long ordeal.

My third and final mistake.

After about twenty minutes a message was brought by two red-faced students (themselves managers in different capacities). I was to go to the wages office where I would be paid up to today and as from today my 'contract' was terminated.

In retrospect, many years later, I understand that my insistence on a pay rise must have been seen as insubordination rather than normal business negotiations. How could they have given in to me after the first refusal? It would make them appear weaker than myself, a mere woman of no great professional or social standing. I could not have seen it like that at the time, but had expected at least a middle road or a gentle paving of the way to some kind of agreement. Even a gentle pep-talk could have pointed out my lack of status and reminded me of the perks I enjoyed and took for granted. These included unlimited tea on the house, and a meal if I wanted it, since every worker was entitled to this on their factory shift system, and meals were cooked fresh each day, not packaged or microwaved!

However, I was definitely put in my place, with no contract and no language school or company to negotiate for me. I wonder now what on earth I was thinking of by challenging their authority.

As my first 'termination' belongs in another book, I will continue with the third time I lost my job, which was also due to my 'insubordination by attitude', although I was never given a reason or even officially informed that my contract would not be renewed.

There had been a large number of 'Native Speaker' teachers newly employed by a State University for its English Language Department. The sudden increase in number of foreign teachers due to the hugely increased student intake must have been quite problematic and unnerving for the resident Turkish staff. Many of them had started work there years before at the founding of the department. As a new Native Speaker to their system, I assumed our input would be considered valuable and we would be able to quickly right all the wrongs which were self-evident in the programme.

Many of us voiced our complaints regularly in the staff rooms and mocked the rigidity of the system. There were other problems too, with new teachers' work permits and even contracts: it seemed that a large number of us were employed at a lower rate of pay and had no health insurance or other perks until the contracts came through from the Ministry of Finance. This took nearly a year in some cases, so quite a large proportion of the original new intake had left in disgust before the spring.

At the start of the autumn term and our second academic year there were just six of us left, all by now on proper contracts until the end of the calendar year. We still complained about the idiosyncracies of the system and felt somewhat aggrieved that our ideas and suggestions were mostly ignored.

However, I didn't realise just how precarious my own position had become, and I had begun to associate more openly with some of the more vociferous mockers and complainers. Despite earning 'brownie points' from the Head of Department by starting an extra-curricular yoga class for teachers and students, and receiving similar permission to start a choir, I felt I was swiftly falling from grace that term.

In fact, although permission was given for the choir to be formed, the hall to practise in was never free at the requisite time, so the project fell by the wayside and the department head made no effort to help us find another venue, simply reiterating that we could always use the hall when it was available.

The atmosphere seemed to be thick with gossip and discontent, and many formerly friendly teachers kept their heads down and limited their time for chat. I had heard that one of my closest friends was definitely out of favour and might be axed, so I foolishly decided to ask the Head when the new contracts might be ready.

I can still see the look of utter malevolence on his face as he literally hissed at me that <u>SOME</u> of us would not have our contracts renewed at all. Slightly shocked, I innocently enquired when it might become clear as to who it was going to be, still thinking of my Canadian friend. The terse reply informed me that we would know at the beginning of December.

The first week of December passed with still no news. So did the second week. Meanwhile another member of our last bastion of Native Speakers took me aside and hinted rather obliquely that I might be on the list to go. I was dumbstruck, as it had never occurred to me that I was one of the 'bad apples' causing problems! My classes were going well and I had no discipline problems with the students, unlike many other teachers. How naïve I was!

On the fifteenth of the month all became clear as we checked our bank accounts for the monthly salary in advance. Only half of it was there for three of us, including my Canadian friend. The kind colleague who had dropped me the hint of my own demise was not on the list, but had told me he would resign if indeed we three were fired. To his credit, he did so and I really appreciated his show of support.

The Head of Department never spoke to us directly or even acknowledged us. Nothing was said, but a couple more slights were made:

My Canadian friend found that someone else was sent to take over her classes, even though she was in the classroom and planned to proudly stay until the end of the month. I think they worked out something between them, seeing as the other embarrassed teacher was one of the Native Speakers retained for the following year.

A secretary was sent to ask me to return my identity card, provided by the university and giving such privileges as access to the university swimming pool, and some discount coupons from the superstore on campus. I refused to part with it, as it was dated till the 31st of December in line with my contract, but offered to return it after that date, knowing full well that the end of the month was a weekend and on principle I would never go back to the university to hand it in. I still have it today.

Being Recruited Three Times

On our return to Turkey in August 1992 after a fifteen year absence, a lot of time and energy went into readjustment and settling in with our thirteen-year-old daughter and eleven-year-old son. Facing the rigours of a brand new school and an unfamiliar education system in an almost unknown language, most of my time was spent on supporting my children and making our home habitable and comfortable.

In the mid-year break in February 1993, my parents-in-law came on a visit of inspection. *Buz gibi!* my father-in-law said approvingly. Literally 'like ice', the phrase meant that he thought everything was clean and tidy and is considered a term of praise. All was indeed neat and tidy for once; carpets, curtains and furniture were not yet old enough to show much sign of wear and tear. Somehow I realised that my home was established and my children were increasingly independent. Their incipient criticism of my Turkish was a sure and welcome sign of their growing linguistic competence.

I needed to define or redefine my own role. The

advancing months gave rise to a sense of boredom and frustration. All fled the nest at 8.30 am to return in dribs and drabs after 4.30. That left me with too much time for cleaning, cooking and shopping. It was time to find a job, not only to boost the family income but to preserve my sanity.

Having had a long-standing and deep-seated desire to be a teacher, I approached the British Council in Izmir. When the long list of private language schools and private high schools arrived, I got out a map of the city and circled all the institutions within reasonable reach of my home. Evening and weekend work was unacceptable as I had no wish to abandon wifely or motherly duties. I drafted fifteen or so letters, setting out my qualifications (a British university degree from an Arts faculty) and played up my rather limited experience of teaching English as a foreign language (summer schools in London and a few months in the Turkish-American Association in Izmir some fifteen years previously). I sent off the letters and waited. It was August by the time I got around to seriously looking for work and I wondered if I had missed the recruitment boat. As we were out of town for the summer holiday, I had given my husband's work telephone number.

One hot and sunny afternoon, some friends arrived unexpectedly, bursting with news. A language school in the centre of Izmir wanted to interview me. Barely suppressed excitement turned to nervousness as the due day dawned. My responses to all the expected questions had been rehearsed ad infinitum. I was ushered into the office of one of the school's co-owners, the female half of the husband and wife team.

She was well-dressed, about forty, and had an air of efficiency about her. She immediately started to tell me about the school rules for taking sick leave and the related procedure, which involved a visit to the local state hospital.

I found her oblique approach rather bizarre and coupled with her lack of questions about my own background, somewhat perplexing. It seemed that she wanted a native speaker and beyond that, their relative competence was of little importance. She indicated that she would probably be able to offer me four afternoons a week, reserving the fifth day for a non-native speaker teacher, as they had a better command of grammar. I did not argue, although if we were to have the conversation again today, I would certainly take issue with her. She then asked me to come in the following day and observe a lesson, to be given by a young Australian teacher. Relieved not to be asked to do a sample lesson myself, I readily agreed.

Arriving in good time for the lesson, I took the opportunity to observe not only the lesson but the student-teacher interaction and to drink in the atmosphere of the school. All seemed relaxed and happy and my young Australian friend, although less than forthcoming, did and said nothing to disillusion me. As I sat smugly listing the ways in which I could have handled the given material better than the teacher, I saw myself installed in a parallel classroom.

A few days later, instead of being invited to sign a contract, a call came asking me to substitute for a teacher in a 5 o'clock class. The alarm bells rang as my morale slumped. I had been promised daytime teaching and saw that this was the thinner end of a very fat wedge. I declined the invitation, at the risk of condemning myself to another year of domestic monotony.

It was now September. Schools were due to open the following week. All was not lost! Another phone call came through from a private high school. This time I arrived with my son in tow, after a visit to the dentist. The principal's office had a breath-taking view of the bay. Here was a smiling face and a courteous manner but once again very few real questions were directed my way and certainly no penetrating ones. Finally he asked me if I had any experience with young learners. Reluctantly I confessed that I didn't. In an astonishing non-sequitur he said I could teach his fourth and fifth years, i.e. ten and eleven-year-olds! He offered me a monthly salary of 5 million lira, more than twice what I would have been earning at the language school but for a full-time job. After a family conference around the dinner table, I accepted.

On the Friday, I met my Head of Department, a bubbly blond, some five years my junior, and all the teachers of the school. A general meeting took most of the morning. Able to follow the proceedings to a degree, I missed some of the finer points and rapidly became very tired with the effort of absorbing so much new information in a foreign language.

After lunch we settled down in an empty classroom to write year plans on vast sheets of squared paper. "This is your book," beamed my HOD before disappearing without any further explanation. An older male colleague had forgotten his glasses and in order to feel useful I spent the rest of the afternoon writing his year plan as his secretary. I went home clutching my book and dutifully wrote lesson plans, only to discover that we were meant to have two weeks of introductory activities before embarking on the text. It came to light some two weeks later that I still hadn't completed my own year plan. By that time I had some idea about how to do it. The following Monday, I was initiated into the *birinci kademe*. This was the section for children aged six to eleven, which seemed to have different rules and procedures. Here I was to share three classes with a young colleague, who was friendly and welcoming. In place of the solid information and help I so badly needed however, she spent most of our brief time together filling me in on school gossip. My learning curve was a vertical line for some time to come.

The next crisis was my first set of exams. Despite promises of help, I wrote, administered and marked papers for my six classes without any input from anyone else. Then suddenly, a nasty thing called an interim report folder arrived on my table mid-lesson, to be completed within the hour.

"I'm teaching!" I protested.

"Just give them something to do and fill in their marks!" was the unhelpful reply.

So the year passed and I found my feet. Thrown in at the deep end, I learned to swim, avoiding the whirlpools of departmental rivalry and navigating the rapids of classroom discipline and parental demands.

At the end of the year, everyone became anxious and depressed. The season for contract renewal had arrived. No collective bargaining here: divide and rule was the order of the managerial day. Each teacher was summoned to that deceptively beautiful office with the stunning view to hear their fate. If required for the following year, salary negotiations followed.

The director said that he was very pleased with my work: flattering words indeed but I couldn't refrain from asking him how he knew as no-one had been to observe a lesson, inspected my plans or checked my exams. He did not offer any reasonable explanation, other than tapping the side of his nose.

This acquisition of knowledge by osmosis, the reliance on gut feelings rather than empirical evidence, I now know to be typical of Turkish private schools and I suspect of Turkish management styles in general. The idea of career development, annual appraisals and such like is pretty much unknown even in the bigger and better run institutions. My school managed to recruit more native speakers during my tenure. They both turned out to be frauds in different ways and had produced references, which had never been checked.

After five years, we parted company over an unresolved financial dispute, with a degree of regret on both sides. Subsequently I worked at two other schools. My next application and recruitment experience included two interviews with the General Manager and a breakfast given for potential employees. This time there was a hint of unofficial investigations into my background among the teaching community, of which I was now an established part. At no time was there any serious discussion of my ideas on teaching but I was bold enough to hold forth on certain issues at one of these meetings. There was no reaction and my request to study a contract brought smiles and laughter. "Plenty of time for that," was the only reply I got. The alarm bells should have been ringing but the increase in salary blinded me till I realised too late that I had jumped out of the frying pan into the fire.

The year I joined that school there was a big intake of foreign teachers. Within three weeks the first had left, simply not turning up to lessons one day and was never seen again. A further two were to last a year, giving foreign staff a bad name. The head did not link the lack of a proper recruitment procedure to the high drop-out rate.

It seemed that the only criteria for advancement were the passive ones of attracting no parental complaints and being totally subservient to management demands. Don't rock the boat and you will go far. Meetings were often conducted in a tea party atmosphere as if the proffered beverages were an attempt to soften the criticism, usually veiled, which inevitably followed. Taking on extra responsibility was considered a reward in itself: there was certainly no financial incentive. When I was asked to take care of the primary English teaching team of some 20 teachers, many of my colleagues thought I was quite mad, as all I had to show for it were early mornings, late evenings and weekends spent on exam planning.

Four years later I moved on again. References were again given with my application but once again not taken up.

"I know all about you," said my next Head of Department with a secret smile.

"Good or bad?" I asked wondering as to her sources of information. She certainly wasn't about to let that particular cat out of her bag. I was offered the job and accepted. Immediately impressed by the greater degree of organisation and clearer division of responsibilities, there is still a lingering feeling of government by whim. You argue with your head of department at your peril. It feels safer to toe the line and keep quiet.

If you are looking for first world standards and workers' rights, you may well be disappointed but if you learn to tread carefully and think things out, you may find a happy atmosphere and a shared sense of purpose and commitment. You will almost certainly be working among people who have great regard and affection for each other. If you are very lucky this personal rapport will also extend into good personal relationships and professional commitment.

Crime and Punishment

It was a new, private university, with freshly painted corridors and big shiny windows. The boss had an aura of confidence and cordiality; at the interview she offered me a choice of six different kinds of tea. When I signed on, I cut my travel time to a quarter and almost tripled my salary. The bait was irresistible.

I was given a nice desk, a whole cupboard to myself, and the use of a shared computer. (In my previous job, there wasn't even a shared typewriter.) My new colleagues were friendly and interesting. Everything seemed too good to be true, which it was.

Before I go on, I must tell you that I am not a boring teacher. I do not say, "Page sixty-one, section five. Read the grammar notes, then do exercises one, two and three. We'll check the answers in twenty minutes." None of that stuff. Instead I might ask, "What was the best thing that happened on the weekend? Tell your partner about it in English." That kind of thing. All of us teachers were eager and creative. The classrooms were bright and airy. We had air conditioning and whiteboards and tape recorders and even videos.

The problem was the students. We catered to a rich and spoiled youth. Unable to meet the entrance requirements of mainstream universities, these young people squeezed into our institution with the help of many expensive private lessons. They attended only because their parents wanted them to have the status of a degree, and when they got it, their jobs would be ready in the spacious offices of family businesses. Their aim was to just pass, by fair means or foul, and to have as much fun as possible along the way.

A few months into the course, I talked to a young woman who was carefully painting her nails in my lesson.

"Why don't you learn some English?" I asked.

"Don't like," was her response. "I not want be here."

"So why are you here?"

"My mother wants."

"What would you like to do?"

"I want stay home. Not get up early. See my friends." She was completely honest, and there wasn't much I could say. Applying nail polish is at least a peaceful activity; it did not destroy the lesson for others. The MM, as I called them, for Motivated Minority, could still learn English. These were mostly scholarship students, as starry-eyed and delightful as good students anywhere. I promised myself fiercely that they would get what they came for – good lessons.

My department was called Preparation English. We provided a year's course to all students entering the university who didn't already know enough of the language. If they passed at the end of the year, they would move on to study their chosen subject for four more years. Attendance at prep classes was obligatory. Teachers had to keep a record and students who missed more than their "absence allowance" automatically failed the course. This allowance was intended to cover minor illnesses and other contingencies. It was an absurd system for a university; they were not little children, after all. They were old enough to keep a job, drive a car, vote in national elections, or even get married. Shouldn't they be able to decide for themselves whether to attend lessons? In any case, their families were paying a lot of money for them.

The attendance rule had major consequences. The worst students would exhaust their absence allowance early in the term. After that they would feel obliged to attend constantly, getting more resentful and frustrated as the weeks passed. Their classroom behaviour became steadily worse. As exams approached, the MM, who so far had not missed any lessons, politely asked if they might revise on their own in the library, because it was quieter.

"I'll have to mark you absent," I said.

"Yes, of course, no problem."

"OK then, good luck."

"Thank you, teacher."

One day I was writing on the whiteboard when I smelled smoke. I looked round to see the habitual sleepers, magazine readers and text-messagers slumped in their chairs, but in the middle of the room was an unusual huddle of bodies, tense with excitement, and a thin spiral of smoke rose from the middle of them. Shouts of triumph and laughter followed. They had lit a fire of paper on the classroom floor. A surge of fury interrupted my exposition of the past perfect tense, and I yelled,

"Stop that! Put it out!"

With much laughter, feet began to crush the ashes. The dark stain on the plastic tiled floor is probably still there.

Apart from such incidents, it was the noise that got to me. Not just whispers, but loud, resonant voices in their own language, discussing TV, football, computer games, anything and everything. It did not matter how hard I tried to present my subject in an attractive way. I was the teacher and teachers must be boring. These students never listened to me, but calmly pursued their own social agenda as if they were relaxing in a pub. Time and again I asked them to stop talking so that the MM could have their lesson, and time and again I was ignored. One day we had the following exchange:

"Ahmet, could you stop talking please?"

He glared at the intrusion, but went on regardless.

"Ahmet, this is an English lesson. Will you be quiet please?"

No effect.

"Ahmet, I asked you to stop talking!"

"Filthy whore!"

The words cut across the room, and for a moment silenced everybody. Of course he said it in Turkish, and he didn't expect me to understand. But you don't live for forty years in a country without acquiring some basic vocabulary.

I filled in an Incident Report Form and gave it to the Coordinator, and it did actually reach the Discipline Committee. Much was made of the supposedly mitigating fact that the student was stating an opinion of me, rather than addressing me directly. In the end he was suspended from the university for one week as a punishment. The time designated fell conveniently in the winter holidays when there were no lessons and students did not attend the university anyway.

The solution to my troubles developed gradually. Restless students began to take breaks during lessons, for cigarettes or coffee. At first they asked permission to "go out". I always said yes, hoping the break would calm them down, which it often did. Other teachers did the same, and the corridors became quite busy. The authorities noticed this and decided that anyone who disappeared for more than five minutes during a lesson was to be marked absent. How unfair! A student could attend 44 minutes of a 50-minute lesson and be recorded absent! However, I thought it wiser not to protest. I simply ignored the rule. That was my first crime.

My second one was to show the absence record to any student who asked, during the official breaktime. The bosses said students should keep their own records, but mostly they were too scatty and disorganised to do that. When they saw that their extra breaks had no dire consequences, they took longer ones. Lessons became more peaceful. The MM and I worked cheerfully together, and I enjoyed my job.

I had told the wanderers to go to the cafeteria or the garden, and not linger in the corridors. But tact and common sense were not their strong points. Soon enough, the Voice of Authority declared that all breaks during lessons were forbidden, except for illness. My attempts at teaching ground to a halt again. For a few days I just sat and looked at my unteachable class. Then I committed crime three. "Go and chat in the cafeteria," I told the loudest group. "Some of us are going to have a lesson. No, I won't mark you absent. I've filled in the record for this lesson, and I'm not going to change it." They wandered off. The MM and I got to work, and everyone was happy. Things went well for a while after that, until we got caught.

It was Friday afternoon, there were three students in my classroom, and they were getting some really good conversation practice. Unfortunately the Coordinator decided to take a look round. On Monday morning she dutifully summoned me to her office.

"I saw only three students in your lesson," she said. "But according to your record, there were seventeen."

"Well, they come and they go, you know. They get restless and sometimes take a break, then they usually come back. I took the attendance at the beginning, when they were all there."

She was not impressed.

While these real crimes were unfolding, I was alleged to have committed others which existed solely in the imagination of my boss. She who had so smilingly offered six different kinds of tea at my interview, became suddenly frosty. Her corridor greetings signalled dislike, and I had no idea why.

I had been asked to edit some exam papers, a task I carried out in my usual conscientious manner. I was therefore horrified when she accused me of leaving "serious grammar mistakes" in these papers. I asked to see the errors, but she said, "I can't find them just now. I'm too busy." In my trusting innocence and state of shock, I mumbled apologies and left. Later I began to think. English is my language, and I do not make serious grammar mistakes. What was going on? I found a friend who was on the exam committee and made investigations. The errors were bad enough, but they were on papers that I had never seen.

Then there was the question of the Incident Reports.

"You wrote at least ten Incident Reports last term."

"Actually I wrote three."

"No, it was more than that. Far too many."

"Can I see them, please?"

"I don't keep them here."

When the long envelope containing my letter of dismissal finally arrived, it was a masterpiece of vituperative imagination. I stood accused of not knowing my own language, of having no teaching skills whatever, of recording exam results improperly. Of my true crimes there was no mention. I now wish I had kept this historic document, but at the time I was so upset that I tore it up.

By the time teachers returned from their summer holidays, I had recovered. I sent out a lot of e-mails that said, "Dear ex-colleague, This is an invitation to Tina's Liberation Party. Come and help celebrate.'

It was a good party.

Children

Images of children are woven into carpets by those who wish to become parents. Compulsory education for children in Turkey has now been extended to eight years.

2 - Primary Schools

Snapshot of a School Day

It is not a good day to ask me how I find teaching in Turkey. The things that are wrong today sum up all the things that are wrong with my teaching life!

Students come to lessons with no homework and even less enthusiasm. Many of them have no notebooks and blame their lack of motivation on the hot weather. My seventh year class has gone into holiday mode although there are still 29 working days to go. The looming exam, together with the awarding of final oral marks, does not seem to make any impression on their adolescent minds.

After two lessons of very hard work, we have managed a discussion in English, at least on my part, and some of my charges have strung together some words in a comprehensible stream. At the end of the 'torture', one recalcitrant apologises profusely and yet again promises to turn over a new leaf. He has promised his mother he will behave and is clearly upset by her distress. She has recently been to school to hear the same bad news.

I go to my fifth year class, hoping for better things. I am rewarded with a great array of shining, expectant faces. We play the game I have prepared. Their eagerness is touching but the scene is marred by a group of gigglers in the corner – all boys! Yes, adolescence is rearing its ugly head here too.

As soon as we get into the flow, there is a knock on the door. The assistant head has come to tell us to go to lunch early as the students are going to watch a play in the afternoon. My double period has been cut off after 30 minutes. Plans go distinctly awry, not to mention my motivation. To cap it all, my reading glasses have disappeared from the teachers' room table.

After a hurried meal, I sit with a secretary as she dials the numbers of two parents I need to speak to. Having imparted the bad news (no performance homework) I recross the scorching playground to go to my sixth year class. As I approach the main building, I spot a high school girl, perched on a third floor windowsill, legs dangling precariously over the drop. Deciding that a shout from below might startle her, I go quietly inside, rush up six flights of stairs, by which time she has of course disappeared and I am unable to identify her. I report the incident to her assistant head, who looks at me with sympathy but a degree of resignation.

Next on my agenda is an eighth year student, who I am coaching as she is to make announcements in English at her forthcoming graduation ceremony. She arrives promptly only to tell me that she is leaving school immediately to go to another appointment. I am unable to hide my irritation as I grumble that my day is not going exactly according to plan.

It's at moments like these that it's a good idea to stand back to remind yourself of all the reasons for carrying on in the job. There are many: after seventeen years I have every intention of signing up for more of the same!

Like parenting, that most difficult of jobs, it is also the one that brings the greatest rewards. It may be an improved exam result, an imaginative piece of writing or a beautifully presented project but very often it is a simple greeting or a friendly smile from a student who has hitherto been too shy to talk to you or ask a question in class. When a student allows you a tiny glimpse of their inner selves, there is a surge of happiness, as though the sun has started to shine on your soul.

The younger children give their love and trust uncritically and completely. I was once away from my second year students for nine weeks due to a slipped disc. As we were only four weeks into the term, there had hardly been a chance to bond with my four classes before I fell ill. My first day back was spent hugging and kissing. As I entered 2D's classroom, the whole class ran to embrace me: not so good for my fragile back but wonderful for my morale! My Head of Department was besieged by parents, demanding my return. Suddenly I found all sorts of friends among them: doctors and therapists of all kinds offered to help.

Although I hate Teachers' Day with all the accompanying hype, I could not help be touched by a gift from a student, who is no longer in my class. He had bought me a pair of earrings with his pocket money and said he wished he had been able to spend more time in my classroom.

Being a part of so many young lives is a wonderful chance to learn more about the culture to which I now belong. As the students describe their lives, they bring so much of their background into the classroom, giving me an insight into their heritage. I can keep in touch with those a generation or two younger than I am. It is a cliché to say that a problem shared is a problem halved but when you can reassure a desperate parent or help a despondent student to overcome a fear of English, then life's rewards are rich indeed.

When we teachers are praised, usually when we can bask in the reflected glory of some student success, we may have a passing moment of deep satisfaction but I am always reminded at such times that it is only as a result of real teamwork that such success can be achieved. I have been lucky enough and been in the job long enough to see some of my erstwhile students joining the ranks of the teaching profession. If I played even a tiny part in the process, it is a source of great satisfaction.

The English language has always been a source of fascination for me. It has so rich a vocabulary, and its wide and diverse literature is an enormous gift. The chance to share something of this cornucopia in the classroom gives me enormous pleasure. At the same time I enjoy being able to share some cultural insights with my students. Having been lucky enough to be a part of two contrasting countries, I know how enriching an experience it is, to see your own native assumptions from a distance and to therefore re-evaluate what was taken for granted.

So life is never dull. No two days are exactly alike and there are worse ways to earn a living!

Exams

During his first year at a Turkish school, I asked my son how his school day had been. When he told me that he had an exam the following week, I was surprised as it was only October. 'It's a test,' I countered. I was wrong and he was right.

In Turkish schools exams are conducted throughout the term at regular intervals, are the length of a single lesson (40 minutes) and are generally not cumulative, thereby precluding the enormous feats of memory that I had undertaken in my school days. If there are fewer than four lessons a week in that subject, there are two exams per term: over four lessons and the number of exams goes up to three or four each term.

I went on to become a teacher myself and worked in three different schools, each with a different approach. The import of exams underwent a change of focus. I now had to write exam questions. In my first school, I was left very much to my own devices. Despite strong expressions of support from my Head of Department, I set, administered and marked the exams for my six classes without any supervision. I found this a somewhat daunting task, heavy with responsibility.

Exams were taken in parallel classes at a time to suit the teacher. On one occasion, a student was summoned to an awards ceremony and I had to release him from the exam room. Such was the poor level of communication. When I caught one of my students cheating, by having an open book on his lap, I was told to allow him to start afresh with a new question paper! So great was the desire to avoid confrontation with parents.

Back in the early nineties, there were no personal computers and at that particular institution, no secretaries to type exam papers, so the questions were hand written and photocopied. After one exam I was confronted by the mother of a boy, who had not achieved the grade he had been expecting. His mother blamed my handwriting! Despite my indignation, my Head of Department hovered nervously behind me, ready to step in if things got difficult.

In my next school, teachers recorded proposed exam dates in the class register. At least this had the virtue of preventing the students having to sit two or more exams on the same day, which is in fact against the rules set by the Ministry of Education. Usually the system seemed to work, but one could still be caught out by class outings or conferences, long since planned but only announced at the last minute.

Then the English department decided to set a 'general exam' once a term. This meant that all the classes would sit the same paper at the same time. This was deemed to be fairer and provide a real yardstick of student progress as well as eliminating the chance for sharing of the questions between classes that had sat the exam and those who had yet to do so. There was also an unspoken aim, which was to eliminate favouritism from individual teachers, who might set easy exams or mark more leniently than others.

There was only one fly in the ointment: I was appointed to write the exams for the fourth and fifth graders and sworn to secrecy. I was not allowed to share any information with my colleagues. Holding the fate of some 500 students in my hands made me distinctly uncomfortable. I worked long and hard over several weekends in order to come up with fair and balanced papers.

The departmental secretary took care of the typing but no one but me proof-read or edited the paper, with the inevitable result that, on exam day, a mistake was found and I had to go round ten classes to correct it.

The next time round I tried even harder and was congratulating myself, when I saw a class teacher, who should have been invigilating, in the corridor looking very distraught. It turned out that a colleague from another year group had been taken ill that morning on the way to a school outing and had unfortunately died of a heart attack. Dire news indeed but I wondered how this news had penetrated the exam room, as the event had taken place after the exam had started. Within minutes the corridor was full of fourth grade teachers, while their charges continued the exam completely unsupervised.

Moving on once again I was pleasantly surprised to find a rigorously organised exam system in place. All exams were on prearranged dates. The exam calendar was given to every teacher and every student so each year group took the same paper at a fixed time and on a fixed date. If the exam fell in your lesson, you were responsible for collecting the papers, supervising the exam and delivering them to the relevant department at the end of the period. Welcome to sanity! What could go wrong?

'Plenty' is the short answer! Although the exam calendar had all the administrative rules on the reverse side, some teachers chose to stretch their interpretation of them. Hence, on the day of the English exam you could find a teacher in the corridor, desperately trying to attract your attention, blithely ignoring the students who could then copy from each other without interference in the meantime.

Students were not allowed to ask questions during the exam as a matter of policy. Understanding the questions and instructions was considered to be an integral part of the test. Some members of staff not only lingered in anticipation of such forbidden questions but also actively invited the students to ask them.

Some forgot to check their timetable and turned up late. Others got bored with invigilation and nipped out of the classroom for a quick chat with the teacher in an adjoining room.

Of course there are always students who create problems too. There are those who succumb to genuine fits of panic: these usually still manage 90 percent or so. Others are always mysteriously ill on exam day. There is no escape but the counselling service may be able to help with nerves. In some classes the talkers are so numerous it is difficult to punish the guilty and if you are bold enough to report the wrongdoers, you have to be prepared for the flack from both students and parents. An incident report must be written forthwith while memories are fresh.

The students sit at double desks and are asked to put a school bag between them to prevent copying. Glancing across at one's neighbour can be a sign of absentmindedness rather than a deliberate misdemeanour. Some class teachers discourage the placement of bags on the grounds that it is a signal of acceptance that students are naturally dishonest.

Invigilation can therefore be very stressful and you breathe a sigh of relief as the final bell goes but your troubles are not yet over. There is no discipline when it comes to collecting the papers. Students immediately stand up and circulate, discussing the answers as the last few desperately try to add a few words to boost their scores, despite the teacher's injunction to stop writing. It takes a considerable effort of will to impose order on the disorderly but relieved rabble before you. Then the teacher must count papers before anyone may leave the room. To my shame I once forgot this golden rule only to find myself summoned to the principal's room, where a student who had produced his maths paper, well after the exam had finished, was being quizzed. I felt as awful as he did. I have always made sure that I count all the papers at least twice since that day.

Then, for the language teachers, there are the oral exams. In particular, there are oral exams at the end of the summer term for prospective students. Here there is a panel of two or three teachers at each level. I have twice been invited to be a 'panellist' and each experience has been interesting. The first time I went along with my colleagues but was taken aback to find that they had done no preparation and had no strategy for asking questions. Prolonged silences were interrupted by two or more voices chiming in with different questions at the same time. So the second time around for me, I suggested we draw up a list of topics and questions and agree a rota for asking the questions. Perfect! All was orderly and we all made our notes for post-interview discussion. Some of our young 'victims' were a bag of nerves, others supremely confident. After a run of disappointing candidates, we were faced with a very confident and handsome young man. 'I love you!' enthused one of my colleagues. After the candidate had been dismissed, I had to point out that such outbursts, while no doubt encouraging for the student, were quite out of place, especially should we decide not to recommend their enrolment.

Such are the mechanics of exam procedure. Setting exams seems to be straightforward enough but it is an area that few teachers receive training in and is not as easy as it looks. As a native speaker I am often asked to edit papers before printing and can therefore weed out spelling and grammatical mistakes. Persuading teachers that the focus of the question is not quite as they intended can be a more difficult task, requiring much tact and diplomacy.

Very young children (and their parents) behave as though their very lives depended on the results. I find this a sad reflection of the pressures of modern life that impinge on the young from a ridiculously early age but I am mindful of the huge responsibility that is ours as teachers.

Drama Club

In June we have 'environment day.' So our second graders (seven to eight-year-olds) dress up as trees and bees and recite poems and sing songs. Parents come to offer support and increasingly to snap and video the event. The teachers are all on hand to encourage and admire and everyone seems to be happy.

Scroll on two years and the children have 'clubs.' For two lessons a week, every child has the right to choose an activity, from chess to football, from basketball to drama.

Ideal, you may think, but here the problems begin. Some parents push their offspring into the chosen club. Sport is oversubscribed. Which little boy does not want to be the next Ronaldo or David Beckham?

The 'performing' clubs compete for the most talented students so the rivalry does not start or end with the parents. Teachers use subtle tactics to 'sign up' the stars. For the English drama club there are auditions. Over the past eight years there have been lavish productions of all the old favourites: Hansel and Gretel, Aladdin, The Princess and the Magic Pea, The Wizard of Oz and our crowning glory, The Magical Pied Piper of Hamelin.

So the starry-eyed fourth and fifth graders come along seeing themselves as princes and princesses or as a wicked witch. The teachers encourage the children to do their party piece before retiring into a huddle to select the club membership. We promise to post the list on the board within a few days.

Anyone would think lives depended on it. Until we actually finalise our list, every foray into the corridor is peppered with anxious enquiries.

"Have you decided?", "Am I in the club?" reverberate around the school.

Once you have a group to work with, the allocation of roles is the next hurdle. Here you may face not only the whims of the students but also parental wrath.

"At home, we always call her 'princess', so can she have the starring role in your play?" Not everyone is so keen. Some decide to opt for football at the last minute or decide that being in a Turkish play will be easier all round. The music teacher may 'steal' the student you have marked down as a witch or a prince.

Finally we manage to start work, explaining the language, getting the students to add mime and gesture to their spoken offerings and teaching the songs that everyone will sing. CDs are distributed, one with the spoken text and the other with the songs. All are enjoined to study their lines and practice the songs. I fear we fall into the trap of concentrating on the finished product and forget that it's supposed to be fun. Our expectations are high and so we all go through periods of near-despair when it is impossible to envisage a production ever getting onto the stage.

Rehearsals continue weekly. If we have a large group (42 students is our record), we split them into groups to go off and practice song and dance.

There are usually four or five teachers sharing this club so we can split the workload. As the only native speaker my role is 'voice coach.' I also edit and simplify the text and work with those in starring roles on pronunciation and intonation. Some are responsible for the music cues and lighting. Costumes and scenery constitute another task. During the first term, when June still seems very distant, some of the teachers unilaterally decide to find other things to do in club hour. Friction is not confined to the students. Come May and June, extra rehearsals are scheduled and intensive work goes on. There is always a magic moment when you can actually visualise the show happening.

When you actually get to performance day, it is hard to say who is more nervous: the actors or the producers. Students of a very tender age are whisked off to the hairdressers to be ready for the big night. Teachers also choose their outfits with care and see if they can sneak in a quick hairdo between school and the evening call. The euphoria, which descends with the final curtain, does not always extend to the post-production analysis.

Praise and criticism are dished out in equal measure, the latter in a more discreet form and usually reserved for the teachers.

Whatever transpires, the students greatly increase their English vocabulary and grow in self-confidence so you feel it has all been worthwhile. I cannot help feeling that it is all a little too serious and that if we were just a little more relaxed, everything would go more smoothly.

Such occasions are a showcase for private schools so Drama nights, English nights, music and dance nights, end-of-year shows abound. At least here we are a team and enjoy the support of the Head of Department. Time and money are not spared in the construction of backdrops, painted scenery and colourful costumes.

At a previous school things were rather different. Teachers had to fall back on their own resources. Two hapless colleagues were charged with producing the entire 'English night' from start to finish with very little support. It was a trade-off, or a punishment, for having one less lesson a week than the rest of us. At least the planning was easier than the previous year where each teacher had produced ten minutes' worth, which then had to be sewn together like a patchwork quilt.

They did wonderfully well, choosing 'witches and ghosts' as a theme and entertaining us all with a series of short plays and sketches. At the eleventh hour the principal started to interfere and, missing the point entirely, (she had no English) came close to ruining the show in the name of neatness and tidiness. She disliked the colourful array of T-shirts on view and said they ought to be of a single colour, like a uniform.

Still further back in my memory is a night where each teacher was given a class or year group to do something with. I spent many hours rehearsing 4A in reciting poems with actions to match. Rehearsals were conducted in their classroom and we spent a long time establishing the order of entrance and the transition of places for each individual poem. Imagine my dismay when the final rehearsal, actually on the stage, saw the principal's wife rearranging the students in order of height! They did well on the night and I was rewarded by praise for their excellent diction. Too many cooks came very close to spoiling the broth.

As I edit and largely rewrite the play for the coming year, I hope that we will have a talented and willing cast, a close–knit production team and at the end, rounds of applause. I suspect that I am being just a trifle optimistic.

Friend or Foe?

Who goes there? Friend or foe? This sums up my experience of being a native speaker teacher of English in private schools in Turkey. Mixed responses may be met in classrooms and teachers' rooms alike. Can the homegrown teaching contingent swallow their professional pride and ask you to advise, inform, or even check their work? Much depends, I think, on their experience of the foreigners encountered. Learning that we are individuals and not a product of some standard mould is a learning point in itself.

If you tread carefully and offer your help only when solicited to start with, you may be gradually involved in the process of correction. If you can quell your outrage at seeing wrongly-worded announcements or even exam questions, you may be able to create some useful input. If non-native speaker colleagues are discussing the finer points of grammar, bite your tongue until invited to give your opinion. Expressing willingness to help may be misconstrued. Once the floodgates have opened, however, you may find yourself spending a lot of time acting as a spellchecker, grammar book and dictionary combined.

Dealing with those in authority gives a different slant on the problem. I once taught in a very large school, where the foreign contingent was equally big.

One of my colleagues was a lady from the North of England with a forthright attitude. She was as blond as a Swede whereas I had dark hair. The Deputy Head, exasperated by trying to pronounce her name, Elizabeth, with its inconvenient final diphthong, claimed that he couldn't tell us apart! At a later date that same Deputy Head called me into his office to complain about the behaviour of another foreigner. Enlisting my support and asking me to act as a translator, he was reassured when I said that I agreed with him and would attempt to bring the offender to heel.

"You are both English," he exclaimed in amazement. "How can you think so differently?"

Before you get too irate at this seeming piece of stupidity, stop and picture your idea of a Turk. Stereotypes are at best misleading and at worst dangerous. Added to the fact that most teachers of his generation had never had the chance to go abroad, such attitudes are less surprising.

Being a fluent Turkish speaker is of course a big advantage but on occasions such as these, it seemed to draw me into the trap of being the bearer of bad news.

In the classroom or among the students in general you may be regarded as something 'different'.

"She's only a foreigner. She doesn't know anything," was the response from a student, whose nose was bleeding, one morning during a summer school. He preferred to rely on the cleaning lady rather than a teacher, despite the fact that I had told him in clearly comprehensible Turkish that the school nurse was already on duty. This is perhaps an extreme example but more subtle clues are there to be garnered and reflect an underlying attitude. This may be because the Turks are fiercely patriotic and the scope of the syllabus is narrow in terms of learning about the rest of the world. The result is that many foreigners tend to have more discipline problems in the classroom than their Turkish counterparts, regardless of their length of service.

Turkish schools have traditionally arranged classrooms with two or more pupils sharing a wide desk, which have either bench seats or individual chairs. Even very young learners are expected to sit quietly and obediently, while the teacher pronounces or leads the lesson from the front of the class. Of course many of the students do their best to wriggle out of this uniformity by sitting at odd angles. Some recline in deckchair fashion with notebooks perched on knees. Others turn their chairs to face their friends rather than the teacher, thereby sending a clear signal as to where their attention is focused.

Occasionally the rigidity is broken up for a few weeks due to the demands of another lesson, such as science, and the furniture is rearranged to facilitate group work.

A few more enlightened institutions have lighter, more moveable furniture or even dedicated language rooms, but these are few and far between and likely to be in the schools demanding the highest fees. Although times are slowly changing with modern technology and electronic boards making an appearance, the ethos continues to be traditional. A colleague who attempted to introduce the idea of a mat for story time landed up having to ask for outside assistance to control her class of eight-year-olds.

I was once interrupted during a class by a member of

the administration. The students were totally absorbed in their pair-work activity: so much so in fact that they failed to notice his appearance. He was shocked at the hubbub in the room and I got a black mark!

As a very new teacher, my colleagues all assumed I knew what to expect, possibly because I was in my forties and age is associated with experience. In fact, I had certain ideas but most of them had gone out of the window by week two. Even now with many more years at the chalk face behind me, I find student behaviour can be a source of stress. Not only do we deal with individual needs and backgrounds but it is rare to find a school where teachers sit down and discuss common rules. No wonder the students get up to tricks when they can. Some members of staff seem to tolerate a low level of noise, while others operate a strict no talking policy with varying degrees of success. You may be seen as authoritarian or a soft touch. While consistency of approach and a clear set of rules goes a long way to alleviate the teachers' problems, there is always something new to deal with. The youngest of children may be manipulative or a class leader. Falling in love knows no boundaries of age. Illness, a change in the weather or a quarrel in the lunch break can affect the level of performance and the classroom atmosphere.

Suffice it to say that you need eyes in the back of your head and all your senses on full alert for every second of your 40 minute lesson. As a parent recently said to me, "I can't cope with one at home. How on earth do you manage 30 at a time?"

The day consists of eight 40-minute periods. There is no streaming so a student may be 'trapped' in his classroom for several hours at a time but there is a seven to ten minute break between each lesson. The resulting corridor chaos and noise can be deafening and intimidating.

Assuming that you survive the day, the days turn into

weeks and you settle into a rhythm of sorts. You learn to balance the demands of students, parents, colleagues and the administration. The advent of a good and satisfying lesson from time to time gives you a sense of purpose and achievement. When these are rare, the teachers' room becomes your refuge and sanctuary.

Here you will find yourself in a predominantly female environment. Male colleagues are a rarity. How they cope with the feminine topics of conversation, I am at a loss to understand. While some close their ears if not their minds, others wear a long-suffering look. Amongst the complaints about the students, discussion of the latest diet, talk of shopping and make-up, not to mention a good grumble about husbands and boyfriends, there is occasional, serious discussion of professional issues. You may be able to compare notes on shared classes or argue about presentation of materials.

Exams are often thrown together like ingredients going into a stew or soup: a bit of this and a bit of that, add some grammar and stir thoroughly, seems to be the prevailing philosophy. If, however, your Head of Department appears, the levity instantly disappears and everyone is suddenly peering intently at their course book. The teachers are also individuals, of course, and many are hardworking and dedicated. On the social side, colleagues form strong bonds and offer each other real support in times of need, personal or professional.

You may find yourself working in anything from complete isolation on the one hand to being rigidly coordinated on the other. The latter can feel like a straitjacket but is preferable to the loneliness of the teacher taking responsibility for the whole show. Despite all the difficulties, teaching in Turkey has been a rewarding and interesting experience. It has helped me to understand much about its history and culture. A school, after all, is a microcosm of its surrounding environment.

Help! Inspectors!

The inspectors are coming! The inspectors are coming! Panic stations! All hands on deck! The cries of distressed teachers, not to mention the administrators, reverberate around the school corridors. I exaggerate: no one actually admits to such feelings. No, we are all mature adults, who are perfectly confident in our professionalism. Nevertheless even the nonchalant can be seen riffling through their files, making sure they contain the statutory picture of Atatürk, without which you certainly can't pass the test!

Minutes of long forgotten departmental meetings are hastily resurrected. You don't have to know what was said and done but you have to be able to produce them in neat copy.

Once the stage is set the tune changes to *buyursunlar*, meaning they are welcome. Beneath the calm exterior there is still an atmosphere of unease.

Even the most blasé, or experienced, if you are less cynical, come up with all sorts of reasons for the time not being ripe. It is too near the end of term (or the beginning), too soon after a holiday (or before), too cold (or too hot), or just not quite a convenient moment for the team to descend on your institution.

They hunt in packs, these elderly grey men. They are almost exclusively male and senior in their profession by definition. If you work in a large school, they come in teams of ten to fifteen. The best rooms are set aside for their offices. No one may disturb this inner sanctum. The dining room has a special corner, with fine table linen and shining cutlery. In short they become lords of all they survey as no one in their right mind would deny their slightest request. Underneath this old-fashioned courtesy, there is a feeling of anxiety. After all we are all human and dread the knock on the classroom door. Protocol dictates that they give warning of their impending invasion but this is often a practice more honoured in the breach.

There is a plus to counteract all these negative feelings: students miraculously change their behaviour and start to behave angelically. Even the most hardened abandon their well-tried disruptive tactics. Lessons are for once conducted entirely in the target language – English! I discover hidden talents under the adolescent uniform of feigned boredom. It simply isn't cool to be seen to be keen on learning.

On one such occasion, I was introduced to the inspector during the first break, before returning to my noisy, uninterested seventh year class.

'I'll just finish my tea and I'll be along in a minute. You go ahead,' he said. This man, who had loomed so large in my anxiety dreams, looked inoffensive enough. In his mid-50s with receding grey hair, he had a warm smile and a friendly demeanour. I returned to my class to spread the news. In despair, I tried to remain calm as the rowdiest continued to strut their usual stuff, delaying tactics, refusing to settle down and making loud conversation. The more helpful tried to silence their peers, sensing my unease. The expected knock at the door came soon enough and produced an abrupt but welcome change. Everyone leapt to their feet and stood rigidly to attention: any visitor would have thought we had become a military academy! The greetings over, the inspector planted himself firmly behind the teacher's desk, ignoring the chair placed discreetly at the back of the classroom for his use.

For once, all ears were tuned into my lesson, as the grey head buried itself in my files and lesson plan notebook. From time to time I glanced across at him. He was peering intently at various papers in the files. Knowing that he had little or no English, I tried to concentrate, while wondering what he was making of my plan, which consisted of severely abbreviated hieroglyphics.

Surreptitious glances at my watch told me that it would be over mercifully soon. I foolishly allowed myself to relax, only to see a glazed look come over a student's face. Reverting to type, he threw a rubber across the room. Unable to react with a shout or a reprimand, I gave him a murderous look and was rewarded with an expression of abject apology. The files on the desk were still more enticing to the inspector than the unfolding events in the classroom so the misdemeanour had gone unnoticed. As the next activity was a vocabulary exercise, I needed to retrieve the necessary papers from my file, which I did hurriedly, feeling like a thief in the night.

The bell rang and the class filed out in uncharacteristic orderly fashion. A few brief questions from the inspector followed: routine stuff about length of service and teaching experience.

"Very good!" he said in his limited English, relieved to find that I spoke his language. "You don't have any trouble in this class, do you?" he added. For a fleeting moment, I was tempted to acquaint him with the reality of the daily grind, the tricks the inventive employ to annoy and disrupt but I quickly suppressed such dangerous notions.

"Of course not, but some of them can be lively this near the end of term!" I replied judiciously.

"They're young!" he countered with a smile. He then left the classroom to select his next 'victim'. I was left wondering who was kidding who.

Of the 170 or so Primary inspectors in the region, only two or three have more than a smattering of English. I was once bold enough to ask one of them what he could learn without this facility.

"Oh you'd be surprised!" he said. He was also middle-aged, meticulously polite, if a touch old-fashioned. He came into a double period fifth year class, arriving half way through the first lesson without warning. After observing carefully for 30 minutes or so, he asked me to give the students a task as he wanted to discuss some points with me. His 'questions' turned out to be a monologue on his son who had been to the USA and spoke excellent English.

The following year this self-same gentleman of the old school visited a notorious second year class, which had a group of unruly boys. The teacher was experienced but quite unable to impose discipline on the five recalcitrants. The small ringleader was in the habit of climbing on the cupboards and had been known to throw his shoes out of the window in extreme rage. He was not going to stop because some old fuddy-duddy asked him to!

The teacher wisely admitted that, having employed various tactics, she was at a loss.

"Leave it to me!" answered the man from the ministry. Sadly chaos continued to reign and he had to admit defeat. To his eternal credit he did not blame the poor embattled teacher.

In my third year of teaching in Turkey, I had my inspectorial baptism of fire. I knew that the inspectors were in school but had been told that they were not interested in foreign teachers. So the knock on the door of my fourth year classroom door came out of the blue. The students were silently doing an exam: I apologised for not having reorganised my schedule and suggested he come to another lesson. Having assured me all was fine, he proceeded to walk up and down the aisles, leaving the already apprehensive students in a state of near terror. He stopped to look over the shoulder of a normally mischievous boy.

Aferin oglum. Hepsi doğru' (Well done my boy, all right).

I was somewhat taken aback as the student in question was not one of the brightest stars in the firmament. Later I saw that 'all right' should have been 'all wrong'. Perhaps encouragement was the order of the day.

While the students busied themselves with the exam, I was asked a few questions. As the inspector didn't seem able to grasp that I had graduated from a foreign university, I offered to fill in the requisite information myself.

On the basis of these ten minutes, I later learned that I had been awarded a score of 90 percent. Marks are not usually broadcast. Some schools treat them as a closely guarded secret. Asking for any form of feedback is greeted with sideways looks as though it is not quite polite to comment on a teacher's performance.

Sometime later another inspector enrolled his daughter in the school with the admonition that we should bring her English up to scratch within a year. The school principal saw this as a great compliment and accepted her with a beaming smile. My colleague and I exchanged a wry look but luckily for all concerned, she proved a willing student and a fast learner.

Once a year the inspectors gather us together to impart the latest thinking and words of wisdom emanating from the bowels of the Ministry of Education in Ankara. These golden snippets either seem to be based on some Utopian school in the sky or state the blindingly obvious. We should no doubt be grateful that someone somewhere is spending time looking after our welfare and making enormous efforts to raise educational standards. We have a long way to go!

This is all in the way of 'routine' inspections carried out by the local team. Inspection by the national team, which comes to a school near you directly from the Ministry of Education, is a beast of a very different nature.

We had been warned, way back in August, that this would be the year of the 'big one'. So you might say we were well-prepared, ready to take on all comers.

Therein lies the rub: we should not of course be in adversarial mode but welcome the chance for an honest appraisal and help with curing our weak points. However as human nature would have it, a competitive atmosphere can be discerned, interdepartmental rivalry rears its ugly head and the inevitable note of panic creeps in. Files are reorganised into one monster creation that you have to carry around for the duration as though your very life depended on it. When inspectors haunt the corridors every teacher carries every possible piece of paperwork to be ready for the visitation. Up to date and correctly completed records will make or break you and despite the niceties, the inspector may descend at any time without notice.

Teachers, of course, need complete and meticulously kept records of student achievement. They must show that they can justify marks given and record all efforts made to help an individual realise their full potential, but isn't classroom performance the real yardstick? Do I really deserve to be marked down if I have no picture of Atatürk, the greatly revered founder of modern Turkey, gracing my folders? So there is a hint of political correctness about the whole procedure. Are the inspectors placemen, recipients of government patronage, and if so, how will this affect their judgement? These questions are in everyone's mind, if not on everyone's lips.

So bright and early on the designated day, a minibus sweeps into the playground and disgorges an assortment of darkly besuited men and women. The first surprise: there are three women and one of them is under 40! – Unheard of in the long annals of inspection.

As they settle into their official and sacrosanct office and demand timetables, the rumour factory goes into overdrive. There is at last an inspector, who speaks English, a 1995 graduate, lowering the average age of the team by a decade or two.

At the end of the first day, the whole staff is called to a meeting. As the conference hall is out of action due to extensive refurbishment, we huddle together in the stands overlooking the sports hall. Down below on the basketball court, the grey men file in and arrange themselves behind a long table. The chief inspector struggles to his feet and starts to mumble into a microphone. It is hard to distinguish anything meaningful as he continues reading legal gobbledegook from his PowerPoint presentation. By the time we get to the meat of the meeting, so to speak, we are so numb with cold and boredom that it is hard to concentrate on the graphs and figures, appearing with great rapidity on the distant screen.

We gather at least that every person employed, in whatever capacity, will be assessed. Besides the inspectors' evaluation (50 percent), every teacher will be assessed by their Head of Department, the Principal, and fellow teachers. We will also assess ourselves and in a departure from tradition, our students and their parents will also be asked their views.

From day two, everyone waits for the news of the inspector's daily programme. Breaktime loses its convivial atmosphere, as at the end of each lesson, you expect bad news. We beg our students to be on their best behaviour and exchange anxious glances in the corridors, particularly if we are actually on duty and thereby accountable for all behaviour.

Our lady inspector wins many plaudits with her understanding attitude and when she offers to help teachers carry their materials to the classroom.

She expresses surprise at the size of the English Department – there are so many of us – she will not be able to see all of us in action at the chalkface.

So the tension increases as the first teachers are chosen. In fact the wait is worse for those of us left hanging from day to day, while those who have been through the fire and lived to tell the tale, are seen sporting smug smiles.

Selected students (how are they picked?) disappear from classrooms to complete their forms. In some cases teachers are politely asked to step outside while the inspectors quiz the students about their teachers' performance. One student greets me with a knowing smile at the beginning of our lesson.

"I've just written about you!" he tells me. Sealed envelopes are sent home to parents on a similar random(?) basis.

We are all given a lengthy survey to complete. We must evaluate our administrators, our departmental colleagues, support staff and ourselves.

The number of criteria is daunting. Welcoming the chance for a real appraisal, I find that many questions are hard to answer truthfully or at least deserve more subtlety than the bare one to five scale allowed. Teachers refuse to give their friends less than straight fives. Having been warned that such perfect results will be disregarded, fours are sprinkled over the survey like grains from a salt cellar. I dutifully fill it all in as best and as honestly as I can, but some answers are unfortunately little more than guesswork. Does the principal use money wisely? Do your colleagues make good use of the counselling services, by referring their students when necessary? Then there is the thorny and contentious issue of dress codes. How, we all wonder, will the students answer such questions. If we obey the letter of the law and dress in greys and blacks, will we win brownie points from our adolescent charges?

If some are assessed by the inspectors and some not, is the end result fair? In fact only about 50 percent of teachers had a visit: the rest were only assessed internally.

After ten working days, we reassemble for the results. This time we are ensconced in the basement, a long, narrow, flat space. We are at least warm but only those privileged enough to sit in the front row (the principal and his assistants) can actually see the screen. So as the inspector talks through slide after slide of questionnaire results, we reach the denouement. Our glorious institution has scored 94 percent. Speeches of mutual congratulation follow. Relieved and happy to be released at 6pm, a sneaking suspicion remains that what has been presented is not real. When, if ever, will individual results be announced or discussed? It is considered impolite to ask such questions.

Within days the rumours start all over again: according to some unattributed source they will be back next year! A collective groan rises from the teachers' room.

However, three years down the line they have yet to appear!

Winding Up and Winding Down

In late June, 'we are just winding up at school,' I remarked to a friend. 'Are you winding up or winding down?' he asked me. An apt question and one that got me thinking about that dreaded time, after the end of the school year and before the beginning of the subsequent one when school teachers have their 'seminars'.

School generally starts mid-September and runs through to mid-June with a fortnight's break between the two long terms in late January and early February. The quaintly termed 'seminars' take place during the two weeks or so after the end of the second term and before the school year begins.

Hours and dates are fixed by individual schools, the most hours being put in by the private sector. For most of us this involves a fortnight after the students leave, clutching their report cards. The seminars start again two, three or even four weeks before the next school year is due to begin.

Joining my first school in 1992 on the Friday before school was due to open, I had never heard about this custom. At the end of my first year, I heard vague rumours about coming in for a further two weeks from 9 to 12 but stoutly declared that I was off on holiday with my family. No one disabused me and I got away with not attending. How I managed this, I have no idea. Gradually the nets have tightened to prevent the escape of stray fish like me!

During this period most private schools have a morning timetable, which releases them from the obligation of providing lunch. State schools often reduce the hours to a token appearance of an hour or two a day at the discretion of the head teacher. You may of course be required to stay into the afternoon if your work is not finished.

My current institution requests the pleasure of my company from 9.30 to 3:00. Lunch is provided with considerable style and smiles.

So, what do teachers do? Some schools actually have teacher training seminars as the name suggests. Some affiliated schools get all their teachers together for a week or so and invite outside speakers to come and share their knowledge and expertise. As a presenter on such occasions, I have found marked reluctance to actively participate in such sessions as the teachers are exhausted at the end of the year. At the beginning of the next year, it may still be very hot and not conducive to concentration.

Even if the temperature is tolerable the staff are more likely to want to spend their time on the nitty-gritty of planning for the coming term.

If there are no seminars, teachers may resort to drinking endless cups of tea and chatting to their friends to while away the time. Some years ago, I was amazed to see the older generation take out their knitting. These days such frivolities are frowned upon. Teachers have now graduated from knitting to surfing the internet. A few are seen to have their noses in books, all of which serves to make them look more purposefully engaged than the knitters!

It is also the hiring (contract renewal) and firing (non-renewal of the yearly contract) season. Every school handles this difficult and sensitive procedure in its own way. In my first school, which was a small family-run concern, the head teacher would call each teacher into his office for an appointment, where he delivered the good or bad news and then, if appropriate, proceeded to negotiate next year's salary. In my case there was always an 'appraisal'. I use the term loosely because it all seemed to be based on hearsay and was highly impressionistic. Flattered as I was to be told after my first very diffident attempts at teaching, that I had exceeded expectations, I couldn't help but blurt out, "but how do you know?" The answer was a big grin and a tap on the side of the nose. So we proceeded to the salary negotiations. In those days of high inflation (early 1990s), one expected 80 – 100 percent rises. Having been told by my Head of Department that I might be offered 20 or 40 percent, I was amazed and delighted to be given 100 percent, without having to argue at all. Relief flooded over me as my bargaining skills fall far short of Turkish standards.

When I moved to a larger school, I found the process was collectivized and thus huge and often unwarranted discrepancies in salaries were avoided. Regardless of experience foreigners are likely to receive the school's standard package, which appears fair but in fact puts the first year graduate, possibly new to the country, on a par with the experienced foreign teacher: another recipe for trouble!

This is also the season of the 'envelope', which contains a polite letter thanking the recipient for their hard work but telling them that their services are no longer required. Polite good wishes do little to soften the blow: the reality is that you have been sacked. This news is rarely imparted face to face and the administration seldom gives any reason for your failure to meet their expectations. Without formal appraisals, you may be totally at loss to understand why you are being fired. Length of service does not seem to afford any protection, as I have witnessed teachers of ten or twelve years standing being summarily dismissed in this way.

Because the process is so opaque, imaginations run riot and the rumour factory goes into overdrive. When someone gets the boot we hear almost as many reasons given as there are teachers present. All sources are said to be 'reliable'. Traditionally and rather cruelly, the unfortunate recipients of the said envelopes had to wait till the last working day for the axe to fall. This year, at my school, they were given an extra week's warning. Some cleared their desks in an hour; others worked quietly till the end of the month.

On a brighter note, the seminar season is also the time of promotions to assistant and deputy headships and even to the top job itself. The application procedure is non-existent. If these posts are filled internally the announcements may be made at this point, giving rise to a new round of rumours and gossip. Speculation is rife as to how decisions were reached. This always takes place behind closed doors in a highly secretive manner. A teacher may be brave enough to hint that he or she would not be averse to such an offer. After seventeen years of teaching here, I try to be philosophical, congratulate my colleagues and hope that we will all be able to work in an atmosphere of mutual respect. A strong and disciplined administrative team can do much to alleviate the burden of teaching.

Apart from these important events, there is the usual crop of meetings to attend and reports to be written. High school teachers also have exams to prepare for students who have the chance to improve their grades or re-sit. These tasks occupy about 50 percent of the time available. For the rest of the time teachers start to look for things to do. The first choice is to clear out cupboards, a process that produces bagfuls of waste paper. Next we tidy up the shelves of resource books, putting them neatly back in an order that will not survive more than two weeks of the new term.

Another few hours have been filled without resorting to the internet. Retiring to the canteen or the garden may be tempting until the head grumbles that nobody seems to be working and we all rush back to the teachers' room where we attempt to look busy. Some years we have started to draft our year plans at this point but as we nearly always had to start again in August when the working calendar is made available, it seems to be rather a waste of effort.

There is a sharp divide between the winding down in June and the winding up in August/September. When you arrive back refreshed by a long holiday the atmosphere is much more business-like and purposeful.

It may take a few days to get into top gear but meetings abound first for the whole school and then at departmental level. Meaningful tasks are allocated, classes are allotted and everyone gets down to the serious business of the year plans.

In my early years this actually involved ruling lines on giant pieces of squared paper. It could take a whole day just to produce enough templates with the requisite number of boxes and columns. From that we progressed to pre-printed plans and now of course to the ubiquitous computer-generated material. Once we have produced our blueprint master plan, we go onto unit and lesson plans but then we hit a brick wall until we know which classes contain which students. This is usually kept a closely guarded secret until the last minute. So the next stage of attempting to gather background information can be hard. If we are to teach years one to five, the class teacher is a key player and will fill us in on any problems, academic or behavioural. Higher level classes are mixed up each year so we have to exchange information with colleagues as best we can. I always hope for some familiar faces to minimise the number of new names to learn, which seems to take longer with each passing year. Learning 200 or so Turkish names and surnames is quite a task!

Then we have to start to get to know the parents but that is something that goes on well into the first term.

Finally we have done everything we can usefully do, typically with two or three days to go before the students return and we are impatient to begin.

Although this September will see me starting my eighteenth year of teaching in Turkey, I still feel a kind of nervous excitement, which only dissipates when I see a sea of even more nervous and excited faces looking back at me.

A Parent's Perspective

As a parent, you slowly acclimatise to the idea of discussing your child's progress – both social and educational – with their teachers. It is not always a happy experience as the detached professional can make observations which don't coincide with your own rosy-coloured view. Some comments may not only be critical of your beloved offspring but also an aspersion on your parenting.

At the London primary school, which my children attended, parent-teacher meetings were by appointment, giving the chance for a private discussion and a genuine dialogue. We always felt able to approach teachers to share background information. Sometimes expert insight helped us to handle our children at home.

Our first experiences of these occasions in Turkey came as a rude shock. Rather than a private appointment at the school, we were all herded together with four teachers to a classroom. There was no semblance of a queue so the stronger-willed or more bloody-minded elbowed their way to the teacher, who was sitting in state. The female staff seemed to enjoy this position more than their male counterparts. The teacher concerned then proceeded to hold forth without fear or favour, dispensing news good or bad, while barely pausing for breath. Thus we learned that our bright offspring were failing hopelessly at Maths and Turkish.

There were a few teachers who attempted to be more discreet but their efforts were thwarted by the system. Trying to be tactful and sensitive was difficult in such a

throng and insult was added to injury as
great success of other students.

As newcomers and with a distinctly po(
Turkish, my children had their difficulties, es
first year. I am not suggesting that it was
teaching staff to cope, but I would have we\   ...ore
advice than the criticism that was all too common.

The following year the system changed. This time we
occupied our child's classroom and waited for individual
teachers to make an appearance. As I waited for the show to
unfold, the English teacher arrived with her husband in tow
as if for a social engagement. At least I could hope for good
news from her and was not disappointed. Nevertheless my
articulate native speaker son had managed to score only 47
percent in one of his early English exams!

Then the real star of the show arrived. We dubbed her
'the queen' but her students were less kind, insisting that she
was a witch, no less. As she slapped her file down on the
table and started to proclaim from on high, I secretly
sympathised with the student viewpoint. As each individual
student's name was read out, the appropriate parent raised a
reluctant hand to receive a report on their child's progress. I
am ashamed to say that I felt embarrassed to be owning up
to being the mother of a very 'weak' student but my
embarrassment turned to rage at the teacher's obvious
pleasure at imparting bad news. She clearly had a power
complex which dominated her relationship with parents and
students alike.

Years later we reverted to sitting in classrooms, as each
teacher made the rounds. The news was now academically
considerably better: this time I found it equally
embarrassing to be an unwilling eavesdropper as a father in
front of me was told of his son's laziness and insolence.

Then there were the oversensitive type of teacher who
bent over backwards to be kind. We were discussing our

aughter with her English teacher one day. They had a good relationship and all seemed to be well. We were by now used to the presence of other parents, some of whom couldn't resist offering advice of their own. Suddenly we were whisked out of the classroom to the relative privacy of the corridor for a private word. It turned out to be a matter of no importance, but as we re-entered the room it was clear that tongues had been wagging and speculation rife as to what could be serious enough to warrant a separate discussion.

When I became a teacher, I asked my head to institute a system giving some privacy. If not appointments, at least the chance to have a queue outside the door, as we talked to parents individually. She refused on the grounds that Turkish parents would not accept queuing, while adding sadly that many parents needed educating as much as, if not more than, their children.

This story has a happy ending. My current school puts one teacher in each classroom. Parents come for a private exchange of views. The door is firmly shut although many can't resist asking about children other than their own.

My children have long since left school but reliving these memories has reminded me of the lack of privacy I found so difficult an aspect of the culture when I first arrived in the country. In the early days of my marriage my mother-in-law told me firmly that I could only expect to be alone with my husband at night! All decisions big or small were sanctioned by the whole family. In desperation I looked up the word 'privacy' in my dictionary only to find it unlisted. With a more sophisticated reference book at my disposal, I find that there is no direct equivalent. One word given, *inziva* actually translates as becoming a hermit or recluse!

Running Water

This motif is the only common one showing movement. It represents the importance of water for life, and invokes prosperity. We have used it here relating to travel, since throwing water on the ground behind a departing vehicle is said to bring a smooth journey and a safe return.

3 - Getting About

Walking to Work

We all know the rule, don't we? Walk on the pavement. It sounds simple but it isn't, at least in Izmir.

I used to walk up the hill every day, because the bus from my house stopped at the bottom, and the university where I worked was half way up to the top. Unless the obstacles were unusually serious, the walk took about fifteen minutes.

Parked cars constitute one hazard to walkers. In Turkey it is routine to actually park on the pavement, and in that part of town it is narrower than the width of an average vehicle. So cars are squeezed up tight against the walls of buildings. Any pedestrian who is more than a couple of inches thick is thus forced to go out into the street to pass them, and has to wait for a gap in the traffic to accomplish this. If you think pavements are meant for people, think again.

Another obstacle is trees. Most people like trees, so the city council works hard at planting new ones. The problem is location. Either they will impede the traffic on the street, or they will block the pavement. In Izmir it must be presumed that all city councillors and their wives drive cars and never walk anywhere, because the trees are invariably on the pavement. A large hole is dug, and the new tree placed in the middle of it. In the early stages you can still walk past, just taking care not to fall into the hole. When the branches grow big, you have to go out into the street and walk round them to avoid having your eyes spiked.

Then there are dustbins, which are usually the same width as the pavement they stand on. Beside them are the bags of rubbish that wouldn't fit into the bin. Animals attack these bags, sniffing for morsels of food and spreading out the contents to facilitate their search. When the garbage lorry finally comes round, it is always in a hurry and of course the men cannot collect everything.

In addition to obvious rubbish, there are all the things people don't want which get left on the pavement, especially in the season for spring cleaning. The rusty iron winter stove, for instance, hopefully to be replaced by a new one in the autumn. That will be good pickings for the *hurdacı* or scrap-metal merchant, who comes by with his horse and cart later in the day. Sometimes there is a mattress or a sofa, or a defunct television.

Then there are cats' breakfasts. This part of town is inhabited by cat-lovers, but there are no gardens and they don't keep animals in their flats. Instead they feed the ones on the street. Regularly in the early mornings, groups of sleek and multi-coloured pussies cluster around the latest offerings, which vary from commercial cat pellets to last night's fish heads and scraps of greasy bread.

While dogs are considered dirty by serious Muslims, cats are holy. Why? Because they bear the mark of the Prophet; they have stripes on their heads because He once stroked a cat.

There are other live creatures competing for pavement space: people. I don't mean walkers in transit, like me; I mean people who live here. Concrete apartment buildings soak up the sun and become ovens in hot weather. That's why the more expensive flats all have balconies and big windows to bring in the evening breeze. But the older buildings, typical of this district, have no balconies on the ground floor, and no garden around them. The lowest level, small, dark and hot, smelling of aging drains, is usually occupied by the *kapici,* or janitor, and his family. His job is to keep the stairs clean and run errands for the residents, fetching drinking water from the shop in big bottles, buying fresh bread, newspapers and cigarettes. For these services he gets accommodation and a very small salary. His wife is probably illiterate and works as a cleaner; they may have half a dozen children.

On summer evenings the pavement becomes the sitting room of such people. Sometimes they decorate it with pot plants inherited from their more prosperous neighbours: graceful palm trees and flowering geraniums. They sit on old cushions on the ground, or on small wooden chairs. In the evenings when I go home, they are all out there. The children play hopscotch or do homework, kneeling with pencil in hand and notebook on the ground. Men play backgammon, women knit. They have glasses of sweet dark tea. *"Afiyet olsun",* I greet them, which literally means "May it be good for you". I circumnavigate the family party, watching out for traffic on the street, and they answer politely, *"Sağ olun! Buyurun!"* which means, "Thank you! Come and share!"

There were times when all the obstacles on the walks to and from work seemed like a nuisance. But mostly they were more of a Cultural Experience. In those brief periods of transit, I learned more about the real Turkey than I did in all the long hours I worked at the university.

School Transport

Most students in Turkey go to school by bus: not the public kind but specially designated 'services'. The British tradition of walking your children to school is largely absent, regardless of how close to school you live. So our youngsters arrive having had no morning exercise and sometimes after a long journey. After going all round the houses and having left home in some cases at an ungodly hour, they may hardly be in the mood for learning. Some, of course enjoy the camaraderie and a small minority actually read or study on the bus. How I envy their powers of concentration!

The actual vehicles involved vary in size from minibuses to 50-seater coaches, all colloquially referred to as 'the service'. Teachers may avail themselves of these services: sometimes a free ride is a part of the contract. This 'perk' may be a mixed blessing, for you exchange the wait at the bus stop for cacophony and babysitting.

In some institutions, the school administration will direct you to your service bus. Others leave you to cope as best you can in a general free for all. It is like bargaining in a market except that you have no money and nothing to offer. Asking a series of drivers if they are going your way and if there is room on their vehicle becomes a wearying and rather humiliating experience. Even when the school authorities point the way for you, some drivers will find some excuse not to take you. Why, I wonder, did a driver take an instant dislike to me? After he had made a feeble excuse so as not to take me, I was told he was recently divorced, as though that was sufficient explanation for his discourteous behaviour. So, in the first few days and weeks of term, you may find yourself going home on a different bus each day, with a different load of companions.

Primary school students (aged eleven and under) now have to have a *teyze,* a hostess to look after them on the journey. These low-paid ladies are generally housewives trying to earn a little extra cash and are long-suffering in the extreme. They collect their very young charges from the classroom door, arrange the seating plan, break up fights and arguments, pacify the upset and generally cater to the children's every whim. Children seem to feel the need to eat immediately school is over, however close to home they are. Woe betide the hostess who is unequipped with wet-wipes, tissues and a plastic bag for collecting sweet wrappers, empty drink cartons, apple cores and other detritus.

As the bus leaves the school premises with its noisy, squabbling load, it is a wonder that the driver can concentrate sufficiently to drive away at all.

With the older students life should be easier but as with all youngsters you just exchange one set of problems for another. This time the poor unfortunate driver is faced with demands for the air-conditioning to be turned on (or off), the radio to be turned on (or off) or the door left open (or shut). As you can see, there is no way of pleasing all of the students all of the time.

If you are a mere teacher, then the safest strategy is not to express your opinion at all. No journey, however short, is possible, it seems, without loud music blaring. If you have developed an allergy to loud noise after hours in the corridors and the playground, let alone the classroom, and are looking forward to ten minutes' quiet relaxation before the domestic onslaught, then the service bus is not the place for you.

In return for a free ride you are expected to enforce discipline, get students to sit down (and stay sitting down) in their allotted seats. In theory any damage to the bus, reported to the driver, can then be attributed to the occupier of the seat. So a task as difficult as the twelve labours of Hercules confronts you every day.

In my experience, the teachers are just as reluctant as the students to spread out through the bus, as the seating plan demands, preferring to bunch up at the front, so that they can exchange gossip in loud voices.

Inappropriate conversations, possibly concerning other members of staff are bandied about without any regard to which young ears may be listening.

Drivers are also a law unto themselves. Some are unfailingly polite. My current edition is so courteous that he gives way to everybody and we are always the last to leave. This does not go unnoticed and the sharper tongues among us start to grumble loudly after five minutes of watching our colleagues and friends disappear into the distance. Other drivers may not like your face as I have already described. Having agreed with one driver on a pick-up point and time, I was amazed and upset to see him sailing past my bus stop one fine morning. He told the school that stopping to pick me up would make him late for school. They accepted this lame excuse. Clearly drivers have a lot of clout!

If you work for a small school, the drivers may be part of the staff and then everything changes. I went to and from school for four years with one such employee and he became a real friend, inviting all 'his' teachers to his son's circumcision party. Always prompt, he was sometimes berated by a sleepy colleague for arriving too early but he took it all in good part.

So we come to the pick-up point etiquette. Students and teachers must be at the designated spot at the agreed time. If you appear late, you run the risk of having to make your own way to school. In fact, many drivers bend over backwards to wait for students, who emerge bleary-eyed, breakfast in hand at the last possible minute. Teachers are generally not shown the same latitude. If the driver waits too long at a given point, he may risk the wrath of those already on board, who are counting the wasted minutes, thinking of the extra seconds they might have spent in bed.

Students can be obdurate too. We once picked up two girls, whose houses were 50 metres apart. Each refused to approach the other, forcing the exasperated driver to stop twice in as many seconds.

While the very young are collected from their doorsteps, older students are expected to make their way to the nearest main road. Parents can be a problem when their offspring are deemed old enough to fit into the 'older' category. Not many seem to be willing to get dressed in time to bring their children to a convenient point for pick up.

Heavy traffic, breakdowns and other mishaps are all acceptable excuses for late arrival at school. This standard excuse may of course be proffered by those who have never been on a bus at all. Or we see students sauntering in well after the first lesson has started, knowing full well that they have a cast-iron excuse for unpunctuality.

Some teachers prefer to get to school under their own steam, despite the expense, in order to arrive in enough time to have a quiet dose of caffeine before the first bell rings. At least you have time to collect your scattered thoughts. Though students may be excused for yawning their way through the 9 o'clock lesson, teachers can afford no such indulgence.

Perhaps the teachers who travel alone are simply avoiding the hubbub of the bus ride.

So at the end of the day, as all and sundry stream out of the school gates, as boys shed their ties and girls untie their flowing locks, as the air is riven with the sound of mobile phones ringing, we climb onto our buses and take a deep breath. It's the end of another day.

Now we have a new system. Teachers have to be in half an hour before the students and leave 20 minutes later, separate transport being provided. While all the students leave promptly after the last bell has rung, the teachers have time to put their books away and pack their bags in a more leisurely manner before going home. It is quite pleasant not to have to rush out of the classroom particularly if the last lesson finds you at the end of the top floor corridor. After the ritual grumbling about the extension to our working hours we have settled into our new routine.

The new policy is subject to review, however, as some of the 'student' services have become impossibly noisy! So if we have to share transport once again perhaps it will no longer be seen as a privilege but recognised as an extension of our duties.

Whatever happens, my journey is mercifully short and I am one of the first to get off.

Night Bus

Late night service shuttle to the garage, packed with travellers of all ages and types. Obnoxious kids not sitting where they're told to, making a fuss, complaining loudly, whining. Bumpy jerky ride through town in the dark of the night; dimly lit shuttle – *dolmus* (mini-van) – and fairly dim city lights. Not like London or big western cities, where the glare is bright white; these are muted yellowy street lamps.

The dimness and rocking of the service bus lull one towards a dozing sleep which is rudely awoken by the driver suddenly switching on the interior fluorescent lights and announcing we are at the central bus garage. "Everybody out now."

Hustle bustle of the mammoth multi-storey bus garage – 'coach terminal' to be correct in English, but somehow 'bus garage' seems more appropriate. The large double-decker buses are sleek and glide into place with a kind of rolling sway, rather like an elephant on huge roller skates. "It's so exciting!" I remember my English friends exclaiming, when they took me to the bus station for a midnight ride from Denizli to Ankara, and saw the hurrying passengers running for their tickets, their luggage, their supplies for the journey, amidst shouts and cries from the various bus companies hailing the times and departure bays for coaches leaving forthwith.

A crowd of around eighty people, old and young alike, surrounds one bus shouting to a young man seated inside at the window. They sing rousing songs, cheer him, someone even playing a guitar. It seems he is leaving for the army, for compulsory military service. What a wonderful send-off! A far cry from London's Victoria Coach Station, where there is muted noise, little fuss and less rushing about; certainly no singing and no rumbustious crowds giving someone a send-off – not even for a wedding.

In the not so distant past one would see the tea man (*çayci*) swinging his tray of tea glasses; this would be suspended from a kind of inverted tripod with a hook to slot one's index finger under; he would rush through the crowds calling out '*çay! çay! çay!*' and quickly dispense tulip shaped glasses of steaming hot tea among the dozens of waiting passengers standing around. These days at the garage it is more 'modernised', with fast food kiosks – although admittedly the fast food looks fresh and appetising in the case of the bakery stalls! The smell of freshly baked buns (or *çorek*) with sesame seeds on them, *simit*, *poğaca* and *tost*, assailing the nostrils with a sweet and yet savoury aroma. (The *tost* is actually a toasted sandwich, usually with cheese inside, and often with salami and tomatoes as well, depending on your taste and the availability of the ingredients at that particular stall.) All are typical snacks, usually found everywhere in town during the mornings and also for lunch, yet they now seem to be just the thing for a long night journey - although one would normally never eat them at home late in the evening!

These sugary, spicy and salty scents are sometimes punctuated with the sweaty smells of the traders and, it must be said, the passengers too.

Luggage is deposited in the *bagaj* under the coach, and a small ticket given in receipt. Sometimes this is a brightly coloured plastic tag with a number on it. The man in charge of stowing the luggage shouts out the various stops on the way so the bags can be organised for easy retrieval. More hustle and bustle, pushing and shoving as everyone wants their bag taken care of NOW. No orderly queuing here, and no hushed respectful tones: people shout across to each other, to uncles and aunts waiting to see them off, to husbands or wives ordering them to go and get tissues or water or snacks; or just shouting generally; having a normal conversation in public; al fresco; in a noisy place.

We climb onto the bus, after being checked yet again by the driver and steward to make sure we are boarding the right bus at the right time, and stumble along the aisle to find our seats. Mercifully these look the same as they did on the plan in the ticket office. This is not always the case. Buses have different makes and models, and the one you chose from may not be the one you are going on. Your seats by the exit may turn out to be three or four rows behind or in front of where you wanted to be. It's best not to have great expectations.

The seats themselves may be narrower than desired, with little leg room, and maybe a foot rest, maybe not. The seat may recline, or may have a faulty reclining button, in which case *Boş ver!* (Never mind!).There is, however, a little pull down shelf, for tea and snacks, or resting a book or magazine to read. Individual spotlights make this easier late at night, and there may even be a fully operational air-conditioning knob which will send you cooling air once the driver has switched it on – usually some time after departure.

More whistles and shouts and the bus starts to glide out of its parking bay with shouts of '*gel, gel, gel!*' (*'come or 'come on/keep going/keep coming'*) from the attendants for the bays, whose job it is to guide the driver out, sometimes accompanied by a thump on the side of the coach as it leaves – rather like a slap on the flank of a horse to send it on its way. And, at last, WE'RE OFF!

Traffic Police

Ten o'clock at night. The strident tones of my husband's mobile phone wake him from his deep slumber on the sofa in front of the TV. A noisy conversation ensues. Short staccato burst of questions in rapid Turkish. I have no idea who he is talking to, but the phrase about 'plate numbers' is repeated many times, questioningly.

Husband replaces phone on the table and slouches back on the sofa, silently. Five minutes later, as I am getting deeply into a crime drama that has just started, he announces:

"You have a traffic fine, dear. The papers came by post. That was my brother. He says there is a fine of 156TL."

As I struggle to keep my temper at the outrageous assumption that any traffic penalty must be mine, light dawns and I understand the repeated questions on the phone.

'What is the car registration number on the fine?' I ask, since we have two cars and both are actually registered in husband's name. He often uses my car, so it is also quite likely that any offence committed might be his rather than mine.

'It's not clear dear. Not written, but it's the Clio.'

I am ready to explode at the assumption of my guilt despite any definite registration number. Did the police just write down 'white Clio sighted doing something wrong' and then somehow the fine arrives miraculously by post – to Hasan's brother's address? Obviously there are some information gaps here.

I rack my brains trying to remember being stopped by the police in the past month, but can find no clues to this mysterious and expensive fine.

Sleep is difficult, as my tired brain wrestles with the problem and I try to remember any offences I may have committed… and worry about how I will find the money needed for the fine.

Next day, late afternoon, as I am about to start my last lesson of the day, my mobile rings. I had been about to switch it off for class, but too late…

Husband's voice comes in snatches of crackle from a noisy place. I tell him I can't hear him, he's breaking up, and switch off. However, I did hear enough snatches to understand that somehow it has been confirmed that the fine is indeed mine.

That night as I crawl through the front door, weary from my day and still recovering from flu, husband calls to me from the living room, where he is comfortably slouching on the sofa.

"Yes dear it's your fine. It's written your name dear. Rosalynd Margaret Elliott. Two twelve oh seven."

I struggle to digest this information and the significance of the numbers (all delivered in rapid Turkish) whilst hanging up my jacket, removing boots and depositing bags of lesson materials, tape recorder, unfinished lunch and yoga clothing inside the entrance hall, as cats tear past me looking for supper.

"What do you mean, two twelve oh seven?" I ask, preparing bowls of cat food to calm the hungry beasts and get them out of the kitchen as quickly as possible.

"Twelve. They wrote it. Month dear."

Again light dawns. It's a date. December. Where was I? What traffic crime did I commit last month? Rapid scanning of my memory banks produces nothing. Oh, wait, there was that red light… and I was going too fast down the motorway that day, rushing to catch the ferry…

But that's ridiculous! Nobody stopped me, but the fine is written in my name. How can that be? The car is registered in Hasan's name, and he's obviously now using his brother's address in Menderes for post and documents since it's more reliable than his old flat where his ex-wife and children live.

We suffered before with a missing receipt for about £1000 which he had paid towards his ex-wife's national insurance for her state pension: the receipt went missing, and even though the records would be on computer by then, the Social Security people refused to count that deposit towards her pension. ('Tuh', as the Turks say, a kind of half spitting sound, pronounced with a 'u' like a French 'eeuu' sound, and roughly meaning 'Oh bother!' or 'Drat'.)

I decide to put up a fight.

"Nobody stopped me dear. I haven't been asked for my licence for ages now. Even last time they just looked and said 'carry on' and didn't note my name or tell me I'd done anything wrong."

"Two twelve oh seven dear, remember. Twelve oh two. Maybe on the way to Bodrum to see Leslie."

"What?? You know I haven't been to Bodrum since June dear. What are you talking about? I went to the UK in December, so maybe it's YOUR fine?"

"No dear. Yes dear. Last year. Oh two. Twelve oh two."

Light dawns and pennies drop with a crash. February. 02.

12/02/07. Now I understand. That was just before I went to the UK last winter. Yes! I remember now!

I had given my neighbour a lift into town to her art class as we bumped into each other leaving home that bright cold day. The roads were confusing around the old town, and despite following her directions after dropping her off I had suddenly come face to face with three lanes of traffic roaring at me, and a policeman on a motorbike waving angrily at me. Trying to escape from the oncoming traffic (and the policeman, it must be said) I quickly turned right into a windy side street leading into the old market area, and stopped. The motorbike followed me and stopped. My heart sank. I had foolishly tried to explain my way out of it and even called Hasan to get him to explain it, but the situation went from bad to worse and the policeman sternly wrote out a ticket, and left. I still had no idea how to get out of the windy street without going back the way I had come and thereby facing the one-way traffic again, and incurring more offences.

Anyway, somehow I managed it and got to my lesson in a very bad mood!

Hasan had been furious with me. How could I drive the wrong way into a one-way street? Didn't I know the routes through the town by now?

Actually, no, I didn't, I'd replied, as I never went into that town if I could help it. The roads seemed to keep changing as they tore down buildings and dug up streets in the name of 'improvements' or 'development'.

At the time of the 'incident' Hasan had paid the fine the next day. So all was settled.

I felt a great weight drop from my shoulders as I realised we had paid already, ages ago, and this was just Turkish bureaucracy whereby the actual written ticket had taken eleven months to reach its destination.

Mystery solved. Not a problem for us anymore. I even remembered seeing the receipt after Hasan had paid it, and putting it in a safe place... now where could that be I wondered...

Hasan checked the car documents but couldn't find the receipt. I wondered if I had put it in with the house documents. Never mind, he said, it will be on the computer records. I'll go and check in the morning.

We slept well that night, no longer worried about finding 156TL in a hurry.

Next morning Hasan duly set off to town to check the records while I slept in, still snuffling with flu but no longer worried about the fine. I would just check the house documents later to find the receipt, just in case there was any question of our not having paid it.

Two hours later husband returned.

"I went to the police station dear. It's the fog lights. You left the fog lights on. They wrote the fine for that."

"What do you mean?" I exclaimed. "I haven't been stopped for fog lights and nobody took my name or details. How can they write a fine from the registration plate yet produce my name on it?"

"They said oh three dear."

"What are you talking about?"

"Three hundred forty-one division one."

By now I feel as if I am talking to a walking talking alien calculator.

"What?" but glimmers of light are flickering. Some kind of statute number perhaps?

"Law number. It's this kind of penalty. For fog lights on."

Again I explain that I have not been stopped for that misdemeanour since 2003, and nobody fined me then, no details were taken, no ticket written, they just warned me verbally and showed me where the switch was so we could turn the offending lights off! I have been particularly careful about that mistake ever since, but have noticed that whenever the car returns from its periodic services, with husband as chauffeur, these lights are in the on position…

"I don't know dear. They said like this. Something wrong I think. I will pay it."

The logic of this last statement escapes me, and I issue further instructions to husband to go and sort it out – surely it cannot be possible to say one thing one day and change the date and statement the next.

It all seems so unfair. The weight is back on my shoulders which are now slumped, and I set to worrying again about how to find the money if it is indeed a true fine.

Two hours later husband returns, weary from shifting all his painting and decorating equipment back home after finishing a job in the village here. Meanwhile he has also been phoning his brother who still has the document which is causing us so much angst. Finally all is becoming clearer:

It turns out that Hasan's brother's wife originally relayed the message and misread the document. Stifling my impatience at such stupidity I learn that the paper is so badly printed it was impossible to read. This is true of the majority of important and official documents in Turkey; they are written on what seems to be re-cycled paper, which is flimsy and absorbent, so the ink is often smeared and the paper may be creased and torn. We have experienced this problem with receipts from the local municipality which are almost faded to transparency, and have resulted in us paying the annual housing tax several times over, as we had no tangible legible proof of paying! Even receipts from the store may have faded ink and no visible date or price.

Hasan's sister-in-law Tülay said the fine was 156TL, but it may turn out to be 'only' 56 lire. It is impossible to read it clearly.

The chief of police, a friend of Hasan's, further expanded on the story by announcing that the fog lamps misdemeanour has no name written on it, only the car registration plates. (So it could have been Hasan after all!)

He also told Hasan that if the fine is paid without delay there is a slight discount, so it may amount to a mere 49TL.

However, it still remains that my full name is written on the posted document, as Tülay originally read it over the phone to Hasan. So it looks as though this paper may still refer to a fine we have already paid, whilst the penalty of the fog lamps is still to be written up, officially stamped and posted.

Thus it becomes a future problem in the pipeline unless we can waylay it by paying in advance, so to speak. This strange method of proceedings all takes place at the Traffic Tax Office, whence husband is now wending his weary way.

So it may all turn out to be yet another storm in the Özlek teacup.

Tea in the Village

This village is in the hills, 600 metres above the outlying suburbs of Izmir. When the summer heat eases off in the evening, we drive up there. There are four teahouses, two of them with a view. Our favourite is closed; that's the one with a wooden platform in the walnut tree. If you climb the narrow board steps and sit up there, you can hear the woodwork creaking and feel the tree sway in the wind. In the autumn you can pick a few walnuts, crack them between two stones, and break the nuts into little pieces to flavour your tea. But tonight this teahouse owner is still working in his vineyard, so his establishment is closed. We go to the other one, in the old school yard behind the horse trough.

Vines and Virginia creeper cover a frame with thick greenery, and in its shade are tables and chairs. We sit down, enjoying the soft evening breeze, and ask the old man for tea. His face is brown and wrinkled like a walnut, and he has a friendly smile.

We are the first customers, so we will wait for the tea to brew, perhaps half an hour. We enjoy the view, the valleys filled with vineyards and fig trees and patches of oak and pine woodland. Down in the deep clefts below the woods are hidden streams of silver water, diverted in places by earth channels and plastic pipes to support vegetable gardens; beans, corn, tomatoes and peppers are grown there.

Beyond the valleys are the shapes of hazy blue hills, and then the pale, gleaming surface of the Aegean Sea. On a very clear evening, you can see the Greek island of Chios in the distance.

The *çaycı*, the tea man, brings us tumblers of cool spring water, and soon afterwards the tea arrives in steaming glasses, together with a saucer of sugar lumps. No surplus wrapping here, no plastic cups or bottles to be thrown away. My daughter gets out the box of chocolate cake she has brought along. The neighbour who came with us has cheese and tomatoes, but no one has a knife, so we ask the *çaycı*. He offers to bring plates, we say we don't need them, but he brings them anyway, and forks as well. We offer him some cake, which he accepts. Then he presents us with plate of freshly washed pears, small and sweet, with thick skins. We sip our tea contentedly and order a second round.

Afterwards we go for a walk, down an earth road that winds between gardens and vineyards. Our neighbour's dog, Teddy, joyfully pursues smells she doesn't find in her suburban home: tortoises, goats, sheep and donkeys. The last of the season's wild flowers bloom along the way, pink hollyhocks reaching up out of the brown grass, and *verbascum,* with leathery leaves and flowers like multibranched yellow candelabra. And there's a scratchy, creamy coloured umbellifer which isn't listed in my book. It has one fake, black insect on each head of flowers, to encourage the real ones to come and pollinate.

We pass olive trees with small round fruit that will swell gently all through the summer, and green blackberries that will never ripen because the dry stream beds have not enough moisture to give them. The bramble bushes do not know this and they cling on through the years, forever hopeful.

The sky turns pink with sunset and we head back to our car, passing the interesting spectacle of a mechanical digger being employed to pick apricots. A boy sits in the scoop of the digger with a plastic bag, and the driver lifts him up to reach the trees. It is probably a council digger that was working on a road somewhere near; perhaps the driver is a relative of the family who own the trees. I am reminded of Sundays by the seaside years ago, where you would see parked cars and vans painted with the logos of various businesses: *Marshall* (paint), *Puffy* (quilts), *Konfor* (furniture). It did not mean that they expected customers on the beach, merely that the person who normally drove the vehicle had a family who fancied an outing. I used to wonder who paid for the fuel. But nowadays there are more private cars around and you rarely see business vehicles used for family trips.

The pink sky has faded to grey when we get back to the village. We back the car in front of the fountain, where a stream of clear mountain water gushes into a concrete basin. Here we fill up the big plastic bottles we have brought along. Why pay for drinking water if you can get as good a product for free? We load the full bottles carefully back into the car. Since they are sharing their space with Teddy, it is important to tie up the heavy bottles so they can't roll around.

We drive back down to the suburbs, with a load of water, a well-exercised dog, and an empty cake box. The planet Venus gleams in the darkening sky above the sunset.

Kindness of Strangers

My many years of living in Turkey have brought lots of opportunities to travel around the countryside, first with eager foreign colleagues and later with my own, Turkish-speaking family. Determined to see the "real" Turkey, we always avoided popular resorts and went to more remote places, seeking out archaeological remains, interesting buildings, or dramatic scenery. On these trips we constantly met and talked to local people, and were greeted everywhere with friendly interest. I am going to tell six little stories. The first four are about my experiences as a traveller; the fifth tells of a misunderstanding that left some bad feelings, and the last is about a glass of tea that changed a person's life.

My first story is from a holiday early in the spring of 1971. We were four young teachers together, with little knowledge of Turkish and much curiosity, who climbed stiffly off a long-distance bus, shouldered our backpacks, and set off through the streets of Tire, a small town, to look for a cheap hotel. In the early evening there were people everywhere, filling the pavements, milling around inside and outside shops, spilling over the road amongst the hooting traffic. On one street corner the crowd seemed even thicker, and out of the crush came people carrying bits of newspaper and licking their fingers. Closer inspection revealed that they were eating *lokma,* a kind of small, brown doughnut. Eager to see what was going on, we wriggled our way forward and were much encouraged by people saying, *buyurun, buyurun*, which is a general expression of invitation to buy something, do something, or go somewhere. In the centre of the gathering was a man, a huge metal bowl, and a cauldron balanced over a blazing gas flame. The bowl was full of thick white dough and the cauldron contained boiling oil. The man scooped up some dough in a ladle and dropped it into the oil, expertly pushing a finger through the centre of the sticky mass on the way. The result was a small and somewhat lopsided, ring-shaped doughnut, which quickly fried to a rich golden brown. A large perforated spoon was used to take the cooked doughnuts out of the oil and dip them into another bowl containing sugar syrup. Then they were dusted with cinnamon and quickly rolled up in a piece of old newspaper, to be passed to one of the waiting people.

"Nobody seems to be paying for them," remarked one of my companions.

"That's odd, but let's ask the price anyway," I said, and did. However, money was declined; the doughnuts, it seemed, were free for all. And they were delicious, hot, sweet and spicy, a delightful welcome to Tire.

Later, when we consulted with colleagues who were more knowledgeable about local customs, we learned the origin of the free doughnuts. Forty days after someone dies, the family hire a doughnut maker and distribute the product, free, to anyone who is around. By eating it, consumers perform an act of worship and help to speed the departed soul on its way to heaven. The fact that we, as foreigners and presumably non-Muslims, were encouraged to participate in this ritual, is typical of Turkish tolerance and hospitality.

In the summer of that same year, a friend and I were walking through the fields near Turunç, a small, remote seaside village in the neighbourhood of Marmaris, when we came upon the fig tree. I had seen fig trees before, but this was a giant, at least eight metres tall. It rose in green splendour into the deep blue evening sky, springing miraculously from a field of dry, yellow grass, and it was laden all over with rich purple fruit. In Turkey it is always acceptable to pick and eat a sample of anyone's fruit when you pass by. This custom is called *göz hakkı*, which means "the right of the eye". So we began to scan the lowest branches, and after some searching located a ripe fig. It was delicious – soft, sweet and juicy, with a rich flavour. One or two more seemed irresistible, but they were too high up and neither of us was tall enough. While we were pointing and stretching and trying to reach, a little girl appeared, carrying a basket. She was perhaps six or seven years old, with untidy hair and a ragged skirt, and bright sparkling eyes.

"You want some?" she asked in Turkish, indicating the tree.

"Yes, please!" we said at once. Immediately she kicked off her plastic flip-flop sandals and began to climb barefoot, carrying the basket. With the easy expertise of long practice, she scrambled rapidly up among the grey branches and disappeared behind the big leaves. After a few minutes she reappeared, moving a little more cautiously as the basket was now full.

"How much?" we asked.

"One lira." It was ridiculously cheap for a whole basket of fruit, so I said to my friend,

"Let's give her two liras." We arranged to return the basket next morning, and left joyfully with our produce.

My third story is also from 1971, but later in the summer, and this time there were five of us. We were heading for Gordion, capital of the Phrygian Empire in the 8th century BC, where they made beautiful bronze cauldrons with bulls' heads on the rims. More famously, this ancient city was the home of the legendary King Midas, said to have been gifted with the "golden touch", and, half a millennium later, it was the place where Alexander the Great was said to have cut the Gordian knot.

We were all crammed into a white VW beetle, and our camping gear was tied onto the roof. When we arrived at the village after miles and miles of bumpy, twisty and dusty earth road, it was already beginning to get dark. We found a flattish patch of dead, brown grass that nobody seemed to be using at the moment, for a campsite. A division of labour was quickly agreed on; some started to put up the tents and others went to find a shop to buy food for supper. I was in the latter group and we soon found somebody to ask.

"Which way is the shop, please?" The answer came:

"Shop? We don't have a shop here."

We conferred. In our naive system of belief, villages had shops. Perhaps the woman was baffled by the speaker's foreign accent and had misunderstood the question. Perhaps she had a personal feud with the shopkeeper and didn't want him to get any business. Perhaps she was senile and didn't know. We should ask again. So we tried the next convenient inhabitant, only to receive exactly the same answer. This was distinctly worrying. In the car, I reckoned, we had half a loaf of stale bread and a couple of very squashy tomatoes. Hardly a supper for five people. And everyone was extremely hungry. The situation was getting desperate.

We decided there was nothing for it but to ask some individual to sell us a loaf, and if possible something else as well. Repeating the enquiry about the shop for the third time, and again being told there wasn't one, we made the request.

"Where are you staying?" The man answered. We indicated the tents, now two triangular boxes in the gloom fifty yards behind us.

"We'll bring you some bread. Don't worry. We'll bring it soon." There was nothing to do then but to go back and hope for the best. We arranged our sleeping bags for the night and tried to admire the moon which was beginning to shine. The bread was a long time coming, and it got really dark. Personally, I had given up hope and was preparing to face a hungry night, but I had not yet voiced this gloomy view to my companions.

And then they came. Two people, an oil lamp, and a large round tray. Bread? Yes, a big fresh loaf, neatly sliced. They had also brought a jug of water and a plastic mug. In addition, there was a large dish of yogurt, a plate of tomatoes, and a wide, flat pan full of hot fried eggs, the kind Americans call "sunny side up", with a thick golden yolk in the middle and a thin crunchy edge all round the outside. In other words, a feast. They declined to sit with us and share, saying, "No, no. It's for you. Do you need anything else? The tray? Oh, we'll get that later." And then they left. You can imagine how joyfully we tucked in, and how the moon suddenly became extremely beautiful.

We were full and sleepy when the man came back to get the tray. When we proposed payment for the dinner, he refused.

"You are guests," he said. "No money." My Turkish wasn't very advanced; I think I said:

"You are a restaurant. You must take money." But he was adamant in his refusal. Then he offered to leave us the lamp, but we had a torch so we didn't need it. We repeated our thanks and said goodnight. As the moon sailed slowly across the sky, we all slept soundly.

The last of my four traveller's tales is a recent one, from 2004. My brother and his family were visiting from Britain, and together we went to Spil Dağı, a high mountain near Manisa, in order to escape from the summer heat. It was not easy to find a nice walk on the part of the mountain where we stopped. There were too many fences, and every attractive-looking field road seemed to end abruptly at the iron gates of somebody's summer villa. The route we finally followed meandered pleasantly for some distance, affording fine views of the rolling fields and red-roofed village nearby. You could see the far-away valley full of haze, and the smoke-blue heaps of other mountains in the far distance. The grass under foot was dry and yellowing, but green leaves and wild flowers abounded at the sides of the path. It was a pretty road and we followed it happily. But then it led straight into somebody's cherry orchard. If no one had been around, we would have just eaten a few cherries and turned back. However, this time we were luckier than that.

The orchard was occupied by two young women in long, colourful skirts and big bright scarves. They had a wooden ladder and buckets, and had come to pick their cherries.

"Kolay gelsin!" We greeted them as one does all working people, "May it be easy!" We were immediately made welcome and kindly invited to eat cherries. Trees bearing different varieties were pointed out to us, and we were encouraged to pick as much as we could eat. Rich, juicy, sweet and sun-warmed, they tasted to me like the best cherries I had ever eaten.

They enquired about our various nationalities and places of residence, and we learned that the two sisters both lived in the city, but spent a month with their parents on the mountain each year to help with the cherry harvest. The elder sister was married and had a baby; the younger was aspiring to take the university entrance exam the following year. We asked her what she would like to study, and she said, "theology". Later we talked among ourselves about this surprising reply. A sad waste of talent? A brave excursion into a world of conservative men? Or was she someone who might one day make a difference in a dangerous situation, her warm good nature tipping the balance away from fanaticism and violence towards reason and tolerance?

We climbed the hill to the top of the orchard. From there, in the hazy distance, the faintest gleam of water could just be discerned: the Bay of Izmir. (On a clear day, you can just see Spil Dağı from the roof of our house, too.) On the way back we ate more cherries. Then we took some photos of the girls, one of them perched on the tall wooden ladder.

This kind of ladder must be heavy to carry, but it is the perfect shape for the job. The rungs are placed between two sides of a narrow, pointed triangle, and a single hinged pole goes down from the top of the triangle to provide additional support on the ground. In this way the ladder doesn't need to lean against a tree and it doesn't wobble when it stands on a rough field.

After expressing our thanks and farewells, we began to make our way back to the car. We were just leaving the orchard when we met the husband of the older sister, carrying a handsome little boy of perhaps 9 months on his arm. When you meet strangers in Turkey (and most of the time at family gatherings, too) men converse with men, and women with women. So now it was my husband Ali's turn to chat, and of course the two men had to smoke a cigarette together. (At all social encounters, Turkish men smoke cigarettes together. When I tried to get Ali to give up smoking, he claimed that it was a social necessity.) The child, meanwhile, regarded us with an expression of fascinated wonder.

"Maşallah", we said, "Praise God". It is very important to say this when showing any admiration for a child, otherwise they believe you may attract the attention of the Evil Eye and bring harm to him. We were invited to eat more cherries, and when we said that we had already consumed as many as possible, the young man insisted that we take some with us. Had we got a plastic bag? We had. So he filled it from their bucket, and then, with more thanks and goodbyes, we finally left. The cherries were eaten in a few days, but the kindness of the family on the mountain is something none of us will ever forget.

My next story is about a kindness assumed and a misunderstanding. This happened in the mid-1980s, after I was married and settled in Turkey. My husband and I possessed a holiday house near Dikili which we sometimes let to foreign visitors in the summer. Arrangements were complicated by the fact that we were usually in Britain when the visitors were there, and none of the neighbours spoke English. One year, our friends Ted and Mary, who had never been to Turkey before, decided to rent this house.

We met them when they arrived at the airport, drove them over there and left them at the house, jet-lagged and a little bewildered. I had prepared a file full of instructions and suggestions in English, in my best handwriting, and put up informative notices all over the house. Things like, "To avoid mosquitoes, please only open screened windows," or "Unfortunately Turkish plumbing cannot cope with toilet paper. Please use the bin provided." And so on. Anyway, we left them alone to digest all this as well as they could, and two days later we flew to Britain.

Ted and Mary later expressed themselves well-pleased with their holiday. There were only a few little inconveniences in the house; one lampshade had fallen down, the frying pan was a bit small, a few more pegs to hang up clothes would be a good idea. But the beach, the weather and the neighbours were all wonderful. The neighbours Mustafa and Sezgi had been so kind, they had invited them out for a trip in their car. They went all the way to the lovely old seaside town of Ayvalık, where they had lunch together and walked around the streets among the old houses. It was a delightful day.

After returning to Turkey we met up with Mustafa and Sezgi. "How nice of you to take our friends out!", we exclaimed cheerfully. "They had such a good time!". But it was at once clear from their faces that something was wrong. Sezgi began angrily, "They never paid us!" Mustafa added grimly, "They didn't even pay for the lunch, much less the petrol."

We asked if they had arranged a price for the outing. They had not. Had they said anything about paying for petrol, or lunch? They had not. It wasn't, they thought, polite to discuss money. Wasn't it obvious that they expected payment? Why else would they have offered to take the foreigners to Ayvalık?

Gradually the background to the misunderstanding emerged. A couple of days before the Ayvalık trip, Ted and Mary had asked Gökhan, the village taxi-driver who was recommended in my suggestions file, to take them to see the famous ancient ruins of Bergama. Gökhan did this graciously and efficiently, asking a fee that he thought the evidently prosperous foreigners could easily afford. Sezgi had seen the taxi arrive to fetch them, and later asked Mary where they had gone. She also asked what they had paid Gökhan. That was actually the beginning of the problem, because Mustafa thought the fee excessive, and was filled with righteous indignation that our guests had been ripped off. No doubt it also occurred to him that here was an easy way of having some fun and making a little extra money at the same time. Accordingly, he approached Ted next morning, pointed his finger firmly to his own chest and said something like:

"Me taxi. No Gökhan. Ayvalık? Ten? (pointing to his watch)." The offer of transport was clear, but it was not surprising that Ted missed the intended implication of "Me taxi."

Our British friends had no way of knowing that a couple of hours worth of petrol, or the cost of meatballs and salad for four people, might be a significant expense to these middle-class retirees. They just assumed that they had nothing else to do and were taking them out for the fun of it.

Because I am British, I felt it was up to me to do whatever damage control I could. I tried hard to explain what Ted and Mary's point of view must have been. I told them that they should have set a clear price when they made the proposal, and I offered to pay the expenses out of the rent we had received, which they declined. In the end, I think they saw their mistake, but they still thought the foreign visitors were very peculiar people.

My final story is about some other people who got things right, but this time the kind ones were the Brits and it was a Turkish girl called Selin who benefitted. It happened like this.

Ian and Moira came from Scotland, where they had a business in antique books. Some time before we met them, they had made their first trip to Turkey and fallen in love with it. From then on it was twice a year, usually spring and autumn. They were enterprising travellers, hiring a car and exploring new parts of the country each time, staying in simple guesthouses wherever they found themselves. Then, one day, they met Selin. She was then fourteen or so, with a mane of black hair tied behind her head and sparkling brown eyes. She approached them on the street of the small town where she lived, and inquired:

"You speak English?" On receiving a positive answer, she continued enthusiastically:

"I study English my school. You make holiday? Turkey good, yes?" The conversation continued for a while, and then Selin asked them to have tea at her house, which they accepted. Selin's mother was round and smiling, with colourful baggy trousers, a headscarf and some missing teeth. They sat on low couches, with cushions against the wall for their backs, while the tea was served, hot and dark, in little glasses, with lumps of sugar to add. They put the glasses on a round copper tray supported by folding legs. Selin had not been learning English very long, but she was eager to practise and quite successful at communicating. Ian and Moira learned that her father worked as a watchman at a factory, that the sitting room was where Selin and her two sisters slept at night, that they had a small TV but no telephone, and that Selin was going to high school next year and dreamed eventually of university. Before they left, Selin asked Moira and Ian if she might write to them, and they exchanged addresses.

Some months later, after several letters had gone back and forth, Selin wrote sadly that she would have to leave school. "My father is ill." She reported. "He cannot work. We have no money for books, or bus fares. We are very sad." Quickly Ian wrote to Selin, offering to help. Then he telephoned me, to discuss what might be appropriate, and how to transfer some money. A system existed whereby you could send money orders from one post office to another; it was used by people who did not have bank accounts. Simple. Ian wrote a cheque for fifty pounds, and paid it into my bank account in Scotland. I took fifty pounds' worth of Turkish liras to my local post office, stood in line for forty minutes, filled in a complicated form, and sent a money order in Selin's name to the post office nearest her home. It worked. Selin stayed on at school, and got top marks. Her father got better, but the family had many problems, and Ian's contributions became a regular occurrence. He and Moira visited Selin and her family again, were given a meal and made to stay the night. Selin had got taller, and her English was more advanced.

Selin got her university place, and studied computer engineering. With her new status she was able to acquire a bank account and a credit card, so I no longer had to queue up at the post office to send her money. Instead, Ian could do this direct from Scotland. He and Moira continued their help until after her graduation, and she is now happily established in the office of a major corporation.

These are my stories. Nowadays, many thousands of visitors come to Turkey every year, most on organised tours that offer sun, sand and English breakfast, with perhaps a trip to Ephesus thrown in. But for more adventurous travellers, the real Turkey still waits, warm and welcoming, full of fascinating places and delightful people.

Flights and Tickets

Home is where the heart is, or so the songwriters would have us believe. If you have lived in another country for a long time, you may start to wonder just exactly where 'home' is. However you feel about it, you will probably have a yen to see the 'old' country from time to time.

In my first job in Turkey, it didn't occur to me that my employer might pay for a plane ticket to the UK, so my journeys remained flights of fancy.

In fact many educational institutions include such provisions in their contracts for foreign staff, the most generous giving a yearly entitlement, regardless of the distances involved.

In my second job, the school had a large number of foreigners from all over the world. The entitlement to plane tickets was reduced to once every three years. Flying people annually to Australia, the United States or Canada was deemed too expensive. I was still happy to have any help at all and so accepted gracefully.

After three years of employment, a number of us decided to exercise our rights. First, one had to pay for the ticket, go and come back and then claim the fare from the school. A number of teachers grumbled about credit card bills and interest accrued. I was just happy to be going to London!

On my return, with a fellow teacher, I approached the administration to enquire as to the correct procedure for claims. We were passed from office to office without getting any satisfactory reply. I began to smell a rat. While some got their refund easily, my colleague and I were summoned to see the owner and director of the school. Here we were subjected to the third degree. My friend's 'crime' was to have flown via Switzerland, surely not the cheapest route. As for me, I had had the audacity to present a ticket without a price on it!

"I can't pay you for that!" he thundered.

"Why not?"

"Because it's not tax deductible."

This man was a multimillionaire with a thriving business at his fingertips. I on the other hand needed the money rather urgently. Discretion was the better part of valour and I withdrew promising to get a quote from a travel agent. I was only claiming the standard fare!

He finally agreed to think it over. In the end we got our money but our 'punishment' was to wait three months for reimbursement. When the payment was finally made the director said he was fed up with dealing with all our claims ad hoc and would institute a proper procedure for dealing with it.

He was even considering getting the school to buy all our tickets in the first place: just what we had been asking for!

Forewarned by this experience, I was ready to fight my corner when joining my current school. They too had long experience of employing foreign teachers. After experimenting with different systems, they had reached the eminently sensibly decision to pay us all a flat bonus once a year. It was up to us how to spend the money. This certainly seems to suit the current staff but if we ever have Americans or Canadians I suppose they may feel a little hard done by.

Water Jug

Before people had modern plumbing, a jug like this was used to hold water for washing. In daily life throughout Turkey there is a nice tradition of offering to pour water or cologne for visitors to wash their hands.

4 - Everyday Life

Early Days in Ankara

1) Arrivals Terminal

As I look back on that first day in Turkey, I see myself standing, leaning against the wall outside arrivals. The grey concrete of the Ankara terminal seems to be all around, reflected in the cloudy, overcast sky and the drab colours of rumpled business suits fluttering around me like birds, as people hurry to their taxis or shuttles or expectant relatives, friends and drivers.

Only I am motionless, waiting. Wondering incessantly what I have done, why I have packed up six bags of varying shapes, sizes and durability to come to this place of unknowns.

How long will my sentence be?

I feel it as a self-imposed sentence, since my gut instinct knew I had to accept the offer, the door which opened to release me from another grey world – although it was a world permeated with flashes of vibrant colour from time to time; a world which spoke of creativity in many directions for myself as well as the different groups I worked with.

I feel lonely as a tree in the middle of a bustling world of purpose. The people rushing off (homeward bound?) are filled with the energy of direction and meaningful existence.

Only I am waiting, left discarded and unnoticed by the hurrying grey figures – now like bats swarming to an unseen light, while I remain in the shadows.

My roots and trunk are strong. I am content, for now, to wait.

I know I will be collected eventually, and I feel my purpose is here – although I still do not know why or how I came to uproot myself from such a deeply-embedded comfort zone as London.

London, a beautiful, rich tapestry of sights, sounds and scents full of extensive memories to be explored and lingered over... but now far away and becoming greyer in my mind.

A finished tapestry put away on a high shelf, the cupboard door closing.

My purpose is here now.

What purpose? Why? How?

Be patient, all will reveal itself step by step. Be here, be now. Just wait. They are coming.

I see a small pale face framed with dark shoulder-length hair, further along the wall, peering, searching. Our eyes meet, and connect.

My heart says, "I know you, my sister!"

She turns away and hurries back along the wall to the far end of the empty greyness.

Less hustle and bustle now. Only a few birds (no longer bats) are scurrying to the last remaining cars and taxis. A sense of calm is beginning to settle on the scene, yet I feel even more alone and unwanted, totally out of place in this world of dark colours, dark faces, dark groups clumped together and united in their sense of belonging – their purpose is clear, as a whole. Individuals are ignored or regarded with suspicion and a lack of comprehension.

"What is she doing here?" I feel them asking each other, "and alone?"

I feel a terrible, aching loneliness inside my strong tree trunk. I reassure it. I am okay. I will always be OK. I can survive... anything... even alone. I will find my way. Be patient. Be calm.

"ROS!" A sharp cry pierces my protective cloud, and a tiny woman appears before me, followed by several other dark female faces.

"INCI!" I cry.

"We have been looking everywhere for you," a torrent of words rushes out from her as we take or shake hands and register each other's faces.

"We didn't know if you were at the international terminal down there, or the domestic one. We have been running backwards and forwards between, trying to find you! Come on, the car is over here. This is Tijan and Yaprak, and Seda – she will be your assistant."

We are hurrying across to another grey area, now lightening and clearing, and discernible as a car park, my bags distributed among the group of dark females with silent formal faces, following their leader, Inci, my new boss.

And I look into two dark pools in a paler face with shoulder length black hair framing her beauty, and an understanding at some level passes between my spiritual sister and I.

I do not know this grey place or these people, my task or my path. I feel isolated and slightly fearful, apprehensive of my future daily life now beginning with these first steps to the car.

Yet, as I recognise something in Seda's eyes, my fragile heart knows inside that I am home.

2) Day Two

I woke the next day groggy from tiredness and the stuffiness of the heating system. The radiator was boiling hot and seemed permanently fixed in the 'on' position, whereas windows seemed to be sealed shut with years of grime and crumbling putty. Outside all was grey, with noisy young figures constantly crossing a grey playground square to enter and exit another dun coloured concrete square block. There seemed to be a uniform lack of colour, everyone dressed in dark blues, browns, black, punctuated with the odd red sweatshirt and tracksuit. A couple of trees almost devoid of their last brown leaves stood wearily in their square and empty beds. I let the dingy net curtain drop back and looked around my room, or rather my quarters, taking in the huge carved wooden wardrobe and the enormous dresser, also wooden but with a heavy marble table top and a gigantic oval mirror, the whole supported on spindly wooden legs. The size of the furniture and the darkness of the wood made it all look as if it belonged to a giant in a fairy story, something out of a dark forgotten era. I hoped I would be able to find my own flat before too long.

The university had allowed me to stay in the department for now, until my papers were sorted, work permit organised and salary coming through. My new boss, Head of the Ballet Department for the State Conservatoire, had found me a room in their section, next door to the teachers' tea room. I could hear the tinkling sound of spoons stirring tea, the scraping of chairs and the rise and fall of excited voices discussing something, punctuated by shouts and cries – probably greetings – as another teacher entered the room.

The language appeared to have no beginning or end to words, and sounded to me at that time rather like Welsh, with its rising and falling cadences. I certainly couldn't understand a single word. Later I was to be grateful for being completely immersed in the sound of Turkish voices, as this early training in the tones, intonation and cadence was to train my ears in the 'integral music' of the language and help enormously when I finally plucked up courage to plunge in and try to speak in Turkish.

I pulled on my tracksuit and socks and forayed out to the bathroom, ignoring the surprised stares of students and teachers alike and closing my ears to all sounds unless I could make out something that sounded like a 'good morning' or 'hello' type of remark or face. The teachers' loos were outside the cosy department corridor and along a much wider stretch of dark pink marble. I had been given a key to the loos on arrival the night before, so I felt quite brave and purposeful as I passed the stares and comments of young girls and boys variously dressed in tights and leotards and obviously getting ready for morning class. To an outsider they probably looked more bizarre than I did.

The loos themselves were protected by a flimsy plywood door, with many jagged holes and marks where it must have been kicked and battered as these lively and excited students squealed and generally ran amok in the corridor.

Inside was a large stone-floored room, no carpet or comforts and no hand towel in sight. There were three stalls, all of them 'hole in the floor' types which I had fortunately encountered before on trips to France in my early twenties. These ones had little taps beside them, with a rather grimy looking plastic jug under the taps. There was no toilet paper. (It took me several years before I finally worked out how to effectively employ the items provided.) There was also no soap on the wash basins. I later saw other members of staff carrying the necessary items in their handbags when they made similar trips along that corridor.

I felt like an alien in an alien world as I trudged back along the corridor, alone in a bubble of my own foreign world. I kept my head held high and tried to look both cool and purposeful as I nearly bolted back into my room and shut the door, wondering what I should do next, and if there was any sign outside of anyone I had met last night. Glancing over at the enormous dresser I saw that someone had been in my room while I was out for those few minutes.

There was a small carton of milk and a kind of bun thing in a piece of plain paper beside it. My heart melted as I realised that someone was indeed keeping an eye on me, and there must be a friendly angel out there waiting for me to get up and make an entrance to their society.

I knew instinctively that it was Seda.

Sensing that the chatter and tinkling teaspoon sounds were abating I felt it might be time to venture out and find someone who could tell me what I was supposed to be doing that day. Maybe Seda was in the tea room. Perhaps the morning break was over and teachers and pianists were going back to their studios for the second class or second group of students to take morning ballet class – a daily necessity for all dancers worldwide, and also somewhat reminiscent of taking confessional, with one's sins of the previous evenings' overindulgence plainly visible in the mirror along with one's reduced flexibility of movement.

Seda was indeed in the tea room, and the last pianist was scuttling off to class with her sheaf of music notes, bidding me a brief 'Good morning and welcome' in clipped English. I was already nervous about the possibility of teaching that day as nobody had given me any instructions at all, but Seda just smiled sweetly and told me not to worry. This was not a very reassuring answer but I smiled back weakly and tried to be patient. Eventually somebody would tell me what I was supposed to be doing, I presumed.

Meanwhile it was time to sample my very first glass of Turkish tea.

Shopping Stories

Wherever you live, it is sometimes necessary to go shopping. If you live in a foreign country, acquiring the things you need brings contact with local people and may be a challenge to your language skills.

Turkey, like other countries, has several kinds of retail outlets. There are supermarkets, department stores, corner shops, open-air markets and street sellers. Supermarkets are almost the same everywhere, so I won't bother with them. Department stores are a little different in Turkey, as the following story will show.

It was an important wedding and I needed to be suitably dressed. I possessed a nice hand-embroidered skirt, but I needed a top to go with it. So I went with my daughter to a department store. There were sales in progress, so prices were low but the crowds were thick. Our first choice was a soft, cream-coloured, knitted top. It was labelled extra large, but looked about right. (I am definitely not extra large). Anyway, we pushed our way through a great confusion of displays and shoppers to the ladies' trying-on area. There was a row of alcoves with curtains in front, all closed, and several women were waiting out in front. On the wall opposite the alcoves was an enormous mirror. Watching the women in the queue ahead of me, I understood this very un-British system; when you had put on a potential purchase, you left your own clothes in the alcove and came out in front to look in the mirror and get advice from your friends. Meanwhile others could use your changing-space, adding to the confusion already inside it. There was nowhere to put anything except a few hooks on the wall, and they were already overloaded with other shoppers' personal possessions and potential purchases. While I was waiting for my turn to try on the new garment, my daughter went back to the rails to see what else she could find. When I finally got into an alcove, the extra large item turned out to be far too tight. But my helper had found something else, in two different sizes, and the bigger one was fine. I tried it on, she approved, and we were both satisfied.

It remained to actually make the purchase. We went together to the pay queue, where a few minutes waiting and a little calculation indicated that the process would take at least half an hour. So I sent my daughter off on her way. I adjusted the positions of my shoulder-bag and heavy unwanted jacket (outside it was cold, so I would need it to go home), pulled up my sleeves as far as possible, and settled down to stand and wait in the stuffy heat. The queue in front melted very slowly, and I began to think about my fellow shoppers. They were almost all female, between 35 and 55, dyed blonde and gloomy-looking. Shouldn't they be cheerful, exalting in their new-found bargains? They bought not just a few items each, but vast armfuls of clothes. Each individual purchase had to be entered separately on the store computer, which explained the slowness of the queue. I began to feel sorry for these women; they had a desperate look about them, as if all they had ever had was youth and beauty, and as it faded, there was nothing left in life. Was this manic shopping for clothes a desperate attempt to stay young a little longer?

My next category is corner shops (which really are almost always on corners). They flourish in Turkey, even in this age of supermarkets. To provide them with customers, there are still a few stay-at-home housewives, there are people who don't own cars, and there are hungry kids going to and from school. Besides, everybody in the neighbourhood wants fresh bread and daily newspapers.

In the 1970s when I first arrived in Turkey, corner shops sold little beyond tea and sugar, candles and soap. Nowadays you can get long-life milk, stock cubes, tinned peas, packets of raisins, potatoes and onions, all the worst kinds of confectionery, washing-up detergent, bleach, drain cleaner... you name it. Often there is cheese and ice cream as well. Sometimes they have a licence to sell beer and raki.

The corner shop is more than a supplier of goods. It is a focus point for the community, a reason for exercise and fresh air, a place to meet neighbours, a place to air one's views and frustrations. Shopkeepers, *bakkallar,* are usually friendly and sympathetic people, characteristics that contribute to their success. Here are a couple of stories about me and my local corner shop.

I had slept too late and woke up with a headache, sleepy and cross. The deserted kitchen table was spotted with milk and jam, the family had all gone out, and a scribbled note informed me that I had to buy bread and feed the dog. Simmering with annoyance at these unwanted tasks, I collected my keys and money and went out to buy a loaf.

The first person I met was Crazy Ali. *Bilseydim, gelmezdim,* he informed me in ringing tones. "If I had known, I wouldn't have come." That had been his refrain for years as he walked the streets, telling everybody. Whether he was referring to this earthly life, of merely to the particular street he happened to be walking on, no one knew. In spite of my bad mood I had to smile and say hullo.

A little further on there was a neighbour working in her garden. Her daughter and my daughter had been great friends at primary school, so I had to stop and say *Kolay gelsin,* which means "May it be easy", the standard greeting for anyone at work. We then enquired politely into each other's state of health before going on to exchange news about daughters.

The little round *bakkal,* the shopkeeper, had bright eyes and a warm smile. Bread? Yes, of course. How were the children? Had we had a good holiday? Was it cold in England? We had a nice chat before I left.

Passing the dustbin on the way home, I met another neighbour emptying her rubbish. More exchanges. This one enquired about my mother, whom she had once met, and I asked after her family.

After twenty minutes I was home and feeding the grateful, tail-wagging dog. I had had four friendly conversations. My headache was gone and the messy table did not matter anymore. Cheerfully I put the kettle on to make a mug of tea.

Now, here's the second story.

One day my German neighbour was in the shop. We had each heard much of the other from the *bakkal,* but never actually met before. There were enthusiastic introductions. Then the shopkeeper regarded us both thoughtfully, and said: "Why did you come all this way? Don't they have husbands in your countries?" The German lady was quick to reply: "Don't they have wives in Turkey?"

Open-air markets are the mainstay of fresh produce retail in Turkey, and are held on different days of the week in different districts. Many sellers buy wholesale and move from one market location to another as the week progresses. Small producers take their own goods to the nearest market whenever they have enough to sell. Thus you may find a stand with bananas from South America next to another with tomatoes from a garden down the road. In spring there are wild vegetables and herbs gathered on the nearby hills. In winter, tangerines and oranges dominate the fruit stands; in summer, peaches, grapes and melons. The customers are as varied as the produce. There are country women in scarves and long skirts and plastic sandals, city ladies with smart hairdos and expensive dresses, and women with ankle-length coats and heads wrapped up carefully to hide every strand of hair. Among men the clothes vary less but the mentalities are just as mixed.

To such a market I arrived one day with two cars full of British visitors. One of them was the delightful Samantha, just nineteen, a university student, slim and blond and picture-pretty. Before exploring the market we sat down for refreshment at the corner teahouse, and only then I noticed. Samantha was wearing extremely short shorts. At any seaside resort she would have been just one more pretty girl, but in a big city market she would stand out most unsuitably. People would stare, especially men. Worse, some of them would touch. It was no use being angry with myself for not noticing her clothes when we left home; I had to do something to avoid unpleasantness.

First, I explained gently. She exclaimed, "You could have told me!"

The hard part for me was facing this entirely justifiable indignation. The easy part was the practical solution. I left Samantha safely hidden behind a teahouse table and surrounded by friends. Quickly I walked past the colourful displays of fruit and vegetables to the clothing section. There I found a rail of long, mud-coloured skirts for conservative ladies: all greys, browns and black. A hand-written notice above the display said 5TL, which was about two pounds in UK currency. I selected the least ugly offering, paid for it, and dashed back to the teahouse.

Samantha regarded the item doubtfully.

"How can I change?"

"You don't. Just put the skirt on top."

We finished our tea and started to tour the market. Samantha cheered up, got out her camera, and ended up taking many of the best photographs of the day.

The last in my categories of retail are the street sellers. There used to be a lot more of them than there are now. When I was first in Turkey, most women stayed at home during the day, so there were plenty of potential customers. The sellers plied their trades with donkeys and hand-barrows and bicycle-carts, and advertised in ringing, rhythmic voices. In the course of a morning you could buy pots of yogurt and plastic sandals, bowls of pudding and leather belts, candy floss and cotton underwear.

Nowadays I live in a suburb where the population is more spread out, and many women as well as men are out at work in the daytime. There are still some street sellers, but they are more likely to have a motor vehicle and a scratchy loudspeaker to advertise their goods. I find them intrusive and rarely buy from them.

My all-time favourite street seller was the grape-man who came down from the hills with his donkey. The walk from the village must have taken him two or three hours. He would come about once a week during the autumn, when the grapes were ripe, with a wooden crate balanced on each side of the donkey. The white grapes were on one side, the black ones on the other. He did not knock on doors, but waited on the street calling out *taze üzüm,* ("fresh grapes"), while the donkey searched the ground for bits of melon peel or tufts of dry grass.

Customers appeared with plates and baskets to carry their fruit. (There were no plastic bags in those days.) The purchases were weighed out on a pair of scales which the seller held up in one hand; on one pan was a single 1kg weight, and on the other he put the grapes to balance it. If you wanted several kilos, they were weighed out one at a time. If you wanted half a kilo, he would weigh out one and then divide it, half and half between the scale pans, without using the weight. In this way customers got just what they wanted, and the donkey had only one kilogram weight to carry, in addition to the grapes and the scales.

I always bought two kilos. The grapes were wonderful, sun-warmed and fresh, sweet and crisp and full of juice. They had been picked in the early morning when the sun was low, and came down to our coastal settlement by the age-old means of transport that needed no engine and no asphalt and produced no pollution. This man's ancestors could have been doing the same thing centuries ago.

Around big cities such picturesque customs have largely disappeared, but visitors who venture into small towns and villages in Anatolia can find them still, with minor differences. The seller will certainly provide plastic bags and probably chat on his mobile phone between customers, but donkeys are still around. The real Turkish countryside is still out there to be discovered.

Cleaning Ladies

For a long time, I resisted having a cleaning lady. Despite having a full-time job, a husband, two children and two homes, I guarded my privacy fiercely.

"She's not coming in my room!" was my son's constant refrain.

"Suppose she steals my things," added my daughter. Naturally, they did not think of offering more than token help with the domestic chores!

A somewhat overweight colleague once asked me how I stayed slim.

"Do you do a sport?" she asked. When I told her that I had a flat and a house to clean, her jaw dropped open. I began to feel that I was being unnecessarily masochistic.

My husband took matters into his own hands and found a willing neighbour to clean our summer house. My mother-in-law was appointed to supervise. Her orders reflected her dim view of my standards, so the hapless cleaner was set to scrubbing from top to bottom, with plenty of bleach.

Cleaners in Turkey are usually employed at daily rather than hourly rate. While some have a regular arrangement, many cleaners are engaged for the one-off, like a spring clean or after moving house. I had no intention of paying for a spring clean once a month, never mind once a week.

The cleaner lived nearby, in what I can only describe as a shack, with her drunken husband and small daughter. She was delighted to have the chance to earn some money and set to with a vengeance. On the third day I got a call: "The washing machine has been on for four hours but it hasn't stopped yet. What shall I do?" Thanking her profusely for all her efforts, I enjoined her to pull out the plug and go home for a well-earned rest.

The following weekend we arrived. First, having unlocked the outer door, in fear and trepidation, I saw that the inner door was stuck. When I finally managed to open it, I saw the carpet rolled up, acting as a very effective doorstop. How had she made her escape? Did we have a budding Houdini on our hands?

Such speculation was swiftly cut short as I surveyed the scene. Every piece of furniture had been moved. The tiled floor had been scrubbed very clean but there were splashes of bleach on the walls and on the coal-burning stove. My cupboards had been emptied and the contents rearranged, the beds remade with blankets long buried deep in cupboards.

In short, I scarcely recognised my own house. It took me two full days to restore order. My accompanying curses led my husband to accuse me of gross ingratitude. I pleaded guilty: I was furious. Needless to say, I never asked her again.

When my children had flown from the nest, I was confident I could cope on the domestic front but two slipped discs left me flat on my back and weak as a kitten, so cleaner mark two arrived.

She was from Diyarbakır, in the South-East, had three small children and was squatting in a newly-built but unsold house on a nearby housing estate. She obeyed my commands and cleaned dutifully. "No cupboards please," I pleaded. She never laid a finger on a single one. Then her husband contracted TB. She spent her wages on honey and nourishing food for him. Eventually they returned home, in the hope of speeding his recovery.

Next on the scene was Ayşe, another Easterner but as bubbly and loquacious as her predecessor had been taciturn. Her cleaning was efficient enough and we got on fine until I received an unusually high phone bill, listing calls to her home city. After a warning and an apology from her, she desisted from calling her relatives but she moved away.

So I went to my local grocer and asked him if he knew anybody in the neighbourhood.

Kadriye arrived in her headscarf and bringing her small son as her chaperone. All went reasonably well until one day she came when my son happened to be home asleep. When I got home, I asked him what time the cleaner had left.

"What cleaning lady?" he said. I had suspected that she was less than thorough but this proved that she was in the habit of leaving after two to three hours, clutching a full day's pay.

At last we struck gold. Fehime was a *soydaş,* one of that unfortunate band of ethnic Turks, summarily deported from Bulgaria in the early 1990s. She was honest, hardworking and thorough. She would come to breakfast on her appointed day and relate tales of her life and the family left behind in Bulgaria. She worked hard to provide her three children with a good start in life and to complete her house here. We chewed the fat and discussed the state of the world. She was uneducated but had learned a lot from the trials of life. It was sometimes hard for me to escape from the breakfast table but she started her chores willingly once I left for work.

We only had one problem: 'no cupboards' to her included the fridge. In Turkish fridge is 'an ice cupboard' so she never even wiped the exterior surface.

Over the years, she continued to come fortnightly from September to June, leaving me to look after myself over the summer break. Then one day, not for the first time, she asked me if my married daughter had a baby yet. This question may seem a little personal but is commonly asked in this culture. When I replied in the negative, she started a tirade about the need to start your family young or the mother would have no rapport with the child. As I was 29 when my own daughter was born and had suffered no such problems, I saw red and told her that I thought it was nonsense.

Perhaps I was less than polite but we parted company on that day.

Now, living alone, I do my own housework once again and do not find it too arduous a task. I hope for continued good health but who knows who cleaner mark five will be?

Dirt Squad – An Insecure Life

Although cleaning ladies may be a prolific breed, their characters are widely variable. My neighbours and I once shared one we had to nickname 'The Terminator', because nothing electrical worked after she had made her rounds that day. She usually managed to disconnect every plug and point encountered, either by pulling them out or by altering the contact somehow, making a loose connection. This was maddening for my neighbours as they would come home to find their computer was 'down' again.

Another one would diligently clean the flat and even feed my cats when I was away, until I got the phone bill and discovered she had been calling home, very long distance, and chatting away to her mother and relatives. After a long deliberation with my conscience (cleaning ladies are hard to find and generally earn a pittance for long hours of scrubbing) I decided to challenge her about this bill. She quickly denied it so we reached a stalemate. More deliberations with my conscience led me to show the bill, - which fortunately was itemised - to her husband, our 'doorman' or caretaker (*kapıcı* in Turkish*)*. I pointed out the numbers I did not recognise and his face went white with shock and anger. He didn't know what to say, but was adamant that they would now have to leave this *site* (meaning 'private housing estate') and job because of the shame and scandal his wife had brought upon them. Hastily reassuring him that there was no need to inform anyone else about this we agreed that he would pay off the amount owed by monthly installments. Unfortunately I later heard that this mild mannered and considerate *kapıcı* then hit her that night, so I felt terrible at having been the unwitting instigator of his anger. I wondered if I should really have said anything at all. Needless to say, she never cleaned for me again and I had to find another 'cat sitter' too.

It was after this event that the 'terminator' arrived, and despite her regular destruction of electrical conduits we got along well enough for a few years until I moved house again.

Terminator was young – about 28 –and had a small son who had a slight physical disability so she sometimes brought him with her if she was cleaning for me in the mornings, as his school 'shift' started in the afternoons. Terminator could fit in several 'clients' a day, doing a few hours here and there to supplement her husband's small salary as a factory worker.

I must add here that a reasonable grasp of Turkish is essential if one is to get on at all well with one's cleaning lady. My first experience of such a marvellous helper had been in Ankara when my Swiss friend and colleague recommended her cleaning lady, Habibe, to me.

Habibe was probably in her mid-fifties with snowy white hair under her traditional headscarf. She would prattle away to me in fairly incomprehensible Turkish while I would struggle to get the gist of it. She was really like a warm-hearted aunty or granny, and would insist I go back to bed with a cup of tea when she arrived before 8am so that she could start on the kitchen and other rooms. In other words, keeping me out of the way. This suited us both. However, I was a little put out when she arrived at a later hour one day and immediately asked if she could watch the TV. Apparently it was 'her soap opera' that she would be missing that day. I grudgingly agreed and felt that I was really being used this time, but sure enough, after thirty minutes she switched it off happily and began her work, explaining it was a crucial part of the story and she hadn't wanted to miss it. A TV addict myself (for hospital dramas) I had to admit I quite understood. It never happened again and when I asked her why she didn't want to turn on the TV at 10am any more she breezily replied that that particular soap had finished now.

Habibe lived in a *gece kondu* – a shanty town, or slum region, somewhere nearby on the hills. I gave her a lift home one day and dropped her off in an area of scrubland with small bungalow-style dwellings which looked rather ramshackle. As it is traditional to give one's cleaning lady a set of clothes to work in at the start of her 'contract' I had given her an old track suit of mine which she'd said would be just fine. I'd also given her a nice long blue knitted cardigan which a close friend had made for me years before. I'd practically lived in it and it was getting worn out. Habibe had admired it and I thought it would help keep her warm in the long winters there.

It lasted a week at her place.

Apparently she had washed it and hung it out to dry and someone in their neighbourhood had stolen it. How could that happen, I'd wondered aloud, and where had she hung it to dry?

"Oh we don't have washing lines," she'd said, "so I spread it out on the bushes outside." Enough said.

Today, hundreds of miles away from Ankara and my first cleaning lady, I am watching, somewhat concerned, as my cleaning lady Lütfiye balances precariously outside the window, perched on a narrow ledge in her socks and Turkish pantaloons as she attacks the window with vigour.

It has always concerned me that cleaning ladies do not earn 'danger money', nor even get paid social security or holiday pay. Theirs is a secret world of householders' cleaning and ironing, hours and days arranged informally and subject to the whims of the lady of the house.

You may well find this particular householder to be cruel and heartless, sending her cleaner out onto a parapet, but believe me, I have even brought extendable cleaning mops from the UK, and tried to get her to use them from inside the house. She says she prefers to do it her way as she's used to it and does a better job that way.

In summer, my poor cleaning lady stays home and waits for the telephone to ring in the autumn. However, if she is lucky, someone will ring her and take her to clean their holiday home. They may keep her overnight there while she scrubs floors and cleans the winter grime off the windows. She may even be lucky enough to do this again at the end of the summer, and these occasional jobs keep her going through the hottest months of the year. She has no other source of income, as her husband doesn't work due to ill health and she has no certified training of any other kind. She is now over 60 so other employment opportunities are unlikely.

They were forced to leave their home in Bulgaria during the 'troubles' there, and came with what they could carry to Turkey. This was maybe fifteen years ago, but they have only just been granted Turkish residency enabling them to get Turkish passports. This means that they have not been entitled to sickness benefit or a pension, and can only now start the long bureaucratic procedures involved in winning these rights. One can only speculate on the kind of life they lead and how they make ends meet, knowing that this situation is not unusual. Thousands of Turkish families are also living on the bread line with no welfare state to provide for them. Supplementary benefits such as single parent allowances, housing benefit, unemployment benefit and so on are not an option in Turkey. They simply don't exist.

Lütfiye calls me from the back room; she has finished the windows and wants to know if I'd like the garden weeding, while she is there. Garden? It hardly qualifies for such a grand name, as it is only a patch of earth outside the back door, but by the time I reach her she has almost finished tidying it up and gives me a big smile of satisfaction. These ladies are worth their weight in gold.

The Hamam

After a week in Ankara a major problem came to the fore: regular hot water.

My 'bed-sitter' in the ballet department, sandwiched between the Tea Room and the Costumes Room, and opposite my boss's office, had only a rudimentary shower: a pipe with no shower nozzle in a sort of shower closet with concrete walls and an enamel floor tray. Every once in a while – officially three times a week, but not running strictly to timetable – hot water would spout out of this pipe, provided the water had not been cut off again that day.

Water shortages are a national problem, and most people face a cut supply now and then, if not on a regular basis. I found that the water was usually cut off after heavy rainfall, when roads were muddy and one was constantly splashed by passing cars. One was not safe anywhere on the pavements, with badly-fitting paving stones giving way under foot and spattering one with murky water. Just the time when one wanted and needed a hot bath and some means of washing one's mud-spattered clothes.

We heard about the Hamam, or Turkish Bath, from the owner of the dry-cleaning shop – a friendly gentleman who spoke excellent English with an American accent. He told my friend and I that he had worked for Polly Peck in Cyprus. His shop also did one's washing and used to deliver it freshly ironed and wrapped in brown paper, in the arms of a small boy who brought it to my room in the ballet department.

We were told that the hamam was just up the road and duly set off with our wash bags.

About a mile later we found it: a dirtyish looking building with the word 'Hamam' on it, and some notice about times. Apparently ladies' washing days were Tuesday, Thursday and Saturday, from 12 to 5pm. Other days and evenings it was used by the gentlemen.

We didn't know what to expect, or what to bring or wear even, and we still had only a few words of Turkish between us. Assuming it would be like a sauna we'd brought a towel and some soap and shampoo in our washbags, so we bravely knocked on the locked door.

We were ushered in, not understanding very much, and sent through to a corridor with rows of cubicles and stairs leading down at the end. Presumably we were being instructed to get ready and then go on down into the basement. The cubicles all had lockable doors, a plastic couch and some rather grimy looking black plastic slippers. We hurriedly discussed how much to disrobe and decided to strip down to our knickers and wrap our towels tightly around us.

Stepping hesitantly out of the door, we were assailed by a large wailing figure at the end of the corridor, arms outstretched and jabbering away in Turkish, which couldn't understand. She looked like a tall Native American

Indian woman, long black hair to her waist, brown/olive skin, dark flashing eyes and clad only in a large baggy pair of black knickers. She was smiling and chattering away so we understood that this was a friendly greeting, like an elderly grandmother welcoming us with her arms wide to embrace us – rather unnerving we thought, but we followed her downstairs, donning a pair of the over-large black plastic slippers which were thrust at us. We couldn't answer any of her continuous questions as we followed her through the main bathing area, so she gestured for us to go through a tiny sliding door into a cubbyhole which we realised was the sauna. It smelt awful. We later realised that the smell emanated from a bowl of mustard-coloured gunge which was evidently used for waxing legs and other unwanted hair.

We crouched on the wooden slatted benches and slowly heated up, light dawning on us that that was the aim, to warm the skin ready for…for what? A crack in the door showed us other ladies of varying shapes and sizes being systematically rubbed down with a kind of cloth held by the 'scrubbing lady', for want of a better word. They were lying on marble slabs, wearing only baggy knickers, which were unceremoniously tugged down so that cheeks could be scrubbed.

My friend Parwin elected to go first, since she looked Turkish, or so our Native Lady evidently thought. Parwin's father was Iranian, although she herself was born in Switzerland and had a Swiss mother. Perhaps her nationality also decided us on making her first, since she had a quick grasp of languages and no fear of not making herself understood.

Watching Parwin being scrubbed made the system clearer: first lie on one's front for the back scrub, one's dead skin being briskly rubbed off and left clinging to the body or deposited as tiny black particles on the slab. After turning onto one's side, then onto one's back, then the other side, one sat up for more scrubbing of legs and arms, and even face!! After this one was sloshed down with the remainder of the plastic bowl of water the 'scrubber' had been using to dunk her cloth in. Instructions were fired at Parwin which she interpreted as meaning 'have a wash off and come back IMMEDIATELY'.

By now we had been moved to little curtained awnings around the bathing room. We had a large marble basin filling with hot and cold water from two taps, and a plastic dish to slosh it over ourselves. The basins had no drainage, and water was splashed around over the marble slabs and floors, running into little drainage channels in the floor all around the room.

Reaching for the soap, a loud shriek erupted from our 'scrubber', so we realised that soap was forbidden. This was instantly explained as Parwin was again installed on the slab, face down, and our scrubber proceeded to soap the whole of her back with a different kind of cloth, a soft knitted one this time. Turning only once onto her back, she was lathered and massaged, sliding all over the soapy marble, with the bowl of soapy water poured over her to finish.

Then it was my turn.

The slab was hastily washed down before I was summoned, and the same procedure followed, punctuated by a running commentary from our new granny. Actually, despite feeling like being scrubbed with a scotchbrite scouring pad, it was invigorating, and after the soapy massage one felt literally squeaky clean.

We realised how exhausted we were on our return to the changing cubicle, and understood the necessity for the couches. We had only been an hour in the crowded steamroom, but maybe this was due to the dehydration, so after paying the ridiculously small amount (sub-divided into entrance fee, monies for scrubbing, and monies for soapy massage) we left to seek out the nearest coffee house where we ordered three drinks each – a water, a juice and a coffee, all at once please. The mystified waiter couldn't compute this, as there were only two of us, but we'd ordered six drinks, so in the end we had to settle for ordering them one by one.

We walked back down the long road to the conservatorie where Parwin took a bus home and I crawled back to my stuffy, overheated bed-sit in the department and promptly fell asleep for several hours. All in all quite an experience!

People in Need

Scene I:

Saturday afternoon. The doorbell rings, or rather, buzzes noisily, summoning me to open it. Outside stand two small children, holding a piece of tattered paper. They both start to speak at once and I struggle to understand the Turkish, picking out the odd word here and there. In my own pidgin Turkish I ask specific questions of the more coherent child until I can work out that they are "collecting donations for their father who has to go to hospital for an operation when they can raise the money". The little anxious eyes and long faces combined with simple shoddy clothing convince me that they are genuine *bona fide* charity collectors, with charity beginning at home.

However I am taken aback at the approach.

One can't help but be touched by their appearance and message, but one wonders about the parents and how they could send them out begging. Do they know they are out begging? Presumably yes. Should that matter? Or is this just a European reaction I am having?

I despatch them with a rather small donation to ease my conscience. The amount they are required to collect seems somewhat excessive and I hope that they find the rest of the neighbourhood generous enough to reach it, since I live in a new development of identical luxury apartment blocks which must seem like an extremely opulent area to those two poor mites.

Scene II:

A peaceful Sunday morning, about 10am, nice and sunny with just a few sounds from the street outside, but a feeling of stillness and calm as can often be found on a Sunday morning.

I can hear someone singing. It sounds as if it is coming from the street, and drawing nearer. Who on earth could be singing so loudly to themselves outside, shattering the peace and quiet? The sound is loud but poignant, like a gypsy song. Have the gypsies come, I wonder? Is a street show being put on outside? Do gypsies in Turkey do street shows?

By now the song has formed itself into long mournful phrases, like a slow ballad, and a sad one. I have reached the balcony and can look down into the cul-de-sac. An elderly man is stooped over, with his wife, presumably, holding his arm as they slowly shuffle up the street towards our set of four apartment buildings. She is holding a blue plastic cup, such as is used in the Turkish baths to pour water over oneself. I can catch snatches of phrases, but the pitiful picture they present is more than enough to understand the message. Some terrible misfortune has obviously befallen them and they are desperate for whatever help they can get.

The song has the piercing melancholy of a thorn bird and goes straight to one's heart. Their painfully slow progress up the road shows only too clearly how they have reached the end of their hope and strength.

I simply cannot believe that this is an elaborate con trick – yet the sinful thought crosses my mind.

Cooking and Hospitality

The Turks have a well-deserved reputation for hospitality. The sharing of bread and water is to share the gift of life with those who cross your threshold. Warm welcomes are extended to you in houses rich and poor, to strangers and friends. The tradition of assisting travellers is an ancient one. Visitors are plied with the best food and drink to be found in the house.

The group of tourists, with whom I shared my first experience of the country, were all invited into a house to drink tea on the shores of Lake Eğridir in Central Antolia. The house itself was a roughly built stone structure with a roof of higgledy-piggledy terracotta tiles. As we were many and the house rather small, carpets were spread on the ground outside the front door to allow all sixteen of us to sit comfortably while tea was brewed. Attempts at communication were made difficult by our lack of competence in Turkish. One of us had a few words. We were made very welcome nevertheless. Smiles and handshakes were the order of the day, as they still are to this day.

The following year I returned to get married and as a newly-wed spent an uncomfortable three weeks with my parents-in-law. They were welcoming and hospitable but I felt uncomfortable with the lack of privacy in the house. It was an old stone building with thick walls but with a wooden ceiling dividing the upper floor from the rooms below. Every sound and conversation travelled through the house. I was itching to find a flat of our own and to start married life in earnest. I had met my husband the previous summer, had spent very little time with him and was still struggling to learn Turkish.

On a warm evening in early May, neighbours gathered in the street when my sister-in-law invited me into the rather primitive kitchen to help with dinner preparations. There were no matches to light the gas cooker, a fairly recent acquisition and the family's pride and joy. I went for the matches.

"Ah, she's learning to cook so that she can look after her man properly!" exclaimed a busybody of a neighbour. While my husband beamed with pride, I inwardly seethed. I had had my own flat in London, given many a dinner party and felt I was quite capable of looking after him and myself.

They were only trying to express their approval of my housewifely skills, something more highly prized at that time than any career achievement. Working women then were a rarity in Turkey. Few people had washing machines and fridges were quite a new thing thirty years ago, so the idea of a working woman, never mind a working mother, was very strange.

Not too long afterwards we found a flat and moved away to the big city. My family-in-law did much to dissuade us but it gave us a much-needed chance to set up our own home and establish our own routine.

One day my in-laws came to take me shopping. Mother and father plus divorced sister and her one-year-old son made up the entourage. We set off to buy curtain material. After a long and hot walk round the central market area and some disagreement about my choice for the bedroom, we retired to my home for a late lunch.

I had not prepared anything before leaving and as everyone was hot and tired, I made a salad and put it with bread and cheese on the table. My Turkish was still rudimentary so I did not catch all the remarks made at the table. Off they went leaving me to start on my sewing.

Later I learned that my mother-in-law had been highly insulted by the offer of a 'sandwich'. A full-blown lunch had been expected. The ensuing quarrel was quickly nipped in the bud by one contrite and apologetic daughter-in-law turning up with a peace offering.

Relations were fully restored by an invitation to a proper lunch at a later date. All was going well until my husband wanted an ashtray.

'There's one on the draining board,' I said. There was a shocked silence while he got up and got it. Apparently I had committed another faux pas by not leaping to my feet to get it for him. Girls in Turkey are brought up to wait on their fathers and brothers and then their husbands.

Paying a visit is to bestow a compliment and in time I learned to take it in the spirit intended. With the universal spread of telephones, people are now able to announce their intention to visit but the onus is on the visitor to ring and say they are coming rather than wait to be invited.

Back in the 70s, there was only one member of the family who had a telephone. It was quite a status symbol but

I wondered who he talked to as no one else seemed to have one. Hence you could not announce your intention to visit but just arrive. It was always a mystery to me how the housewife in question would be totally unfazed by the sight of six or more hungry visitors on her doorstep.

One day my mother-in-law gathered together her children, their wives and attendant children to visit her older brother in the neighbouring town. The first hurdle was overcome when a suitable minibus was pressed into service for the journey.

On our arrival my uncle and aunt beamed from ear to ear, delighted to see us all. It was my first visit to their very old and rather ramshackle house. The front door was made of very old and cracked wood with a few metal bars to hold it together. The floors of each room were on different levels and so there were large steps between the kitchen and the living areas. The walls were a metre thick with small windows set into them. The building was one of many abandoned by Greeks fleeing the Turkish army in the 1920s. It didn't look as though there had been much modernisation since that time but my uncle clearly had great affection for his childhood home, despite its lack of mod cons.

Now I discovered how these visits really work. The younger women of both families disappeared into the kitchen to prepare the feast while the oldies relaxed, shouting occasional instructions to the 'cooks'. The only male contribution to the proceedings was the decapitation of the rooster from the backyard. The men then absented themselves from the house only to return at dinner time and claim pride of place at the table. It was my status as a foreigner, rather than being a new bride, that precluded me from helping in any way. I also suspect that they considered me incompetent when it came to producing instant meals for large parties. Plucking a freshly-killed fowl was a skill I did not acquire for some considerable time.

There was a large garden/yard at the back of the house with a few fruit trees, a water pump and a primitive toilet. I was expected to sit demurely with the older women in the front room. As the ladies exchanged gossip about mutual acquaintances, and shared family news before moving on to comparing aches and pains, I longed to learn the cause of laughter emanating from the kitchen. So it wasn't really a case of guests and hosts but generations playing different roles: the elder taking their ease while the younger set to work. No work for the men of course!

There were so many of us that we ate in shifts, the men eating first and then the women in order of 'seniority.' We did not sit around and savour the meal. Conversation was limited to before and after dinner but no one spoke much during the meal itself, apart from orders issued by my aunt.

The young women who stood throughout the meal and served each course at breakneck speed (no one's plate was allowed to be empty for more than a few seconds) waited patiently to eat themselves.

Finally when all had been sufficiently fed and watered, we all sat and enjoyed a few moments of relaxation together but not before the washing up had been dealt with and the tea brewed.

When the family returned the visit, my mother-in-law sent word to *her* daughters-in-law, who were expected to drop everything in their own homes and come and cook for the visitors.

In the light of all this experience, I should not have been taken unawares when the family next chose to visit me. I had heard through a series of messengers that my husband's grandmother would be brought to my house for lunch the following day. Anxious to please and not being much of a dab hand at instant catering (no chickens in my backyard!), I set to work and prepared a meal. Then I waited… and waited… and waited. I put the uncooked food in the fridge and made something else for supper.

The following day I was called out of the shower by a ring of the doorbell. They had finally arrived. Hastily donning something presentable I opened the door. There was no explanation for their delayed arrival and I didn't mention it.

All went well until we sat down to lunch. Should I play waitress or sit with them, English style? I decided on the former to be on the safe side. Then they started to pick at the food, which was clearly not to their liking. The stuffed green peppers had not been made in the traditional Turkish way.

Trying hard to stifle my irritation, I served the ritual glasses of tea and we seemed to be back on track. On subsequent occasions I got more used to sudden invasions but never quite overcame the feeling of panic that I had back then.

Amulet

A written quotation from the Quran is wrapped in cloth and worn around the neck as a protection against illness.

5 - In Sickness and in Health

Sick Leave

Being generally healthy and blessed with a strong constitution, my encounters with the Turkish Health and National Insurance system have been mercifully few and far between. "Nothing is as important as good health," my father wisely told me. His words were tucked away somewhere remote at the back of my mind. He was also in the habit of praising the British National Health Service, something now very much out of fashion. So when I came back to Turkey, I was in for something of a shock.

One weekend, about six weeks after starting a new teaching job, I developed sharp sciatic pain. Deprived of sleep, I felt unable to face the classes of eager eight-year-olds which were waiting for me, so I got my husband to drive me to school to see the school doctor. Thereby fulfilling the first rule of sick leave: however ill you are, you have to put in an appearance.

I was confident that he would agree to a day off: beyond that I would have to attend a state hospital as an outpatient.

The austere middle-aged man whose office I entered was less than sympathetic. In his dealings with students he had never been known to smile. He didn't so much as give me the once over but examined the prescription, which I had already acquired from another more understanding doctor, grunted his approval and dismissed me with a one day certificate.

Of course I was over-optimistic. The sciatica, which had been troubling me intermittently for some four months, did not improve and indeed it deteriorated into two slipped discs, which left me in terrible pain and very immobile. So commenced our battle not only with health but also with the system.

No one helped me to understand the correct procedure to follow. In fact I have found on many occasions that the personally charming Turks turn sullen and unresponsive when putting on their 'official hats.' You are expected to be *au fait* with how everything works. As my husband had always been self-employed, he was not much more knowledgeable than me in these matters.

Visits to various private doctors and clinics were torture for me as well as leaving our finances depleted. No one was satisfied with X-rays taken the week before, and needless to say each diagnostic test and examination cost money. Had I been patient and gone to the state hospital, I would have had to wait weeks for the same attention.

The only cure appeared to be bed rest so I lay down and tried to be patient.

After the first two weeks I was due to be paid my October salary or at least the seventeen days' worth that I had actually earned. In those days foreigners visited the cashier's office on the first of the month to be paid in cash. So we rang the school and asked if my husband could come and collect the money on my behalf. 'Out of the question!' was the reply.

There had been no calls from the school administration or indeed from any of my colleagues during this time. When a friend did get in touch she told me that everyone thought that I had run away and wasn't coming back!

That apparently was the official line given out by the school to stop the parents asking when I would return.

One afternoon we drove to the school, where I lay on the back seat of the car while my husband tried once again to go and get my money. Word travels fast and I was soon surrounded by curious onlookers. The Head of the primary school came out of her office and was very attentive. I mustn't rush back, she would do what she could to help, and I was to ring her if I needed anything. She was true to her word and rang me regularly during the subsequent seven weeks while I was still on sick leave.

In the end I had to hobble into the office myself, leaning on various arms and bits of furniture before I was able to collapse back into the car and go home.

Before we actually made our escape a member of the personnel department accosted my husband to tell him that I as I had not been to an approved state hospital, I was deemed to have resigned. "Fair enough!" he replied with sarcasm. "If you think my wife is fit to work, come and have a look!"

The employee in question retreated in haste with a distinctly uncomfortable look on his face. It was explained to me much later that the school was worried about an inspection of their employment records and that they could be fined for gaps in my National Insurance contributions. Many employers try to employ workers (including foreign teachers) without registering them properly and thereby saving themselves a small fortune in insurance payments. Hence the 'procedure' requires that if you are sick for more than a day you present yourself at a state hospital for examination. Imagine having a bad dose of flu and instead of wrapping yourself up in a nice warm bed, you find yourself standing in a drafty corridor awaiting your turn.

When you are pronounced fit to return to work, you may claim an amount of money from the state, which is a percentage of your salary.

Your employer is supposed to make up the remainder but many do not comply. Travelling that distance and standing or sitting in the said queues was beyond me and so I missed out on any kind of financial compensation and angered my school authorities into the bargain.

A colleague struck down by a particularly nasty virus, which wreaked havoc in the teachers' room, arrived at school one day looking so white and exhausted that I didn't recognise her. Notwithstanding, she was told that she had to come back to work forthwith as she was no longer 'ill'.

One day, when I was finally feeling better, I went into school to negotiate my return. The parents of my students had of course been concerned at my absence. My Head of Department was now effusive in the extreme and welcomed me with open arms. We agreed that I would start work within ten days to give me a chance to exercise my wasted muscles and build up some strength. Suddenly I seemed to have become their favourite teacher rather than a foreign pariah.

Not all schools are so unsympathetic. In my next job there was a doctor with a friendly face. I consulted him a few times over the years with minor ailments. The first time he wrote me a prescription I took it to the chemist. As a working teacher you pay only twenty percent of the cost. The pharmacist informed me that it had to be written up in a special ledger at school: once again I had fallen foul of the system because no one had told me what to do! They promised to contact the school nurse and gave me my medicine without delay. How refreshingly sensible I found that!

Having experienced all this, I was better prepared when I had to have a mole removed. My first port of call was my school doctor but it was holiday time so it took a few days to track him down. He sent me on to the accountants office where I got a *vizite kağıdı*, a piece of paper which proves that you are in employment and therefore entitled to a pay a small proportion of the cost of your treatment. With my sister-in-law to help me with the paperwork, I arrived at the hospital to see a dermatologist. The door to his clinic was forbiddingly shut. She went off to pay the token fee. Then we joined the milling crowd all waiting to present the receipts to the clerk, who had yet to appear. The corridor was stifling in the heat of August. When the lady in question arrived she could barely open her door for the mass of people surging forward, all claiming first place in the queue. My able helper now proved worth her weight in gold and got me seen. As I exposed the offending mole for examination, the next patient was already in the room and pressing the clerk to be next. The doctor and clerk shared a tiny office, which was also the consulting room.

Having been told that I was making a fuss about nothing, I got an appointment to have the mole removed the following afternoon.

This time I waited with two other patients also waiting for minor surgery. We were told to go and wait in what turned out to be the recovery room for patients who had had operations. As the first woman disappeared behind the next set of doors, I was left sitting opposite two comatose patients, one of whom started to come round with a series of moans and groans. Soon I was summoned to the operating theatre, which looked suitably equipped and spotlessly clean. Soon it was all over. They then announced that they had no appropriate pathology facilities so could I please take the removed tissue to another hospital. Needless to say it was a long way off.

Undaunted, determined to claim my rights, and congratulating myself on getting things done for free, I set off the following morning, bright and early. By the time I found the place and the pathology department, the fierce heat was already putting a damper on things. The receptionist refused to accept my offering and said I would have to join the queue upstairs and be referred to the lab by one of their own doctors. 'Upstairs' was seething with people, all in various states of distress or ill-temper.

Once again I ploughed on, stood quietly in a total of three queues only to be told that in order to be seen I needed another piece of paper from the school doctor and accountant!

My courage failed me. I practically ran out of the gate and down the hill, jumped into a passing taxi and went to a private pathology lab, before heading for home. Calling for the results a few days later, which I am happy to say were satisfactory, I felt I had let myself down in some way and was ashamed at jumping the queue but you have to be strong to start with to survive in this particular jungle!

In the last few years, the government has made great efforts to streamline the system and things have improved to a certain extent. As at all times of change, information does not always flow as freely as you would like and there are conflicting reports as to which pieces of paper you need where. I have to confess to having invested in private health insurance and it works miracles!

When I was on my very first round of job interviews in Turkey, I was surprised to have one employer begin the interview by outlining the procedure for sick leave. Of course I didn't take it in at the time, but perhaps it wasn't such a bad place to start after all.

Pension Prospects

I started working in Turkey, in a language school, in August 1977. I was so delighted to be employed, both for financial reasons and as a means of escaping domestic boredom, that I never even asked about national insurance contributions. A month or two later, when I was given a pink card with my photograph on it and told to treasure it, I duly filed it away and forgot about it. Much later on, the card was lost during a burglary but I got a replacement (green this time and with a waterproof plastic covering).

Suddenly I found myself thirty years older! Pensions now became a source of concern so I set off one day to the labyrinthine offices of the Social Security headquarters in Izmir. I was with a good friend, who had done her research and got the name of a high-up official, an assistant director, no less. She had tracked him down through a colleague, who was distantly related. It is common to find a *torpil* or a useful contact, before embarking on any expedition to officialdom.

Süleyman Bey was charming and polite. He sent minions to various other offices in the building, while we sat in his office in comfortable chairs, drinking tea. What's more, he found a record of my first local employment and looked up more recent records. 'You can retire whenever you like,' he said. This confirmed what I had thought to be true. If your first contribution was made twenty years previously, you are aged 50 or more and have worked for 5,675 days, you can retire with a state pension.

I only had to bring in the records of that first job and all would be well. He then detailed the various bits of paper, photographs and so on that I would also need to complete my claim. He sounded a note of caution: although he had unearthed a record of my first employment, there didn't appear to be any payments made in my name. It is illegal to employ people without making such payments but many employers do try to do just that. He started talking about my legal rights and assured me that I could sue them and win.

Not overjoyed at the prospect of a legal battle, I left the building happily enough and set out to the language school. Then the problems began. At first they told me there were no records of anything so far back. The pink card had been lost. Would I have to fight them in the courts after all? They promised to ring me as soon as possible.

My next port of call was my first private school, in which I worked for five years, starting in September 1993. Once again there seemed to be large gaps on the computerised records but I was reassured by the paperwork, which clearly showed my contributions and had the National Insurance office stamp on them.

Armed with photocopies I retraced my steps to Süleyman Bey's Office. As polite as ever, his tone changed. These employers had only paid eight percent to cover health insurance and had not included anything towards retirement. As I had not been a Turkish citizen at the time, they were within the confines of the law. Now I suddenly realised why my name was on a separate sheet from all the other teachers and employees at the school.

The picture now looked very different. Contributions were paid by the employer three times a year or every 120 days. When you started a new job they were not obliged to start paying until after the first 120 days. So my record started in January 1994, although I had worked from September 1993. They had in fact paid the full amount for me in the first third of 1994, thereby establishing my 'entry date'. They then realised they were 'overpaying' for this foreigner and reverted to the health only provision until I got my citizenship. At the time they didn't seem as pleased as I was, at getting my citizenship, which released me and them from tedious and costly applications for residence and work permits. Now I realise that I was about to cost them more money! It didn't occur to me to ask any difficult questions back then. I had simply assumed in all innocence that they were making pension contributions.

My current school had been punctilious in making all the requisite payments but there were two separate months missing in 2004. The system now works on monthly payments, in line with salaries. Delving into the archives revealed one month, which was duly entered onto my record. The second was nowhere to be found. After several requests for information, I was asked to put my request in writing. When this produced nothing helpful, I decided not to pursue it any further although I knew I had been fobbed off with a less than satisfactory explanation. An upshot of this exercise was that I got to see the earnings of the rest of the English department, as I was given the relevant sheet, with my own name highlighted. So much for privacy!

The moral of the tale seems to be that you should always ask questions at the right time, before you sign a contract, and check up to see that people are keeping their word. As for me, I will have to face the rigours of the classroom for another few years.

Süleyman Bey had a final word of caution. "What I have told you is valid as the law stands today. Come back and see me in 2012. Things are constantly changing." This unusually helpful civil servant has unfortunately moved on, so I will have to find another brave friend to help me when the time comes.

Dentists

In Turkey, dentistry is taken very seriously and one can find dental practices on almost every block. What is more, most dentists here are human, friendly and will chat to you, explaining exactly what they are doing – before, during and after treatment. They may also offer deals for paying by installments, deals for cheaper materials for the treatment (for crowns, false teeth, fillings etc.). They may even become your friend. Almost certainly you will have found this dentist through a friend. In this country, who you know is definitely more important than what you know.

The first time I approached a Turkish dental surgery was in Ankara. My teeth had been playing up and I needed a check-up. It was months before my annual visit to the UK, so I asked my trusty assistant Seda who told me she went to the father of one of her ballet students. She duly arranged an appointment for me after her own check-up the next day and we set off in the evening after work. As a child I hated going to the dentist and still feel the butterflies in my stomach whenever I go for a check-up. However, as soon as we walked into the surgery we were offered tea and coffee, soft drinks and cookies. What a surprise! Food and drink immediately before a dental examination! I can never say 'no' to a cup of tea, so I readily accepted and sat down on the plush leather sofa while Seda went in for her treatment.

There was the usual selection of expensive magazines that can be found in many dental clinics and doctors' practices, but I was delighted to see the walls and shelves adorned with 'mind toys' – steel shapes with a delicate balance that when set in motion continue to see-saw *ad infinitum*; the row of small balls suspended on strings which will click-clack from one end to the other continuously once started; pictures on the walls that had 'faces within faces' depending how you looked at them; the strange architecture in a painting that revealed a totally different picture if one viewed it from a different perspective. It was a beautifully furnished and decorated waiting room, so that one felt calm and relaxed while waiting for one's turn in the chair.

Seda was still being treated when the dental nurse came out and ushered me into the treatment room. The dentist was so passionate about his work that he wanted to show me what he was doing to Seda's teeth. She didn't seem to mind at all as he showed me how perfectly her teeth fitted.

Fitted? I was flummoxed. Seda was about 23 years old and had a gorgeous smile showing gleaming even white teeth. Her own, I had presumed. I discovered that all her teeth had been removed in her teens as they were falling out, and she had a marvellous porcelain set. I later read that it is common for people in the Middle East to lose their adult teeth early due to a lack of calcium in the soil. Perhaps this was the case with Seda, as I later met many young people with a similar story of losing teeth to porcelain ones.

After admiring the dentist's handiwork I realised my teeth would also be on display when it was my turn. Maybe this was just as well since my Turkish was minimal and I would not have understood much at all.

An abscess was diagnosed and antibiotics prescribed. Nothing could be done until the swelling had subsided. I was advised to '*Come back in a week. No charge today.*' Seda was, after all, his daughter's teacher.

A week later this dentist was either busy or out of town or something, but he recommended a friend who could deal with me and who also spoke English. This was a bonus, so one evening after work we set off to dentist number two, in another part of town. This clinic was more functional than luxurious; a small waiting room, old chairs and coffee table, a dusty lino floor and dog-eared magazines. However, Mr. Dentist himself was an entertainer, making jokes in English and Turkish and generally moving the show along. After looking at my problem he explained that only half of the offending back tooth was infected and that it would be a shame to extract all of it. He proposed drilling through half of it and leaving me with the good part which could be crowned at a later date as it would still provide a grinding surface for the tooth above. I had never heard of extracting *half a tooth* before, but it sounded logical and he promised that I would not feel a thing. Even the drill was not an ear-splitting shriek and Mr Dentist chatted to me in English all through the surgery, cleaning the two remaining root canals swiftly and thoroughly while he cracked jokes and entertained non-stop. A highly professional job. I had no time to get panicky and he kept me feeling at ease all the time with his light-hearted patter.

When my UK dentist saw the work six months later he was astounded. 'Quite a radical treatment', he professed, admitting it had been cleanly done and was an original solution to the problem, since 'saving the tooth, where possible,' is the dentists' Code of Honour.

'Saving the patient any pain' was dentist number three's code of practice. I needed a filling and this time turned to the lady who had given me two lovely kittens from her cat's new litter. She was a friend of a friend of my current boss, and also happened to be a dentist. It was only natural that I should go to her for treatment at that time.

Dentist three, as I shall call her, was very kind and patient. Too kind. The basic filling took three days.

First she gave me a spray anaesthetic so that I would feel less pain when the needle went in with the real anaesthetic. A foul sickly taste filled my mouth with this spray and I wanted to gag and spit it out, but couldn't. The needle then gave the same sharp prick that it always does, but I was relieved that now I would feel no more pain.

Not so. She had only given me a pre-injection dose. That meant that after ten minutes wait I had to have another injection, the full dose. This one was not felt at all, to be sure, but it did seem unnecessary and did prolong the agony, so to speak. Up to now all dentists had given me just the one shot, and it had been fine with least pain and discomfort and all over with quickly. However, I think that today anaesthetics are different and doses are adjusted so that one's mouth and jaw recover from the numbness much faster.

Anyway, it had taken nearly an hour of this preparation before Dentist three started drilling. And drilling. And drilling. I was there with mouth wide open for another couple of hours. I know that she was being so careful and painstaking for my benefit, but it really did become jaw-achingly unbearable. When she had finally finished drilling and filling she told me to come back the next day. To finish it. My mouth dropped open again, but in surprise. Was it not finished? Oh no, it had to be cleaned and polished, to be more comfortable for me.

Next day, with frozen jaw from the previous day's torture, I duly showed up to be polished off. This meant another hour of opening and closing my poor aching mandibles for testing the bite and roughness of the filling. I realise she was doing her best for the end result, but this was the slowest and longest dental treatment I have ever had in my life, and thus the most prolonged form of torture.

I never returned to Dentist three after that day – she had given me kittens.

Dentist number four was also female, and a friend, and even an English student of mine. I will call her 'Güler'. This

173

was after the move to Izmir. We had been studying English for about a year when my teeth started playing up again and Güler offered to have a look.

Güler was extremely fussy about cleanliness in her practice. Galoshes were provided at the door, and one had to hop around on one foot to slip these elasticated blue plastic 'socks' over one's shoes before being allowed to step over the threshold. I wondered how the elderly patients managed, since there was no chair provided by the door to achieve this one-legged manoeuvre. During inspection of my teeth I was given a stern lecture on flossing. Apparently my teeth did not meet her high standards and she produced a mirror and dental floss and showed me how to fastidiously perform the flossing technique. Three times a day was the requisite.

Next, the brushing technique. Again, I was subjected to a seminar on my shortcomings at brushing my teeth. By now I felt about two inches high and two years old. Not a dental strategy to be recommended for keeping clients.

More was to come.

Güler tapped and prodded my teeth, and after several 'aahs' emitted from my throat, she found the culprit. A porcelain crown was needed. The tooth would be shaved down to a stump and a beautiful crown fixed on top. She could do me a special deal and I could pay by installments. She would also make sure that it was the right shade of off-white, to blend in with my other less than perfect teeth: no screaming differences of colour with a white crown shining out like a beacon among the yellowing crowd.

However, she hated the look of my silver-grey fillings and was plotting to replace them all with aesthetically pleasing off-white ones. Seriously.

I had to laugh at this, and assured her that as I hardly ever saw them, they were no trouble to me. They rarely got viewed by others, unless guffawing open-mouthed or visiting the dentist. She grudgingly agreed to bide her time on this matter and meanwhile my treatment began in earnest.

First, the shaving down of the offending tooth. This necessitated the nasty-tasting anaesthetic spray, unfortunately, and then:

The cattle prod.

Güler asked me to let her know if I could feel anything when she touched my tooth with a kind of small rod. I was expecting a slight tap and maybe a dull ache somewhere, but *'Yeeeoow!'* I nearly jumped out of my skin. The electric shock was so unexpected that I started sweating and my heart was racing – and I am not one to make a fuss about medical examinations. I was just totally unprepared for it – a kind of throbbing pulse shooting through my tooth and whole body, rather like touching the low-pulse electrified fences around cattle fields which discourage the beasts from straying. But touching them with one's teeth?

I really hated that thing and protested loudly, but Güler assured me that every dentist used it, for without it how could they assess how much anaesthetic to inject? "So what did dentists do in the olden days before this was invented?" I snapped back. "What happened to good old-fashioned common sense and experience? Calculations based on knowledge and expertise?"

Güler sighed and agreed not to use it again, but was unsure that she could select the correct amount to numb my mouth and jaw properly so that I would not feel pain.

However, a few taps on my tooth with the normal dental tools assured her that the nerves were asleep and it was safe to proceed. Next she donned a kind of motorcyclist's crash helmet, a white one with a visor. She peered into my mouth from behind her safe screen and proceeded to drill away at my sleeping tooth until only a spike remained.

There followed several measurements with the plasticine-flavoured blue stuff they use to take an impression of one's teeth. Another nasty taste, but an unavoidable procedure. This 'measuring' was done at least three times, and repeated on two subsequent trips for checking. However, my new crown arrived within only ten days and was fitted and checked fastidiously. I will give Güler her due as she gave me an extremely affordable price and easy payment terms. It worked out much cheaper than anything I could have found in the UK. The work was highly professional and she made sure it fitted perfectly – both in size and in colour. She was a perfectionist, and thorough almost to a fault: after my final fitting my teeth were cleaned and polished and I was subjected to another lecture on how to brush them correctly, with me holding the mirror in front of my mouth so she could show me exactly what to do, three times a day and after eating anything.

I 'suffered' a couple more perfect porcelain crowns at Güler's hands, including that earlier half-tooth left over from Dentist number two. However, the long journey (nearly two hours) to her clinic, coupled with the feeling of not being clean enough (tooth-wise) or up to her high standards, encouraged me to look elsewhere for a more sympathetic dentist. I found one closer to home through one of my yoga students whose daughter was a dentist. Özge (pronounced Erz-Gay) had recently returned from five years practising in Northern Cyprus. She was opening her own clinic which was also on my regular route to and from the city.

I didn't find Özge until my teeth were bothering me again; receding gums, I'd thought, but really too sensitive and painful whenever I ate or drank anything. Arriving at the clinic I was welcomed into a small flat on the first floor which had been converted into a dental practice. It had a tiny kitchen, a small reception room, another smaller kind of 'box' room, a bathroom, a toilet, and the main room which doubled as her office and surgery. This room was complete with desk, computer, dental chair, music set, and dozens of plants crowding into the corners by the window. It also had a balcony, so one could watch the outside world from the dentist's chair, as if one was sitting in a garden. I was able to watch one of those intrepid cleaning ladies doing windows on the fourth floor of the apartment block opposite, balancing on one foot inside with one foot out on the ledge as she rubbed away at the outside panes. It quite put my own fears into perspective that day in 'the chair'.

There was soft calming music playing and a couple of budgerigars chirruped in a cage on Özge's desk and she ushered me into the kitchen to see... her black and white rabbit, happily munching lettuce leaves on the floor. She was looking after it for a while for a friend, apparently.

As she offered me "tea, coffee, herb tea or a soft drink?" She also asked me what kind of music I liked and immediately changed the CD for even more beautiful sounds to relax me.

Özge chatted away merrily while she inspected my teeth, relating stories of her mountain hike the previous weekend and how she loved to do these treks in different regions every weekend. They would go by coach overnight to southern Turkey and spend the two days walking up the hills and wooded mountain slopes, just being 'at one' with nature and staying in cheap pensions or with friends, or even camping.

By now she had found a filling that needed attention, but decided to check it with an X-ray. I was surprised that she stayed in the room and even held the small card in my mouth with her own finger as she pressed the X-ray machine's button. When I asked her why she didn't protect herself she just shrugged and smiled. A cavity was confirmed and Özge pinned up the negative and explained all the tiny markings, which I really didn't understand. She told me we could do the filling now or leave it till another day – she understood my over-sensitivity to dentists. I agreed to have it done there and then and she got out the nasty spray anaesthetic for the pre-injection, but after I protested she replaced it on her tray and agreed to give me just the one injection. No problem.

No 'cattle prod' either – she never used one, she said.

I was told I could stop the procedure any time I needed a break by just raising my hand. No dentist has ever given me that option before, so I was amazed. During a 'wash out' with the 'pink drink' I remarked that it tasted much more of fluoride than I remembered from the UK. perhaps they added more chemicals these days? Özge affirmed sadly that this was so, and suggested she change it for pure water if I preferred. Again, I was surprised at being given the choice. Moreover, Özge never forgot these points, and every time I went for a treatment she had replaced the pink drink with spring water and never got the anaesthetic spray gun out or 'double-injected' me. What is more, she always remarked that I had good teeth, that they were healthy and strong and that I looked after them well.

Looking something like Pocahontas, with her long black plait and huge brown eyes, this last dentist has shown me more kindness, sympathy and courtesy than any dentist I have ever known, both in Turkey and in the UK. She is quite simply the most beautiful of the lot.

'Detached professionalism' is not the norm in this country of contrasts, so although I would not have thought it possible to become friends with one's dentist, Turkey has shown me that 'Nothing is as it seems'.

New Eyes

When the eye doctor at the big university hospital first suggested a cataract operation, a big lump of ice abruptly expanded in my stomach. "I'm not ready for that yet," I faltered, and afterwards I tried to put the horrible subject out of my mind. What brought it back was my brother; aged seventy (six years older than me), he got them done in Scotland and was so thrilled with the results that afterwards he reminded me about it with every phone call. Meanwhile my eyesight got worse. I missed buses that I should have caught, and bus stops where I should have got off. Reading became more and more strenuous and I did it with one eye shut to avoid the extra, blurred image of the other weaker one. I could not see stars, or birds, or read the signs to find a toilet in a public place. My brother persisted; "When are you going to ask the doctor? Hurry up! Be sensible and do it soon. Don't just forget about it!"

So when the doctor repeated the suggestion, I said "Well, maybe." She took me next door to the surgeon who advised me to go ahead. He assured me there was no general anaesthesia and no overnight stay in the hospital, and he said I wouldn't feel a thing.

The next step was the special deal. In Turkey, all expensive procedures are special deals, but this was more special than most. My grown-up daughter had given English lessons to the eye doctor's daughter, so I received privileged treatment. The surgeon, who was said to be the best in Izmir, was employed at the hospital only in a teaching capacity. Theoretically, he was not allowed to do operations there; he did them at another, private, hospital. If I wished, I could go there, but it would be much more expensive. Alternatively, they could bend the rules and he would do it for me at the university hospital. "Tomorrow, if you like," he said. I thought that would be a bit sudden for my family, so we settled on two weeks later.

We began the preliminaries. "We" means my daughter and me. Patients in Turkish hospitals usually have a companion, called the *refakatçı*, to accompany them. In the case of an overnight stay, this person is an essential nursing assistant. This did not apply to me, but I was glad of the companionship. It was useful to have someone who could easily understand hastily gabbled instructions in Turkish, and read the signs on the walls in that vast and daunting labyrinth of buildings. We went to the hospital three times, and spent sixteen hours queuing in various places to get the paperwork done. The actual medical procedures involving eye measurements, a blood test and an electrocardiogram took a total of half an hour.

The fateful morning came. I was not allowed to eat or drink anything, so I lay gloomily in bed while my daughter and husband had breakfast. The latter dropped us at the back gate of the hospital; my daughter navigated the stairs and corridors expertly to the correct department. I was given eyedrops and told to wait. Then there were various surprises. I had to wear an identification wristband of pink plastic. I had to take off all my clothes, my glasses, my watch and even my wedding ring, and wrap myself up in a green cotton hospital gown. It had straps to tie round, but one of them was missing so it didn't tie. I was ordered to lie on a trolley. Couldn't I walk? No, definitely not, they said, because I was going to have an operation. The file of precious paperwork lay on my stomach. Then I was wheeled on a long journey involving many corridors and a lift. The orderly was cheerful and chatty; I asked him how many kilometres he walked every day and he said about fifty. When I commented that he must get very tired, he said it was good healthy exercise. He came from the east of Turkey, and he liked Izmir very much.

I was parked in a small room where about eight green-wrapped bodies on trolleys were waiting in a row. Somebody asked my name, and checked the wristband. I got some more eyedrops, and confirmed that it was my right eye that was to be operated on. I wondered how many surgeons would be at work this morning, and whether I would have to wait for all the green parcels that had got there first to be done before me. Also, would I get the right surgeon, since he was not actually supposed to be doing this at all? Then he appeared briefly and said good morning. I could not see his face without my glasses, but the voice sounded right, which was reassuring. They took me first. A room full of bright lights and shiny machines. It was icy cold. I thought, if I shiver in the middle of this, it won't be good for my eye, so I complained. The anaesthetist said it was cold to stop the microbes and prevent infections, but I could have a heater. He got busy gluing electrodes all over me, and then placed a thick light-weight pipe, which had hot air blowing into it, on top of me. It helped, and I didn't shiver. Then a blood pressure monitor on one arm. More eyedrops. When he said he was going to give me an intravenous sedative, I protested. "I don't need it", I told him. Rather to my surprise, this was accepted. Then they put a porous cloth over my face and cut a hole in it to access the eye. Disinfectant was smeared around firmly, and some mechanism prevented my blinking. I kept the other eye shut defensively under the cloth. The work began. It was uncomfortable, but did not hurt. They had said it would take between ten and twenty minutes, so I visualized a large number and counted backwards to pass the time. I lost track of my number listening to the surgeon giving orders to the assistants; he did not sound very pleased with them.

They taped a hard plastic cover over my eye and I slid onto a trolley for the journey back to my daughter and personal possessions. There I was to wait for the surgeon to come and check. I was hungry and thirsty, and very grateful when the hospital supplied a carton of *ayran,* a drink made of yogurt and water. Lunch, they said, would follow later. We were in a room with about four women, some had had eye operations and some were waiting. One who was going to have a cataract done had been hungry since the previous evening; they wheeled her off soon afterwards. The university hospital gets tricky cases from far and wide; these women had travelled long distances and did not have husbands with cars. They had worse problems than me, but they were cheerful and friendly, and curious. My daughter chatted with them; I was too tired to contribute much but I enjoyed listening.

The surgeon arrived and pulled the plastic cover off. I tried out the new eye. It saw some pink haze, and the clear outline of the bottom of the door. The weak eye that had seen nothing but hazy splotches for years could now focus! The surgeon examined it, pronounced everything okay, and said we could go home. There would be another check next morning.

Going home was easier said than done. It was by then eleven o'clock. My daughter got hold of the bill and took the cash, equivalent to about £260, to deposit at the bank nearby. Then she went to see the doctor dealing with discharges, who said she was far too busy with admissions; we would have to wait till the afternoon. Lunch came down the corridor on a trolley, and the companions fetched it for the patients. The steel tray had enough for us both, but there was no cutlery, so one of our roommates lent us a couple of plastic spoons. It was more tasty than I expected, or perhaps that was just because I was so hungry.

Time passed. I fell asleep for a while, the women in the room chatted and dozed, my daughter read her book. Finally, we escaped at about three. In the hospital garden the air was sweet and fresh, the sun was shining and the trees were green. Everything was tinged with rainbows; I saw as well now without glasses as I had before when I was wearing them.

Next day the new eye still felt like it had a piece of grit in it, and this lasted a couple of days. Conscientiously I applied eyedrops, two different kinds for the first week, five times a day and ten minutes apart. The morning after the operation the eye functioned beautifully, showing me a bright, clear world that I had never expected to see again. The fuzzy images produced by the other eye got in the way, though, and I knew at once I should get that one done too.

We went back just three weeks later. Do it within one month, the surgeon had said, and the paperwork would be simpler. It was; it took seven hours instead of sixteen. That included the time waiting for discharge after the operation. The second round was similar to the first, but I did not escape the intravenous treatment. The anaesthetist (a different one) this time consulted the surgeon, and then reported, "The prof wants it." End of argument! I felt the pricking and squeezing of the actual operation more than with the first one, but the discomfort afterwards was less. For two days everything looked foggy, then it cleared. Getting the check-up a week later, I looked down the long corridor in the hospital and was startled by my perception of its length. After years of disuse, I had my binocular vision back: I could automatically compare the images of my two eyes to judge distances.

A month later, I am still in awe of my new ability and the technology that created it. When I wake up each

morning, I check that my new eyes still work. I can see stars
and flowers and faces. I can read and write better and faster.
I can also see rubbish and wrinkles, and am assailed by the
banal messages of advertisements which used to be
incomprehensible. Life is never perfect, but I'm not
complaining.

Dealing with Death

Turkey is a very large country and as such has many
regional variations in all aspects of its culture. Having lived
in Izmır for 30 years or so, I now realise that it is not simply
regions or villages which determine behaviour. Migrants
bring their own culture with them and this, in time, becomes
synthesised with the local variety giving a rich pattern to
customs. Death rituals are no exception.

When my husband died suddenly, my UK family were
very surprised to hear that he had already been buried by the
time they got the news the following day. Funerals are
usually held on the day of the death, if it occurs before eight
or even nine in the morning and on the following day at the
latest. Having to wait for close relatives who, these days
may be coming from abroad, adds to the grief and stress of
the bereaved. Presumably this tradition was born of
necessity when there was no means of preserving bodies in
excessive heat. The news is given to the local mosque,
where it is promulgated in a special announcement called
the sela. In fact, like all loud speaker announcements it is

often difficult to distinguish the name but news seems to spread by bush telegraph very swiftly.

The body is usually taken to a hospital mortuary but will be washed and prepared for burial by relatives of the appropriate sex. Some families then want the coffin to come home on the way to the mosque, where prayers are said for the dead. Until quite recently, women were barred from funerals, only visiting the grave at a later date. These days, the prohibition is breaking down. The coffin is carried in turns by all the able-bodied men from the mosque to the cemetery, so you may see enormous numbers of people processing through the streets. After my father-in-law's funeral, I joined a procession to the graveyard for the first time. Accompanied by other family members and many friends, I witnessed the burial. Here the body is removed from the rough and ready coffin and buried in a white shroud. The coffin is then used again.

The bereaved family is expected to provide refreshments for the mourners and so neighbours rally round and continue to send food to the house for a week or so, to cope with the steady stream of visitors. Women gather in the house of death to read the Koran or recite prayers in order to ease the path of the soul to heaven. The family is so busy trying to provide food and drink that it has little time to grieve or reflect but it seems to be a comfort to many. Keeping busy may be a way of alleviating the initial shock and disbelief. After a week or so people start to return home.

On the third day *helva*, a sweet concoction of sugar, fat and sesame flour or semolina, is made and distributed in the neighbourhood. This may also be sent to the place of work of the deceased. The day of the funeral is day one rather than the day of the death, if they are different.

On day seven there are prayers led by the *hoca* or local priest. These may be held in the mosque or at home. People attending are then given a hearty meal. Parties of 60 or more are not uncommon. On the fortieth day, *lokma* is made and handed out to passers-by, who line up for their share of these sticky doughnuts covered in sugar solution. Thus the general public consume this treat without having had any connection at all with the deceased. The original idea was to feed the poor and so ties in with the giving of alms, a central pillar of the Muslim faith. Day 52 sees more prayers and sometimes more *helva* or *lokma*. This ends the first sequence of death rituals.

Anniversaries are marked by prayers or more *lokma,* with some families keeping up this tradition for many years after the death, but ceremonies generally become more muted and more private as time goes by.

A local family who originally came from the Black Sea marked the tragic death of their son by walking to the grave every day for 40 days although this was clearly very distressing for them. Older people are very concerned to do everything 'correctly' so as to be acceptable to God. Nowadays, I am told by many that contrary to popular belief, none of these rituals are detailed in the Koran and are merely traditions whose origins are lost in the mists of time. People so wedded to rituals are unable to explain their significance.

In the old days, such events served to reinforce community ties as much as weddings and births, but in these days of growing affluence and working women, some now prefer to farm out the making of *helva,* as they are able to pay for these services.

So at these unhappy times one is able to get another insight into the culture and traditions of a different land.

Afterword – Brushes with Death

I have never come closer to death than here in Turkey. A surprising statement, but meant in the sense that death becomes part of everyday life in this country, and is quite a public ceremony.

Attendance at funerals is expected, so when a relative dies one is automatically granted *izin* (permission or leave) to attend the funeral.

This is usually also the case with colleagues and friends. With Turkish families being generally large and widespread this can mean several days a year needed off work. I used to teach a busy manager of a hypermarket who seemed to attend a funeral nearly every week. My husband also goes to a funeral nearly every month, since he comes from a very large family and his circle of friends and colleagues is extremely widespread. Causes of death range from traffic accidents to illness and simply old age.

My initial 'brush with death' came after my first three months in Turkey when I took a trip to Istanbul, staying in a cheap and friendly hostel right in the heart of Sultan Ahmet where the famous Blue Mosque and Aya Sophia are found. With two other girl friends we had a wonderful week before returning to the UK for eight weeks' summer vacation. My friends' boyfriends knew the receptionist, Sefo, at the hostel and he had taken us all out and showed us some of the nicer cafes in the area. We had agreed to spend a few more days there on our return to Turkey after the holiday. One month later I received a phone call from one of our group: Sefo had been killed one night, attacked by a psychopath. Imagining this to be some kind of robbery or even Turkish mafia crime I was then informed that the madman was an American tourist. We were all shocked at the futility of this death. Sefo was only in his twenties and had seemed to have all his life ahead of him, with dreams and ambitions to be fulfilled. Our return to Turkey was subdued, and we visited the grave one day to pay our respects. The cemetery covered a huge and sprawling area, but the helpful attendant remembered this particular funeral well as Sefo was so young and had been brutally killed by a *yabanci* (foreigner); his girlfriend was Irish and she had been beside herself with grief, we were informed.

My first opportunity to attend a Turkish funeral came within the next year when a former distinguished choreographer had died after a long battle with cancer. She had been a dancer with the State Ballet Company and become a noted choreographer in Turkey. Although she had been living in the United States for many years she was to be buried in Ankara and was flown back for the funeral. I imagined a small service and burial with friends and family present. Not so. The whole Conservatoire had the morning off so that hundreds of professors, colleagues, students, their friends and families could flock to the State Opera where the coffin was to be received before going to the mosque and then the cemetery. Everyone could pay their respects and literally say goodbye.

Having totally misunderstood that this was *not* a private affair but a very public one, I did not attend, and later regretted the chance of being part of this amazing solidarity in life and death. However, at the commemorative ballet performance later that month the audience paid homage by standing for one minute's silence before curtain up. Such 'one minute silences' are often observed in remembrance of important public figures as well as colleagues. They may take place before concerts, theatre performances, public meetings and even in schools and universities before classes or general assemblies.

I was to experience another public send-off and the huge emotional response it engendered in the mourners when a good friend was killed suddenly on her way to work one morning. It was a bizarre traffic accident comprising a set of coincidences which resulted in the tragedy. Figen and her husband had taken her son to the station that day in the husband's car, as Figen's own vehicle was out of action. Her son sat in the front this time because he was to be dropped off first. Figen had stayed in the back after waving goodbye to her son since the remaining journey to the university where they both worked was very short. Slowing right down as they approached Figen's office block, a school service bus suddenly zoomed up behind and crashed into the back of their car. The back door flew open on collision and Figen was thrown out across the road where her head hit a tree, killing her on impact. Her husband suffered severe head injuries as his head hit the windshield.

The funeral was held the next day, and the coffin was duly brought to the university outside Figen's department. When I arrived, the campus was swarming with hundreds of people – colleagues, students, family, friends, and all who had known Figen or heard of her through the university. It was a highly emotional setting. Then her husband arrived, head still swathed in bandages. I managed to make eye contact with her son, who was a private student of mine, but could not get through the crowds to be with them.

Then the driver of the service bus also arrived. Figen's husband lunged at him, shouting accusations and angry recriminations. He was restrained by the strong arms of colleagues but everyone was crying by now, including myself. What a senseless waste of a goodhearted human being. Words are inadequate to describe the feelings boiling over amongst the multitude that day.

The coffin arrived and made a kind of tour of duty through the centre of the crowd and was carried off to the mosque, with close friends and family following by car.

I had a friend from the UK staying with me at the time and she had accompanied me to the funeral. We had only been able to briefly greet other close friends of Figen's, but I think my friend was also overwhelmed by the show of support, the hordes of people – no flowers at all, just human beings.

People

These figures from woven kilims look as if they have a problem communicating. Here they illustrate various language problems we have encountered.

6 - Language Pitfalls

Hazards in English

The meeting had ended. Twelve or so teachers who taught Upper Intermediate Grammar began to file out of the door. Just before reaching it, I glanced back and said to Çiçek, my boss,

"Are we meeting at four again next Wednesday?"

"Of course!"

I muttered some response and digested the put-down as I walked down the corridor, shocked. Çiçek (a name that means flower in Turkish) was always scrupulously polite to everybody. And I thought we got on really well. What had happened?

After thinking about it, for a while, I understood. There is a Turkish word *tabii* that you use to answer requests like "May I open the window?" or "May I sit here?" In dictionaries, this word is translated as "of course". However, in Turkish the same word is used to confirm information politely. It is a response to sentences like "The exam is on Monday, isn't it?" In English we say, "Yes", or "That's right". "Of course" carries a critical message that the listener should already have known the information, creating a put-down. Çiçek did not know this; she just made a mistake in English. I was relieved when I worked this out.

When you speak any foreign language, you have to guard against mistakes that may give the wrong impression.

It is also useful to have awareness of what misleading errors people may make in your language. In the following paragraphs, I will describe a few more pitfalls that Turkish speakers of English may encounter.

"Welcome to Turkey!"

My friend Hatice beamed across our dinner table at Lyn, who had arrived from London the night before on her first visit. Hatice was an English teacher, and spoke clearly and confidently. Lyn was delighted to meet a real native, and soon asked her,

"What do you think I should see in Izmir?"

"Oh, there are so many places! Of course you must go to Çeşme with the wonderful beach, and have a *kumru* sandwich by the sea. Then there are the famous ruins of Ephesus, with the restored Roman houses and the amazing library, and then..."

At this point I felt it was necessary to interrupt. I had to explain that Çeşme is a seaside town seventy kilometres from Izmir, and Ephesus is over a hundred kilometres away. Worthy as these places are of being visited, they are most definitely not "in Izmir".

Confusion arises because in Turkish the same name is used for the city proper and the surrounding administrative area, which is something like an English county. I have friends in Yorkshire who do not live anywhere near York; we distinguish Gloucester from Gloucestershire and so on. Turkish speakers who overlook this point can give very misleading ideas of geography.

"How was your weekend?" I asked a colleague one summer Monday morning. "Was it nice in Çeşme? Did you go swimming?"

"Oh it was lovely! The sea was too warm!"

"Do you mean the water was nice for swimming?" I asked cautiously, "Was it a comfortable temperature?"

"Yes, yes. Wonderful!"

"In English we would say 'very warm', not 'too warm', if you enjoyed your swim."

"Oh yes! I forgot."

The distinction between 'too' and 'very' is one of the most forgotten items of vocabulary in English. Mostly I don't correct people I talk to, but with colleagues it is difficult to know what to do, because they are continuously teaching their errors to the next generation of students.

Tourists who visit Turkey have varying reactions to young children who run after them calling loudly,

"Hel-lo! Vot iss yur nem?"

This particular item of conversation is on page one of every textbook of school English. The little ones, who do not yet have English lessons at school, have learned it from the bigger ones who do, and as far as they know that is how you are supposed to talk to foreigners. The situation gets even trickier with older speakers. If a young man, for instance, addresses a lady visitor in this way, she is unlikely to respond positively.

When I taught English to students of *turizm*, I tried to show them ways of approaching people politely. For example:

"Excuse me, do you speak English?", and then, "I'm studying English. May I talk to you for a minute?"

There is much to be gained from local people interacting with foreign visitors outside a commercial setting, both as language practice and cultural interaction, and it is sad that teachers and textbooks provide no guidance on how to start.

There are innumerable pitfalls, but these examples are enough for the present. I must finish this with a few words of advice to English speaking visitors. If someone appears to be rude in Turkey, give them the benefit of the doubt; you are far more likely to meet poor language skills than any deliberate insult. On occasions where information appears ambiguous or unclear, don't guess. Repeat it and ask more questions until you are sure what the person is trying to say. Finally, do use opportunities to talk to local people. They are generally hospitable and interested in foreigners, and you can enrich your visit a great deal by making some acquaintances.

A Comedy of Errors

When I first lived in Turkey, stories of amusing language mistakes were circulated in the foreign teachers' community. Here are a few examples from the three of us.

A couple of new teachers, both girls, were walking along a street one evening when a greasy looking young man approached them. Hoping to discourage him, one of the girls tried to remember the word for "go away". Unfortunately she mixed up *git,* which means "go", with *gel,* which means "come", which had the opposite effect.

The next anecdote is even more embarrassing. A young British woman went to stay with a Turkish family, arriving after an overnight bus journey. After a polite welcome and some breakfast, she felt really tired and wanted to say "I want a bed", *yatak istiyorum.* Unfortunately she confused the word for bed, *yatak,* with *yarak,* a particularly rude term for "penis".

*****

A friend of mine was on holiday with her husband in South West Turkey one summer. They had been out sightseeing all day and arrived at a restaurant hot and dusty and dying of thirst. My friend gasped out 'Water! Water!' as they sat down and a waiter approached. He rushed off and returned with a glass which my friend seized and gulped down gratefully, only to choke and splutter as the liquid hit the back of her throat, turning her face red as she struggled to breathe, swallow and recover.

They had understood she had asked for 'Vodka', not water, or '*su*', as it is known in Turkish.

*****

As a newly-wed, I undertook to do the shopping, while my husband worked long hours to earn us a living. He gratefully agreed to this new arrangement, which freed him from being despatched to the market with a string of orders.

There was only one problem: I had little or no Turkish. Undeterred I would set out armed with my well-thumbed dictionary and head off down the street. My first port of call was always the local grocer, a large kindly man, who patiently answered all my questions, even directing me one day to a reliable dentist after I had broken a tooth on an olive stone.

I can't remember why, but one day I found myself needing some vinegar. Trusting to my old friend, the dictionary, I walked into the shop and asked for *Şirke'* ("sheer-keh"). The grocer looked perplexed and produced a bag of sugar! I tried again but got the same response. Resorting to sign language didn't seem to help until I spied a bottle of the desired liquid, lurking on a remote top shelf.

'Ah, *sirke*!' ("seer-keh") he beamed, and I immediately realised that in adding that fateful cedilla, he thought that I had been asking for *şeker* (sugar), and not *sirke* (vinegar).

*****

When I first met my Turkish husband he was working as a painter-decorator, but he told me he was really a chef. So for his first Christmas stocking filler I bought him a real chef's apron with his name embroidered on it. In those days his English was not so fluent, and I later learnt that the word "chef" (or *şef* as it is written in Turkish) means "manager" – literally "chief". Thus I discovered that he used to be the manager of an Italian restaurant, not the cook!

*****

Our handsome, sprightly and athletic Russian ballet master, who had recently arrived in Turkey, tried to buy a loaf of bread one night at the corner shop on his way home, but instead of asking for fresh (*taze*) bread he confused the word *ekmek* with *erkek* which means "boy".

*****

I was enquiring at the theatre ticket desk for a matinee performance the following month and required a box, as there would be a group of us coming to see the opera. Now in Turkish, the letter "c" is pronounced like a hard "j", and unfortunately I said "Lojman ariyorum" meaning I was looking for "lojman" or "lodgings" instead of a *loca* (or 'loggia', as it is spelt in Italian). After some strange glances among each other I realised my mistake as they corrected my choice of words, and we all burst out laughing at the idea of a group of foreign ladies camping out in a box at the Opera!

English-Turkish Lesson

One of my first introductions to the complexity of Turkish and the importance of choosing one's words carefully came at the end of a lesson I had given to a small group of university level dance students, explaining their homework while walking together along the corridor to the tea room.

On setting them a task I had explained what they had to do and finished with my usual "Did you all understand?" or the Turkish *"Anladiniz mi?"*

Looking at their blank faces I felt perhaps they didn't, but an older graduate student from the Music department happened to be passing and had the temerity to call out to me "Ros, it's rude to say that to them. You have to say *"Anlatabildim mi?"* (meaning "Have I explained it enough / Did I explain it well enough?").

He went on to announce that this was the polite way to talk to students and not to imply by my crude English-Turkish that they were in any way unable to understand and were therefore stupid and unintelligent.

At the time I was shocked by this graduate student's impudence and took umbrage; I was embarrassed that he had tried to put me down in front of my students. I was also incensed that I, their teacher, should have to imply that I couldn't explain things clearly enough to the poor dear students by using the apparently required Turkish expression; this seemed to me a gross unfairness to teachers and an example of how students got their power!

Many years have passed and I have gradually come to accept that this apparent over-politeness is necessary so as not to hurt feelings and to achieve better communication with others, regardless of whether they are students or people in higher positions of authority. It is almost impossible to give a faultless instruction to more than one person at the same time - an instruction which can never be misunderstood or misconstrued. Exam papers bear witness to the countless different ways in which students can interpret the questions; moreover, one only has to listen to two different witnesses recounting what they saw or heard at an accident to understand this. Perhaps by giving the "benefit of the doubt" to the students by saying *"Anlatabildim mi?"*, one can make them powerful allies.

What's In A Name?

When I was at school, way back in the mists of time, my exclusively female teachers were addressed as Miss or Mrs followed by their surnames. Reports signed with a preceding initial were the only clues we had as to their first names. 'H. Chapman': Heather? Hazel? Hilary? Such questions were hotly debated in the back row of the fourth form. When I became a teacher myself, not on the distant shores of Albion but here in Turkey, I was surprised to see that one's given name was in the public domain and certainly no secret. Even the informality and forwardness of the younger generation did not extend to them being on first name terms with their teachers however. I became 'Celia *Hanım*, hanım meaning 'lady'. Male colleagues were accorded the title *Bey* to follow their names.

Armed with this knowledge, I was careful to address my new colleagues as Derya Hanım and Erol Bey. Just to confuse me, within my own department, these titles seemed to be unused. Even my Head of Department was happy to be addressed simply by her name. Anxious not to make a faux pas, I was relentlessly polite until such times as I felt I knew enough not to offend anyone by omission.

It so happened that my teaching partner in the Primary section of the school shared a first name with the redoubtable deputy head. Referring to them both as "Figen Hn" (Hn is the commonly used shortened form of hanım) began to cause confusion. "Bizim Figen?" – "Our Figen?" was a constant refrain when I reported dealings in the teachers' room.

Gradually the pecking order became apparent and I also learned to distinguish between the *sen* (for close friends and family) and *siz* (formal) forms of address, so difficult for English speakers to remember. Moving to a new school some time later, the Principal punctiliously addressed me as Bayan Celia. I felt singled out and distinctly uncomfortable. "I'm the same as you," I protested weakly. Anger simmered gently beneath my calm exterior until my half-Turkish daughter wisely informed me that a courtesy was being extended to me as a foreigner. I have learned to accept both forms of address with equanimity.

Later still, I worked with a more newly arrived foreign colleague, who simply refused to use the courtesy titles, Bey or Hanım, however exalted the status of the person being addressed. Whereas the recipients of his remarks seemed to be unphased, I saw other listeners bristle and feared that we 'foreigners' were being branded as unintegrated or even downright rude.

After many years in the job, I still make mistakes, but I think that I generally err on the side of caution and am convinced that sensitivity to such cultural niceties goes a long way to towards promoting good relationships in our working and social lives.

Studying Languages

I would never describe myself as 'good at languages', but studied French to 'A' level standard at school, and took Latin 'O' level, with half a term of basic German – now mainly forgotten. I was always afraid to speak in a foreign language, fearing laughter or ridicule. Short trips to France only confirmed my lack of linguistic skills – and I didn't congratulate myself on reading skills and general comprehension in the foreign language. If one didn't speak it, then one didn't know it, and speaking it was too terrifying to contemplate with all the possible errors one could make.

This attitude was forcibly changed when I came to Turkey to help build a Benesh Choreology Department for a university's Ballet Section. Despite being assured before I came that 'everybody spoke English' it was apparent on arrival that hardly anyone did; moreover, those that had learnt some English were also too afraid to try and speak it.

I worked with an interpreter/assistant feeling foolish – she might as well have been teaching 'my' subject outright, instead of their paying me such a high salary to do so.

Working first with Turkish language books either lent or acquired I discovered how hard it is to learn a language without a teacher. After two years of stubborn resistance to the new 'useless' language I was 'getting by' in, somebody lent me a simple course book – so simple I felt I already knew it all; I could read it in three sittings en route back to Turkey from UK summer holidays. On arrival at the university I greeted students of mine using this simple Turkish I knew from before and had just re-read. The effects were astonishing. All the students were impressed that I had somehow 'learnt Turkish' during the summer. The key point seemed to be the use of short meaningful phrases rather than longer grammatically correct sentences. This is an obvious point to make in learning to speak any language, but it can take students years or even a lifetime to appreciate and put into practice.

I was thus sufficiently inspired to enrol at a language school for one month. Classes were five days a week with four lessons a day, from 9am to 1pm – tortuously intensive, to my mind. The groups were mixed ages from Middle-Eastern students in their late teens to middle-aged ex-pats and foreign business men. However, the Head of the school took pity on me and invited me to sit in on her own classes – who were due to take the final diploma exam that month. The flexible attitude of both the head and my own teacher opened my eyes to different styles of teaching and learning. They treated us like friends, and these two teachers are still my good friends twenty years later. I don't know any teacher from my past schools and universities who would have behaved in a similar friendly way, including teachers in the adult evening institutes, yet this Turkish principal regularly ordered a round of coffees and teas for all the students who made it to the first class of the morning, just to help us adjust to being at our desks so early in the day to learn something we hadn't really wanted to do but now needed. She paid for these welcome hot drinks from her own pocket.

Thus, my lack of grammar was painfully adjusted and I somehow acquired the confidence to use my pidgin Turkish – everywhere. This opened doors for me quite dramatically. Students and people I met anywhere invited me home to meet their families. Contacts were easily made and friendships cemented. Shopping and visits to the dentist or doctor became a pleasure instead of a trial and the cold Turkish walls of my self-inflicted prison cell came tumbling down. Turks of all ages and occupations complimented my Turkish as soon as I spoke one sentence. Can one imagine an English person doing this to a foreigner struggling to say something in English?

This was yet another eye-opener in the business of education: Turkish teachers are so encouraging of their students and so polite with their corrections, making sure they do not embarrass or wound the student with their words.

In terms of job opportunities, my horizons opened up too. The Choreology Department having been established, my work was finishing at the university, but I had fallen in love with the country, its people, climate and ancient ruined sites. I didn't want to return to cloudy rainy Britain. With my developing language skills, the hobbies and part-time jobs I had been doing, with ex-pats and their children – such as yoga, tap dance, piano teaching and clarinet teaching – now became available to Turkish students. I found the confidence to teach many different things using Turkish – something I would never have envisioned for myself before, even in a European language such as French. Having to shout in Turkish to make corrections to a class of twenty teenage tap dancers, while simultaneously demonstrating the routine, was not one of my natural talents.

My career has changed several times since then, from choreologist and tap dance teacher to English teacher to yoga teacher and now Bowen therapist, and the majority of my work is with Turks, so learning the language to some degree of fluency has been more valuable than I could ever have imagined when I first came to Turkey.

Although the language I had to learn is not commonly found in a university prospectus, I would say that the benefits are the same for any language learned; confidence is built up; horizons are widened; understanding between cultures is deepened.

Response to Responsibility

Recently I had a row with my mother-in-law. Nothing very unusual about that but the circumstances got me thinking about conflicting attitudes towards children and child-rearing.

My son was to receive his Master's degree at a graduation ceremony in Ankara. We had discussed the time and date but reluctantly I had had to admit defeat: the distance (560 kilometres) and my work schedule would not allow me to be there, which was a great disappointment for us both.

During a visit to the family home, I phoned my son to offer my good wishes. My mother-in-law, never one to miss a chance to put her spoke in, waded in. As my husband's death had deprived her grandson of his father, the least I could do was to be there to witness his moment of glory.

For once I did not bite my tongue but gave as good as I got. She had touched a nerve and made me feel like an unfit mother and I was deeply hurt.

"Do you really think I don't want to go?" I cried.

In the ensuing uproar, each of us retreated to a different part of the house to shed a few tears. Her daughter and other daughters-in-law rallied round to reassure me. I was a good mother and had supported my children to the best of my ability, both emotionally and financially. I should learn to take the rantings of an old woman in my stride.

When my husband's sister went on to thank me for looking after her niece and nephew so well, I began to see the whole sorry affair in a different light. She said that she had never had a single moment's doubt about their welfare. Comforting words at the time helped to smooth my ruffled feathers but in the cooler light of the following day I rejected the idea that I had only done these things as some kind of surrogate for my family-in-law.

When a child is born in Turkey, parents are congratulated of course. As well as *Ömürlü olsun*: may it have a long life, you also hear, *hayırlı evlat olsun!*: may he/she be a good child to you. This expression suggests that children have the responsibility of being good to their parents.

Parental responsibility seems to be prolonged into your offspring's adulthood. So my colleagues try to prevent their children from spreading their wings. Even when it comes to the choice of university, they like to have their offspring within reach, if not living at home. So there is commiseration with a mother 'sending' her son overseas to study in Paris, while I alone congratulate her, delighted that he will have the chance to broaden his horizons.

I have long taken the view that after your children reach a certain age, it is no longer desirable or even possible to control what they do or how they do it. We both tried to make sure that they made informed decisions but the decisions were theirs to make.

I am still regaled with questions such as why we 'sent' them to universities in different cities. Even now that they are both earning a living, I am asked when I will marry off my son or whether it was difficult to give my daughter away in marriage. On some issues we just have to agree to differ.

Dragon

In mythology, the dragon guards treasures. With lion's feet, a snake's tail and fiery breath, the dragon has power over earth, air, fire and water.

7 Heat, Crime, Fire and Earthquake

Surviving the Oven

Family life here progresses quite cheerfully, but the links with home are still strong and we go back to Britain every year. Every time we come back from a trip, it's the same thing. Of course we always travel in summer, because that's when the holidays are. So it's August when we get off the plane in Izmir. The grass around the airport is parched yellow-grey, and the heat hits you like a faceful of wet, boiling concrete.

I am usually quite an alert and active person, but at thirty degrees my body sags like a sandbag and muscles melt, so that the smallest movement requires enormous effort. A comparable paralysis affects the mind; attempts to think and plan are overwhelmed by the immediate discomfort of the sluggish body dripping all over with sweat. Sleep is elusive; the open windows bring some movement of cooler air under the concrete roof, but they also bring cacophonies of barking dogs, voices of street revellers, the TV from the neighbours' balcony, and the moans of traffic. I lie awake and think about cool, green, quiet Britain, and passionately wish I was still there.

In the midst of all this misery, a few positive experiences emerge. The first good thing to happen on arrival is the welcome of our dogs. I do not look after them, but still they love me, with illogical canine generosity. They greet our homecoming with a tremendous outburst of excitement and affection.

The next good thing is usually when my husband Ali emerges from the garden with cobwebs and leaves in his hair, carrying a basket of grapes. Look, he says, we grew them. Not the best quality (they are partially wasp-eaten and mildewy), but still, we grew them, and when you have washed off the dust, the best ones are delicious. I am reminded that in Britain there is never quite enough fruit. It is so expensive, and you always have to try not to be greedy. Here in summer fruit is cheap, and apart from the offerings of the garden, we buy as much as we can eat. Some pieces always go rotten and end up in the chicken run, and it doesn't matter.

The suitcases get emptied, somehow, although piles of papers and odd clothes will lie around for a long time. It is too hot to put things away properly, just too much effort.

An absolute minimum of domestic activity is all we can accomplish.

Going out to the dustbin, or watering the plants, we see neighbours. Their greetings are enthusiastic. "Welcome back! How was your holiday? Come for coffee!" I begin to realise that this is actually a place called home, rather than an alien planet. In truth, it is both of these things, in varying proportions. As this period of adjustment passes, the alien planet perception declines, while the home perception gets stronger.

I use the strategies developed in previous years. First of all, sleep in the afternoons, in the coolest place you can find. If Ali is out, that's the basement. If not, the sitting room. The thing is, he snores. It's one of the dark secrets of our marriage. There are a few others, which I won't write about here. The afternoon sleep, preceded by a chapter of a good book, breaks the monotony of the long day in the oven. It also frees some capacity for action for those times when I can actually move around without feeling ill: early morning and evening twilight. The sun rises at around seven. From six-thirty to eight is the best window of opportunity, when my body and mind feel normal and I can do things.

Once the suitcase is empty, I use the early hours to begin tidying the plants on our flat roof. There is a great tangle of vegetation, living and dead; leaves and earth are everywhere, together with mysterious bits of plastic and paper that have probably blown in on the wind.

I locate the shears, broom and dustpan, and find suitable containers for organic and inorganic rubbish. The work gives me enormous satisfaction as I discover unexpected shoots and buds. I rearrange, nurture and display all those living things, that, like me, are surviving the oven.

When the handful of tomatoes from the local shop is exhausted, we embark on an evening trip to the big open-air market. This is a family enterprise, and we take the car. Together we can buy, and carry, anything we want. The stands of gorgeous produce progress in untidy rows, shaded by a forest of wide, colourful umbrellas. Those who have not rented stands spread their goods on bits of canvas on the concrete ground; those with clothes to display hang them in festoons from strings and poles, like giant cascades of brightly coloured flowers. On market day the whole world is here. From almost ragged to downright posh, from covered head to sexy cleavage, from babe-in-arms to grey beard and walking stick. This is the Turkey I love, in all its diversity and enthusiasm, busy, active, absorbed in the age-old activities of buying and selling items needed for daily life.

Ali makes most of the purchasing decisions, in the style of his father, so I am free to observe and enjoy the surroundings. I notice a beautifully symmetrical pyramid of green beans, decorated with yellow plastic flowers. An extra large potato features a smiley face drawn on it in felt tip pen. As well as prices on display cards, there are various notices in praise of the produce. Peaches are *çok tatlı,* "very sweet", Melons are *bal gibi,* "like honey", and a box of dry carob beans is imaginatively labelled *Turkish viagra.*

Another important event in my adaptation is the first swim in the sea. This is in the morning or evening, to avoid the frying heat of the daytime sun. It feels cold getting in, because I am not used to it, but in a few minutes I relax totally into the soft, silky salt water. Here at last I can move freely without feeling hot, I can roll and wriggle and splash and stretch and actually get tired muscles, and feel wonderful. When I see the foreign tourists, I always have a sense of privilege. Those people have flown thousands of miles and paid lots of money to do this, while for me it is only a short drive from home.

Did I say home? Yes. I do live here, actually. We invite some friends. I make my contributions to the dinner quite early in the morning, while I can still move around comfortably. I make a few cold dishes, the things they call *meze,* like green bean salad or mashed aubergine with yogurt and garlic. In the evening Ali does a barbecue on the roof, fresh sardines or homemade meatballs. We drink the traditional grape spirit, *rakı,* which goes milky when you add water, or some rough homemade wine which is still left from last season. We talk about our holidays, discuss the latest political bad news and chat about plans for the autumn. "When the weather gets cooler..." we say.

One morning I wake up, and the light is different. What's happening? I feel a wild surge of hope as I grope for my glasses, roll out of bed and go to the window. Yes! It's true! There are clouds in the sky. They will probably vanish in an hour, but more will come, to give a respite from the grilling sun. And one day, it will rain.

Burglaries

Turkish people have a well-deserved reputation for warmth and hospitality. In country areas, strangers will invite you in for a cup of tea or to share a meal. Nothing is too much trouble. Officialdom, however, has a sterner face. If you have to deal with the civil service in its various shapes and forms, you are lucky to raise a smile. Are post office workers trained to keep straight faces, I wonder? If you are unfortunate enough to end up in hospital, checking in is a formidable procedure. The police have a reputation for brutality.

I have become a frequent visitor at my local police station: no, I haven't turned to a life of crime, but I have become a victim. My house has twice entertained uninvited guests in the last three months. The first time they broke my pathetically inadequate, wooden front door and made off with my computer, carefully concealed in a new winter coat.

As I arrived home from work at the usual time (my routine was my downfall), I cried with shock and disbelief and immediately rushed to a neighbour who offered tea and sympathy and called the police. I was too stupefied to perform this simple act for myself. Suddenly I found my home overrun with well-wishers, some of whom I have said no more than two words to, in as many years. Indeed one of them has not given me so much as a good morning since we nearly came to blows over a repair to the communal electricity supply two years ago. Another offered to call the local carpenter to affect a temporary repair of the battered door. They offered me shelter for the night in case I was too scared to be alone. I thanked them all for their kindness and sat down to assuage my ragged feelings. When the police arrived, the neighbours came in uninvited and started, in that very Turkish way, to give all sorts of good advice to all and sundry. I longed for them all to go. Having decided to have a shower to wash away the negativity along with the day's grime, I had to hastily dress to receive yet more visitors wishing me *geçmiş olsun* (may it be over).

On the advice of a dear friend, I was soon safely ensconced behind a steel monster of a door. Having been constantly regaled with tales of break-ins and deadly deeds perpetrated by intruders, I counted myself lucky to hold on to any sense of well-being. As the police advice was also along those lines, I decided to give in gracefully, dig deep into my pocket and try to put the whole thing behind me.

The burglars had ransacked my lounge and two unused bedrooms but left my own room, where my jewellery lay inadequately hidden, quite untouched. It is not a vast collection but of course the inevitable happened and three months later, the second gang (or were they one and the same?) effected an entry over the balcony and through a window. My few precious pieces of gold were not spared their unwelcome attentions this time. Curiously they also took two financially worthless items while spurning a valuable ring. The financial loss was insignificant but I felt all the usual gamut of emotions: shock, disbelief, rage and an uncharacteristic desire for revenge.

On each occasion, the local police force have sprung into rapid operation and have been full of concern. They arrived swiftly and the second time with wry smiles and inquiring looks. "Don't we know you?" they asked. The constant chatter of their walkie-talkies relayed events to the station commander. If I hadn't been so upset I might have felt flattered. Once they learned that I am of foreign extraction, they started falling over themselves to apologise for their fellow countrymen's behaviour. I was surprised, to say the least, to be treated with kid gloves. On my subsequent visits to the police station to give statements and collect the necessary documents for insurance claims, they offered me tea and further commiserations. As one officer was typing my words, others came to engage me in conversation. They were interested not only in me personally but in the English penal code. No doubt the severe punishments meted out in Europe deter the casual burglar. When I told them that I had been burgled twice in the UK, they expressed surprise. They bemoaned the fact that my burglars, even if caught, are likely to walk free in a matter of days or weeks. One officer started to talk of Turkey's application to join the European Union. I left the station with a personal message for Tony Blair, no less. Despite my protestations that I had no special access to Downing Street, I was duly charged to deliver the officer's personal opinions.

Next came what I can only describe as the battle of the insurance. I little expected this to be much of a problem once I had come to grips with procedure with the help of their very helpful local agent. After months of waiting, they finally agreed to a payout but not before demanding the title deeds to the house and my late husband's will. As the deeds are in the names of me and my children, the money finally arrived, after numerous increasingly irate telephone calls. It was to be paid in three separate amounts. In accordance with the will, my children got the lion's share although neither of them resides with me!

A year or so later, one of the policeman, who had come to my rescue, was kind enough to stop and give me a lift home when he saw me walking home on a very hot day. He told his colleague all about me: he had remembered all the details.

My shock has abated but as I prepare to put bars on my windows, I feel the injustice of being the one who will live in a cage. The whole experience has served to remind me with some force that stereotyping is a dangerous and pernicious thing. You may find goodness and caring or indifference and hate anywhere in the world.

Fire on the Hills

One summer, as we returned from the beach in Kuşadasi, my friend remarked on the plume of smoke rising from the hills in the distance behind our holiday house.

"Must be a forest fire," we mused, and "I wonder how big it is, or if the forestry fire brigade has seen it or if anyone is doing anything about it."

At the time it was just a smallish grey cloud of smoke, and we weren't very worried, particularly as we could now see and hear the helicopters coming, dangling heavy loads of water from the sea to douse the fire. It was even mildly exciting, on that long hot sunny day at the beginning of August. My friend remarked that her friend was working in the hotel behind our '*site*' (private housing estate), so she telephoned her to get more news, but there was no reply.

We thought no more of it an hour later, the choppers still coming and going with their loads as my friend took her leave of me and went home. By this time there were two or three plumes of smoke, and I assumed this was due to the dousing with water. 'It will all be over by dusk' I thought.

Other householders and their children were gathering at the far edge of our estate to watch the drama, although we could only see smoke in the distance.

'Nothing to worry about' I thought, 'It won't come anywhere near our site'. It never occurred to me to worry about possible threat to homes or people since the area was uninhabited forest and wooded hillsides, and seemed to be miles away from any houses or farmland.

All through the evening the helicopters kept up their flights, bringing more and more sea-water until darkness fell. 'Perhaps the fire is out by now', I thought, as I tried to doze off now that the noise had abated.

It may have been my imagination, but that night seemed much hotter than normal, and the walls of my bedroom were even hot inside. Sleep was difficult with the heat and lack of any breeze, but I was sure that the lack of wind would have helped to put the fire out, now that all was quiet.

However, in the early hours of the morning the choppers started up again, like angry wasps swarming overhead, and I began to worry more. 'Fire still not out. Oh dear. It must be bigger than I thought.'

I went out on to the balcony to see if the plume of smoke still looked the same, and was mildly shocked to see the balcony, chairs, cushions and everything was covered in tiny fragments of ash, like a dusting of grey frost over it all.

I began to get an inkling of how serious this fire might be, although I still didn't realise exactly where it was. The plumes of smoke had spread out a little wider by now, but no flames, and no change in colour. I was convinced it would soon be put out.

As indeed it was, by the end of that day. We later learned of the hundreds of trees destroyed on the hills around *Meryemana*, much wildlife killed, and the apparent miracle that the fire had stopped just short of the chapel itself. (*Meryemana* is the sacred chapel dedicated to the Virgin Mary. Every year, thousands of tourists flock to this site in the hills above the ancient ruins of Ephesus, and for some it is an annual pilgrimage, as it is supposedly the place where Jesus' mother Mary spent her last years, having been brought to the region by St. John.)

It appeared that no one had been injured in the fire and the woodland was mainly owned by the state as a kind of national heritage, so there were no reports of damage to property. Rumours were circulated as to the cause of the fire, but it was generally agreed that arson could be ruled out. However, the loss of wildlife and trees made this a major national disaster and local feeling was that it would take many years to replace the woods that had covered these hills so densely.

Nevertheless, only a few months later when we visited the region with friends from abroad, it was astounding how much work had been done by the local forestry authorities: the burnt dead wood had all been cut down into hundreds of logs which were neatly piled up in batches ready for removal; the woodlands around the sacred site were tidy and free of any debris. As we drove up the winding road to the chapel the sun's rays cut through the branches of the many trees still standing, like swords of light piercing the darkness of the woods. These brilliant rays of sunlight added to the eerie feeling that this special place had indeed witnessed a miracle that night of the fire, and that a spirit of hope shone over the area now.

Earthquakes

On a mild but dark evening in December 1977, I was teaching English to an adult class at the Turkish-American Association in Izmir. I was rudely interrupted mid-sentence by a roaring noise, followed by a violent shaking of the floor beneath me. As the lights went out, a young woman student started to scream. At first I thought of the London buildings shaken by the tube trains passing below. It was a few minutes before I gathered my wits sufficiently to remember that there were no such trains in Izmir. By this time one of the students, a calm young man, had lit the emergency gas lamp, conveniently provided on a high shelf in the classroom. Reality dawned as the students streamed out of the classroom and out of the building. Seized with fear, the shock made me move in slow motion. I collected my belongings from the teachers' room, seeing and hearing my colleagues in various states of distress, as if in a dream. I wasn't sure whether we should leave or if class was to resume as the shaking had passed but no one seemed to be in a fit state to continue so I left without a word.

The earthquake had lasted a mere five seconds, I later learned, but each second felt like an hour at the time. The previous year, the city of Managua in Nicaragua had been devastated by a seven second tremor. Thousands of lives had been lost. At the time I had thought that a few seconds was mercifully too short for anyone to realize what was happening. My opinions underwent a swift revision.

I made my way downstairs to the street, wondering what terrible scenes would meet my eye. To my great surprise, everything looked much as usual.

How could such trauma leave no outward sign? Relief would come later but at that moment was kept at bay by the more powerful emotion of shock.

Like a robot, I made my way to the bus stop. My husband chanced to come by, driving a coach-load of factory workers home from their shift. As I climbed aboard without speaking, the chatter of voices died away.

Kahraman asked me what was wrong: unaware that I looked as though I had seen a ghost, I explained with some surprise, the cause of my early departure from my lesson. The passengers were equally surprised as they had felt nothing on the road. Their cheery banter soon resumed but I felt unable to take in anything they were saying.

Returning to lessons the following day, the story swapping started. Every narrator tried hard to cap the tales related by their colleagues. Washing up water had sloshed onto floors, light fittings had performed unsolicited dances and chimneys had collapsed, missing the passers-by by a hair's breadth. Some of these tales may have been tall but it was a reminder that buildings rather than earthquakes kill and maim.

A week later we were in the middle of Kemeraltı, Izmir's busiest shopping district, when people started to pour out of the surrounding office blocks. Panes of glass shattered high above our heads, sending deadly shards to the pavements far below. The after-shocks can go on reverberating for some time. Such was my baptism of fire and my introduction to one of the less attractive features of life in Turkey.

Before my second visit to Turkey, the year before, there had been a powerful earthquake in Erzurum in the east of the country. My mother, immediately anxious, had tried to persuade me to abandon my planned trip. "Izmir is perfectly safe," I replied airily. Once again revised ideas were the order of the day. The pictures on the news were striking, however, for showing that the major municipal buildings, such as the local authority and the police station emerged relatively unscathed amidst the rubble that had been private homes. Hence the second lesson was learned: when builders obey the law when construction takes place many lives can be saved.

Living back in London, where my children were born, we had a family outing to the Natural History Museum where we discovered a newly opened attraction, an earthquake simulator! As everyone climbed on to the shaking platform with great glee, I found myself glued to the floor and unable even to watch them. The real thing had proved quite sufficient for me.

Back in Turkey, the passing years have done little to reduce my feelings of terror and panic to any great degree. A state of seeming tranquillity has been cultivated for the sake of my own children and then for my young students.

On one occasion when my mother was visiting us here, the very solid granite kitchen work surface started to behave as though it had a mind of its own. I calmly put down my knife and stopped chopping vegetables and looked over to the table where my mother was sitting quietly playing cards. She showed no reaction and indeed later said she had felt nothing. How I envied her!

The prevailing philosophy, much promulgated after the havoc wreaked in Istanbul in 1999, is to be prepared as these seismic events are unpredictable and uncontrollable. We are now inundated with advice. Children drill in the classroom, diving under desks or standing in doorways when the alarm goes off. More recent research suggests that this advice is counter-productive.

One morning I was at school very early and there was only one other teacher in the staffroom. When the characteristic rumbling began soon followed by shaking, we fled to the playground where students were beginning to arrive. Persuading them to stay out of the building was quite hard. They thought it was a joke!

After a few hours, which saw us back in lessons, they took us seriously when the aftershocks began. At first I tried to calm the students, saying it would all pass. This did not seem entirely credible as the walls refused to be still so we left the building in a less than orderly manner. The phone lines jammed with anxious parents making hurried enquiries about their offspring.

A teacher reported the blackboard arched away from her as she was trying to write on it. Some of her class were hysterical but others were secretly pleased to be out in the playground instead of being behind a desk. After an early lunch, school was abandoned for the day. On my way to the bus stop, I heard and saw a newly built house shiver and shake: an unnerving experience. The remainder of that week saw us more outside than in. When a free Friday was announced, I took myself off to Istanbul to calm my shattered nerves.

Many families have emergency supplies packed in bags by the door. We are urged to fasten our larger items of furniture to the walls, to prevent being crushed by falling bookcases or wardrobes. Despite all these measures, I have become markedly more nervous during the years I have lived alone. Not usually subject to irrational fears, I find it especially difficult to come to terms with those shocks that strike in the early hours. In April 2005, violent and noisy happenings threatened to throw us all out of our beds at 3am. My neighbours from across the street piled down their stairs, coming close to breaking a few limbs on the way. In fact many injuries are caused in this way or by people jumping off balconies. Strongly advising me to sleep in my ancient and battered car, they then drove away leaving me alone. After a very short time I decided to go back to my nice warm bed although sleep proved somewhat elusive.

At school the following day we found a smattering of students had actually come into school after the night's adventures. My first act was to ask the Head to postpone a scheduled exam. He thanked me for making the request and readily agreed.

Some six months later, after a similar night time adventure, I found the street full of people and the offer of a blanket and car seat quite comforting. I didn't know whether to feel contempt or a sneaking admiration for those among us, who decided to risk dying in their beds. Despite the cold and discomfort, a new kind of neighbourliness sprang up. A sense of camaraderie developed. I found myself invited in by people I had barely spoken to previously, although the constant accompanying television diet of seismic news was less than comforting. Some families may take to their cars or tents for months at a time after such events but most of us gradually return to normal, as long as we are lucky enough to have a house undamaged by the quake. It is easy to misread the signs as superficial plaster cracks may look alarming where serious damage to buildings is not always apparent. It is best to have an engineer take a look and take samples of the reinforced concrete but this cannot always be done in a hurry or in a reliable way.

As with all such happenings, especially in this lovely country, there are myths and folklore which makes many instant 'experts'. The disturbances deep in the Earth's crust, you may be told, are related to hot weather or the phases of the moon. An eclipse of the sun was blamed for an Iranian earthquake not so long ago. There are also the religious fanatics, who tell you that it is all a sign of God's displeasure at our dissolute ways.

After each of these disturbing events we desperately hope that the constant release of seismic energy will stop it building up like the steam in a pressure cooker. Then time does its work and we forget, or try to, just how terrified we were. Life goes on, we say to each other philosophically, until the next one overtakes us of course!

Hands on Hips

Representing nurturing and fertility, this symbol dates back to mother goddess images of 5000 years ago. For us it symbolises the importance of family on special occasions.

8 - Special Times of Year

The Tenth of November

Many moons ago, when I was still very new to teaching in Turkey, I was very put out one November morning, at finding myself standing on the pavement, waiting in vain for the school bus, which had failed to materialise at the usual hour. I lived some twelve miles from the school and so this was more than a minor inconvenience.

Having boarded the next bus, which was packed with people and belching black smoke, my silent anger turned into anxiety. I would definitely be late for my 9 o'clock lesson. Would my feeble excuse be accepted? Would I face a dressing down or even be asked to leave forthwith?

I was very inexperienced and the only foreigner at the school. Some of my colleagues regarded me with a degree of suspicion, if not hostility.

To add insult to injury, I had a steep hill to climb after alighting from the bus: more delay in reaching my final destination. Try as I might, my legs refused to keep up with the pace my head was demanding. I paused to catch my breath and allowed the beautiful cerulean waters of the bay, reflecting the azure skies above, to give me a few seconds of peace and calm. The noise of revving engines and the filthy exhaust fumes emanating from the traffic climbing the hill soon put paid to my reverie.

To my great surprise, a taxi drew up suddenly beside me and the driver got out. He kept one hand firmly pressed on the horn. Other drivers copied this odd behaviour, setting up a great howling noise all over the city.

A glance at my watch told me that as I had feared, I had missed my class by five minutes. I hurried on, only to be told by a fellow pedestrian to stand still!

This annual ritual, with which I have now become familiar, marks the exact hour (9.05am) of Atatürk's passing. He died in Dolmabahçe Palace in Istanbul on 10th November, 1938. The Turks do not use the word 'died', in this context. Atatürk, founder of the modern Turkish Republic and its first president, is said to have closed his eyes on this inauspicious day.

So on 10th November, school buses leave half an hour early to ensure that the students are ready for the ceremony of remembrance. Everybody assumed that I knew.

I have worked in two other schools since then and the sentiments are the same. This year students gathered once again in the autumn sunshine to mourn the loss of the great man. The youngest laid flowers in front of the bust of Atatürk, which has pride of place in every school playground. Poems were read, massed choirs sang and thanks were given for the leader, who was instrumental in forging democracy from the rotting corpse of the Ottoman Empire.

Atatürk's picture is omnipresent. Every office and shop, no matter how small, has a portrait of him on its walls. The message is clear: separation of spiritual and temporal power is at the heart of the Turkish constitution.

On this remarkable occasion, the whole country stands still for a few moments and is united in a gesture of respect, as at no other time.

Teachers' Day

Today is the 23rd of November. I view tomorrow, the 24th, with more than the usual sinking feeling. For tomorrow is Teachers' Day: Atatürk's gift to those of us engaged in this benighted profession. While it is nice to have a day of one's own, a mark of recognition, mixed feelings lurk somewhere beneath the surface. Teachers do command a degree of respect but this is not reflected in the pay and conditions of the majority.

The whole day has become besmirched by commercialism. For a start, you arrive at school to find massed ranks of flower sellers at the gate. Students, rich and poor, feel pressured into buying: a single rose or a large bouquet are de rigueur. Some parents push the boat out and more elaborate and expensive gifts are proffered. The cynic in me suspects that the size and price of the present are in direct inverse proportion to the success of the student.

Once inside the building, lesson time is largely taken up with the presentation of presents and the kissing of hands. (Younger people kiss older people's hands as a mark of respect in this culture.) As a new teacher, I was overwhelmed by a whole class of eleven-year-olds, lining up to greet me, until I realised that the students just kept rejoining the queue in an attempt to keep it going for 40 minutes and so avoid having a lesson at all.

Then there are the shy apologisers, who feel they should have bought something. There is an immense embarrassment on both sides. On your return to the Teachers' Room, there are surreptitious glances, to see who has accumulated the biggest bunches of flowers or the best presents. Again I feel acutely uncomfortable amid the cries of, "however am I going to get home with all this?"

The least well off students may feel compelled to make the biggest show. One former student, who had been abandoned by her mother, had also mislaid her father, leaving her to the tender mercies of a grandparent. Knowing that she had to scrimp and save only added to my embarrassment as she presented each of her English teachers with a sweater. They were of the same style but in different colours and rather badly made but we all wore them to school the next day just to see the smile on her face.

At my current school, the students have a half-day, while we are herded to the conference room to endure hours of speeches, poems and choral singing. Last year some had the temerity to leave after two or three hours, only to be severely reprimanded by the local director of education. "Atatürk gave you this day!" he thundered. "How can you insult him by leaving before the end of the ceremony?"

So tomorrow, we will sit through it all before coming home with the contents of half a greenhouse and who knows what unwanted presents.

Every year I ask my students to give their money to a worthy cause and reward me with their undivided attention – ten minutes would be a start! Maybe one day my words will sink in. I live in hope.

Direct vs Indirect Requests

This piece is actually about Turkish public holidays, known as *Bayrams* by foreigners combining the Turkish word with an English plural ending.

When I first arrived in Turkey it was early February, so New Year festivities had passed and although I was looking forward to Easter, nobody else was aware of its existence, this being a Muslim country.

Later that year, after one *Bayram* in the summer, I learnt that they were three or four days in duration and were preceded by a half day off to prepare. These religious festivals shifted back ten days each year. In other words, they were not aligned to a specific date like Christmas Day is, but followed the Muslim (lunar) calendar year. Having appreciated this, it seemed common sense to me to plan ahead for these *Bayrams*, as they seemed to disrupt lessons, programmes, plans and normal organised living and working. I duly rearranged my lesson programmes well in advance at all levels so that we would not lose valuable teaching hours or fall behind schedule at the next *Bayram*.

However, I had failed to organise for all contingencies – such as transport.

One week before the half-day holiday was due, two sweet-faced choreology students approached me for *izin* (meaning 'permission', as in 'leave of absence'!). When I asked why, they hung their heads and sadly explained that they had to go to their villages for the *Bayram*, and there were no coach tickets left for the day before the holiday started; they could only find tickets for this week, or only for today! I was sure they were trying it on, but being a new teacher and not Muslim, I didn't want to do anything wrong or destroy their chances of being home for the holiday. Of course I agreed to the first request.

Then two more came. At this point I went to ask my assistant what the protocol was. She looked surprised at first, as if she had never encountered such a request in her many years of teaching there.

Quite possibly she hadn't, as Turkish people will usually defer to a perceived 'higher authority' when asked any question at all; she may not have been in this position before.

However, when she talked to the students it became clear that there was a possible problem with some of their travel arrangements.

Needless to say, quite a lot of them escaped a week early and also returned a few days late ("we couldn't find any coach tickets" were the sorry pleas). Moreover, when they did arrive, they appeared late for the lesson, bleary eyed and pale, complaining of lack of sleep on the ten-hour-all-night coach journeys from Zonguldak or wherever, and could they please have *izin* to go and get some sleep? Of course I said yes.

In subsequent years I planned and organised and wrote myself copious notes so as not to be caught out again by students' subterfuge. Needless to say, every year they found an even better excuse to escape from lessons earlier. Forewarned may well have been forearmed, but the end result was the same.

The Drums Of Ramazan

To the rear of my block of flats, there is a building site. Two brand new blocks are nearing completion: the worst of the mess, noise and dirt are over. Putting the finishing touches, such as a low-level wall round the perimeter, can still produce an unwanted assault on the eardrums, especially as the workers start early in order to beat the considerable noonday heat.

On Monday 1st September, 2008, I was rudely awakened by a rhythmic banging noise in the early hours of the morning. My first thought was to curse the builders and their horrible sledgehammers. A bleary-eyed glance at the clock revealed the time: 3.04am. Even builders are not that industrious! The first day of Ramazan, the holiest month of the Muslim calendar, was upon us.

The noise? Lone drummers tour the district, intent on waking all and sundry. Those who are *niyetli* (intending to fast) have reliable alarm clocks and mobile phones these days but the ancient custom of the drum continues. For the rest of us, we have to grin and bear it, turn a deaf ear and go back to sleep.

Easier said than done: you are not only treated to this peculiar serenade for the few minutes it takes for the drummer to actually pass your front door, but you hear the advance and retreat of the drumbeats for up to half an hour before and after their deafening crescendo.

On the second night of this cacophony, I actually got out of bed, as if to catch the culprit, such was the feeling of malevolence in my heart. Across the field beside my flat, the drummer advanced confidently, totally unaware of my hostile stare.

To add insult to injury, the many dogs chained up in neighbouring gardens, reported the drummer's approach in the time-honoured manner.

Once aroused, the canine community get into their nocturnal stride and sleep is once more effectively banished. The noisy protests continue long after the drummer's departure.

He produces a singular rhythm by beating a large bass drum on either side with two differently shaped drumsticks, one being much thicker than the other. The instrument is strapped onto the drummer's body at a rakish angle to complete the effect.

With sunrise at 5am, you may wonder why we are woken at 3. Scarcely enough time to rise, cook and eat and complete the ritual washing necessary before praying. All has to be accomplished before the deadline of sunrise. Some fasters then read the Koran while others sink gratefully back into bed to catch a few hours sleep before the day begins again.

Those who have no job to go to or no children going off to school, may choose to stay up late, eating a final meal at 2 or 3 in the morning before retiring to bed. They then sleep as long as they can through the following day. With fifteen hours of daylight, Ramazan is tough this year and will get harder for the next few years, as the holy month moves back ten days each year.

On the festival that ends the fasting, the drummer puts in a final appearance. This time he may come in daylight or in the early evening. He knocks on your door for remuneration. A few years ago, a fellow foreigner offered to pay the poor musician, only if he promised not to approach her house the next year!

Here in Izmir, many people carry on their lives as usual. Within the same family there may be fasters and eaters, living side by side. Cafes and restaurants now stay open during the day, although some stop selling alcohol. Swallowing a hasty gulp of water on the bus or in the street makes me feel slightly guilty but no one comments. When I visit friends, they generously continue with the norms of hospitality and produce food and drink, even if they are fasting themselves.

So I resign myself to broken nights and look forward to the end of Ramazan, when all join in the celebrations and say goodbye to the drummer for another year.

The Festival Of Sacrifice

In the early days of our marriage we lived in Hatay, a crowded bustling district of Izmir. I was used to the streets being full of shoppers and street vendors at all hours, not to mention the crazy drivers with one hand permanently on the horn. In October 1977 strange things began to happen. Every piece of open ground filled with sheep. I saw sheep on balconies high and low; tied to railings in the street. This was the prelude to the festival of sacrifice (*Kurban Bayramı*), an important date in the Muslim year.

All the sheep were to be slaughtered on the first day of the festival, which commemorates Isaac's escape from being sacrificed by Abraham. I was of course familiar with this bit of the Bible but had never imagined that it would be re-enacted in a modern metropolis.

Imagine my surprise and shock as I witnessed the slitting of an ovine throat in the road outside my house as I made my way to the local grocer.

It was only *arefe*, the eve of the festival. The smell of blood and freshly killed meat filled the air the following morning as we picked our way through the carcases strewn over the waste ground we had to cross.

Muslims believe that meat is only fit to eat (*helal*) if every drop of blood has been drained from the body immediately after slaughter: hence the chosen method of despatch.

Once we reached my husband's family home, he was much in demand as a butcher, a service he performed for many years. In expert and fearless hands the animal dies quickly and with minimal suffering. Then everyone pitches in and the animal is hung from a convenient branch to be skinned and quartered. Families may delegate the work to itinerant butchers or the animals may be taken to the local abattoir. Joints of meat are distributed to friends and neighbours, especially those not affluent enough to have their own animal.

Some people shield their children from the killing but I have seen very young ones watch the whole process quite unperturbed. The skins may be dried and salted or given to charity. Throughout the day special vans circulate the neighbourhood to collect the skins.

Once the mess has been cleared away, the rest of the celebrations begin. Lunch usually consists of liver fried in the sheep's own fat. This is not a taste or indeed a smell that I relish but for my vegetarian daughter it is a day to stay firmly indoors, with the windows tightly shut.

Other animals may be killed. Four families can share a bullock, seven a camel, although the latter is now much rarer, at least in the West of the country. Many poor families struggle to comply with what they see as an integral part of their faith. The celebrations continue with a round of visiting. There is a strict protocol with the younger generation calling on their elders. Children wear new outfits and receive gifts of sweets or money.

A few years ago my father-in-law brought home the designated ram (only male animals are sacrificed). He had left it late in the day in the hope of securing a bargain. Everyone went out to admire the unsuspecting victim, only to discover that it had a broken horn. Panic ensued: was it acceptable to offer damaged goods to God? Would offering a less than perfect specimen entail untold disasters? Immediate reference was made to the holy Koran but alas to no avail. My mother-in-law had learned how to intone the Arabic words and prayers but did not understand what she was reading.

Being too late to find an *imam* (a Muslim priest), a neighbour was summoned. He was old and frail but had a reputation locally as something of an expert on such matters and an arbiter of religious disputes. He equivocated, no doubt not wishing to offend either of my parents-in-law, who were by now locked in a vitriolic argument about the poor sheep. Eventually the verdict was announced, the sheep replaced and everyone was happy, except of course the replacement sheep!

Sacrifices may also be made at the inauguration of a business, to celebrate the birth of a child or even after a death. Some Turkish friends who killed a cockerel on the doorstep of their new high street shop in London were amazed to find themselves the subject of local protest and a critical article in the local paper.

Helping the poor and distributing largesse is the humanitarian face of Islam. The worry over details and preserving tradition shows that the essentially conservative nature of the people has not really changed over the years.

New Year's Eve

The first Christmas I spent in Turkey was in 1987, and it was a normal working weekday. I seem to remember my boss at the university offering me the day off, but as everyone else was working it didn't seem a very good idea to stay home alone. (I was working at a State Conservatoire under the control of a State University.) My flatmate was also working that day, for a newspaper which was printed in English, and other friends – whether Turkish or British – were also going to be at work. Apparently New Year's Eve was the important event, although it was misnamed Christmas by Turkish friends and students. "Happy Christmas, teacher" they would call out in the corridors, on December 27th, 28th, 30th, January 1st, oblivious to my corrections as I tried to make them understand the reason why Christmas was on one important day only, and that that day had already passed.

Thus it was that the three of us – myself, one Turkish friend and one Swiss-Iranian – decided to celebrate that first New Year's Eve by going out for a nice meal in a smart restaurant intending to eat and drink ourselves merrily into the New Year. We got dressed up a bit – nothing too glamorous – and set off for our restaurant, only to find it was 'Closed for the New Year'. What a surprise! After a few more similar abortive attempts we finally found one of our favourite restaurants actually open with people enjoying their meals. Success, we thought, and never mind that it was only a fish restaurant. We settled down to have an entertaining night, but were rather disconcerted when the restaurant seemed to be emptying even before eleven o'clock. Nevertheless we thought we would still have a good time and ring in the New Year even if we were the only customers.

However, this was not to be! Shortly after eleven some of the lights were switched off – for atmosphere we thought – and the remaining waiter became more and more agitated as he tried to rush us through our meal and get dessert and coffee out of the way as quickly as possible. When we asked him what the hurry was he confessed to wanting to get home to his family in time for New Year.

The penny finally dropped. It was not normal for establishments to stay open for New Year unless they had a special (and expensively packaged) evening's dinner and entertainment planned and booked in advance.

How very foolish we felt, walking down the deserted streets back to our Turkish friend's flat, to drink in the New Year at home with a bottle of pink sparkling wine which we had managed to pick up on the way!

You may wonder why our Turkish friend did not explain any of this to us, and herein lies a lesson in both Turkish diplomacy and their flexible thinking. Far be it for them to speculate, criticise, or just offer alternative suggestions to honourable foreign friends. I have had many similar experiences since that night, demonstrating an unwillingness to give a personal opinion without first checking with someone more senior and passing any decision-making on to them. 'Theirs is not to reason why', and so on. They simply have an amazing acceptance of things as they are.

Turkey for Christmas?

I was in London for Christmas in 1975 and then again in 1978 and I felt that Christmas about once every three years was about right. Having left the starry-eyed excitement of childhood far behind, and having no great religious belief, I find that the commercial hype leaves me cold. Back then, even New Year was a quiet family celebration in Turkey. Today, regrettably the shopping rush has hit the newly wealthy and growing middle-class. Those enduring Christmas symbols of Santa Claus and decorated fir trees are now identified with New Year in this predominantly Muslim country.

In 1978 back in London my husband had his first experience of Christmas. He joined in the family rituals and tucked into the unfamiliar flavours of turkey, cranberry sauce and that concoction we call Christmas pudding. As a Muslim he was worried about the role of Christianity in the proceedings but I was able to assure him that, while for some the occasion was a holy day, for many of us it was simply a chance to get together and have a good time.

Settled back in Turkey in 1992, we made an effort to preserve the Christmas traditions for the sake of our two children. They were delighted to celebrate twice within a week: once with us on December 25th and on the 31st with their aunts, uncles and grandparents. Over the passing years, our Christmas gradually disappeared and fell into disuse as it was just another working day for us all.

In 1993, Christmas was a Saturday so the issue of time off did not arise. The following two years passed uneventfully. My only difficulty lay in explaining to my family and friends in the UK that there were no bank holidays for us. In the spirit of 'When in Rome...' turkey disappeared from the menu until it reappeared as part of the New Year feast. For several years we raised our own: I was even brave enough to help my husband prepare the freshly-killed bird for the table.

It was not until I was joined at my school by a fellow foreigner in 1996 that I ever thought of my 'right' to a day off. At her insistence we enjoyed our Christmas tea party, exchanging token gifts. The management were happy to let us go for the day and politely wished us well.

Changing jobs in 1998, Christmas was written into the contract for the large foreign staff: there were 21 of us. We were entitled to a day off, which I gratefully accepted. We newcomers were surprised and pleased to learn that the school would go so far as to give us a present. On December 24th all of us collected our festive carrier bags, which contained a box of chocolates and a bottle of wine. We foreigners had a reputation for being fond of the demon drink, in some cases quite undeserved. One year the school even put on a dinner for its foreign contingent and we gathered with our partners in attendance. The cold sprouts and the turkey and rice were not as appetising as they might have been but we appreciated the gesture and the efforts that had been made to brighten up and heat a corner of the vast school dining hall.

With a change of management, first the dinner and then the present disappeared. "If I give you a present at Christmas, I will have to give the Turkish staff a present on their religious holiday and I can't afford that," complained the new owner.

Moving on once again in 2002, I had no particular expectations. After all, it's not as though the school had a holiday. If we take the day off, some hard-pressed colleague has to take our lessons. As they professed a willingness to do so, I enjoyed a free day for the next couple of years. A large basket containing an assortment of soft and alcoholic drinks and various goodies was duly presented and enjoyed by all the family. For the next four years, the tradition continued happily.

A year later, we received no present. Economy was the order of the day: no problem as far as I was concerned.

So it was quite a surprise in 2007 to be invited to the principal's office at four o'clock on Christmas Eve. The call had reached me verbally and had been repeated from two different sources but as the four of us were leaving the teachers' room, I pointed out to my friends that there were only three names written on the board but mine wasn't among them.

"I'm not coming," I said, half in jest. "The principal doesn't want to see me."

"Don't be daft," was the tenor of their reply but I had a slight feeling of unease as we walked down the silent corridor to the seat of power.

As we opened the door of the secretary's office, her face fell. Something was clearly wrong. The door to her boss's office was firmly shut but she ventured inside, while we waited uneasily. After a brief interval the principal emerged to apologise for the delay but our presents were late arriving and would we please return to the teachers' room and she would let us know when to come back.

Back in our own room, we were all speculating as to the true nature of the problem. The idea that they had, through some miscalculation, only got three baskets to offer instead of four, seemed too bizarre to be true. Someone asked me,

"Celia, when did you convert to Islam?"

Suspicion and alarm started to chase each other round my head.

"Who wants to know?" I replied. Having no real religious affiliation, I nevertheless guard my privacy on this subject.

To my horror, I learned that the principal had contacted the head of personnel to obtain a copy of our Turkish identity cards to ascertain our stated religion. Mine states that I am a Muslim. When I became a Turkish citizen some nineteen years into my marriage, it was assumed that, as the wife of a Muslim, I must also be one. It didn't bother me: what I believe and feel are my own business.

Even then the penny was slow to drop. As school finished at 4.10, we retraced our steps. This time the secretary was behind her desk but the door to the inner sanctum was unfortunately open just enough for us to hear voices within.

"But it says Islam."

On hearing these words, I turned on my heel telling my friends that there was clearly a problem and that problem was me. As the final bell had mercifully rung, I gathered my belongings and made my way as fast as possible out of the building and indeed off the premises. Having received a basket from the self-same principal in the past, I was at a total loss to understand why she had felt the need to go through such a procedure.

Fighting back tears of humiliation and anger, I decided to work the following day.

Although I had told no one of the incident, December 25th brought commiserations from friends in the department: how could she behave so badly?

After a couple of lessons, I found a note on my desk, asking me not to leave for the day without seeing the Primary Head. Uncertain as to how to respond, I postponed the inevitable as long as I could but he tracked me down. Descending the stairs, I admonished myself and tried to be calm.

He apologised for the 'mistake', and hoped that I would accept a basket as a token of the school's good wishes for the festive season. How could I refuse such charm and generosity? His concluding remark gave me food for thought. Changing my identity card to alter my religion to 'Christian' could be arranged and he would be glad to help me to do it at a later date. He had a parent waiting, so could we discuss it another time?

With my morale decidedly restored, I left his office. Then it hit me that he too saw Christmas as a purely religious celebration. The concept of Christmas being a time for all and sundry to share and enjoy was out of the question. My Turkish family had accepted me easily but had always assumed that I would become a Muslim. After all Christianity was also monotheistic and shared a common background in the Old Testament.

When I finally admitted my atheism, they found the idea beyond belief.

The present, on closer examination, revealed a card with the principal's name on it but she had not seen fit to give it to me herself. Was she frightened of losing face or did she consider me dishonest, trying to obtain a present under false pretences? I am sure I will never know. All I do know is that she continues to ignore me in the corridors, choosing not to hear my 'good morning' or to see my smile.

I can now see how the incident unfolded but the sense of discrimination still rankles. The present is of no importance. The only thing that remained for me to decide was how to behave in 2008, should I still have a job!

I worried for nothing. The following year austerity was again the order of the day and no one received a present or so much as a 'Happy Christmas.' Then the principal left the school leaving the primary head in charge, a charming and urbane man.

To my surprise in 2009, we four foreigners have been given a sumptuous basket of goodies. Very welcome you might think but there was a sting in the tail! Our head, beaming fiom ear to ear and wishing everything that we could possibly wish ourselves, asked each of us in turn if we were Catholic or Protestant. I found myself professing an allegiance I do not have.

The Turks really can't deal with the concept of someone having no religious belief!

Ram's Horns

The hooked shape of ram's horns represent power, strength, and heroism. These characteristics are essential to gain entrance to a Turkish university and study successfully.

9 - University Life

Classroom Experience

I try not to remember one particularly bad experience teaching a group of private students at a university. Their course was identical to the university students' preparatory year in English, but as they had failed the university entrance exam they were taking it as paying students, presumably hoping to retake the entrance exam the following year. They would then try for another exam to exempt them from doing this prep year again.

Some of the thirty or so students were well-mannered and pleasant, hardworking and classroom-trained. The majority were, unlike most adult Turks, unruly, impolite, tardy, unprepared for class and even downright rude.

The aim of the class seemed to be, for these ones, to arrive as late as possible but still in time for their soft-hearted teacher to let them sign the attendance sheet; they would then behave as badly as possible so that they would be thrown out of class. The sessions were 45 minutes long, four sessions to a morning, and I had to teach four different groups like this from Monday to Thursday.

If I didn't throw them out, they would read the newspaper openly on their desks, chat to their friends (obviously not quietly) switch on their Walkmans and put on the headphones, perhaps throw chalk at each other, or paper darts, or just get up and saunter out as they pleased.

I remember one particular day of this torture when I totally lost any professionalism I may have had left, and swore something unprintable at the worst offender who was talking back at me. He wasn't even in my class that day but had stopped in the doorway with a group of his cronies to observe and poke fun at the class.

Sticking his head through the door he had looked fiercely at me and hissed that it was up to me to respect the students first, before they would ever return any respect. By allowing myself to respond so rudely I had lost any remaining dignity and control of the class that day and also felt totally demoralised by his remarks.

I think that was the beginning of the end for my work there. Despite the tempting salary – more than the full-time university prep teachers were earning, as it was private and on an hourly basis – I found myself frequently sending in substitute teacher friends to take my classes. I lasted there just two months, and suffered severely in terms of self-respect and confidence!

Interestingly, the same horrendous students would be really quite sweet outside the building in the grounds when I met them, reverting to "normal" displays of Turkish politeness and asking how I was, saying Good Morning or Good Afternoon, and '*Afiyet Olsun*' (meaning enjoy your meal/bon appétit) when they passed in the corridor if it was lunchtime. Such a paradox of behaviour. It begs the questions of their classroom manners and attitude, their family life and personal problems. Even the heinous offender caught me in a break to ask my advice on a book he was reading in English, 'The Celestine Prophecy', which was actually a New Age book in vogue at the time.

So I suppose they can't be ALL bad, can they?

Supervising an Exam

In Turkey there is enormous competition for university places. Students take a nation-wide entrance exam in which they score a certain number of points. Every department in every university has its threshold of minimum points. The result is that students with high points have a wide choice, but lower down the scale they have to go wherever they can get in. Because of this, many end up studying a subject which has nothing to do with their personal interests.

This story, from about 2002, concerns a recently established, private university. The entrance points for easy departments were low and many students attended only because their parents wanted them to have the status of a degree. Theoretically, everything was taught in English. I was a teacher of English language, but one of my duties was supervising exams in other subjects.

Bright and early one Saturday morning, I arrived at the exam office. The room was silent and the door locked. I had been told to come "at least half an hour" before the start of the exam. I looked at my watch; there were 35 minutes to go. I sat down and waited. Colleagues began to arrive, and we chatted and grumbled. Fifteen minutes before the starting time, a young woman appeared and unlocked the door, and we queued up obediently. She consulted a list, told us which rooms to go to, and gave everyone a class list and an exam report form. On this we were to record any incident that might take place during the exam, sign it, and hand it back when the exam was over. We were also supposed to be given the question papers, but she told us that they would be delivered to the exam room instead.

This particular exam was for students in the Department of Fashion and Design. I found my group. They were rushing around shouting and giggling, waving photocopied notes at each other and speculating what the questions might be. I told them to put their bags and notes on the shelf at the front of the room and sit down, which they did, in tightly clustered groups of friends. Spreading them out by giving individual orders took some time, and then began the tedious process of checking all their student ID cards against the class list. By the time I had accomplished this, the starting time had passed by five minutes, several students were still missing, and the question papers hadn't arrived yet.

We waited another five minutes. Then a man appeared, papers in hand. He did not say hello or introduce himself, but proceeded to distribute the questions. A hush fell over the room, soon interrupted as first one, then another late-comer put in an appearance. I descended on them to do my duty.

"Please leave your bag here. Can I see your ID? Please sit here."

There were four or five of them. Not till after all that did I notice the unnaturally bent heads at the far side of the room; their eyes were not focusing on the desks in front, but on their laps. There was a whole row of them. My fellow supervisor noticed it too, and was the first to pounce, seizing one of the illegally consulted photocopies as proof of guilt. Others were hastily dropped, stuffed into pockets, scrunched up and thrown in various directions. There was a great deal of confusion, which the rest of the class made good use of to consult urgently with their neighbours.

We collected several more of the forbidden references, checked under all the desks and on the floors, and slowly restored a semblence of silence. I managed to write down some names, and was surprised that my companion in authority took little interest in this. Soon afterwards, he departed from the room.

Some time later we had another visitor; this one said, "Good morning." She was evidently the course teacher, and proceeded to give the class a long speech of advice, in Turkish, on how to answer the exam questions. When she had finished, students' hands went up all over the room, and she then visited them individually, giving detailed consultations each time. As I watched her, I thought about the exam report form, and wondered if I should record the behaviour of the course teacher on it, as well as that of the cheating students. I thought about how I would enjoy wording it, in formal and pompous English. Surely it was my duty to support the integrity of the institution I worked for?

The rest of the time passed without further excitement. Students began to hand in their papers, sign the list as required, and depart. The man who had been with us earlier returned.

"Shall I write up the exam report?", I asked, "Or will you do it?"

He looked surprised.

"The report? Oh, the 'exam report'. That form. No, don't write anything on that. You just have to sign it, that's all."

"But they cheated! We got those photocopies! They can't get away with that!" I was horrified. He explained patiently:

"If you put it on the form, then there's a record. It becomes official. I mean, it will be on the student's record. That's bad and we don't want that."

Didn't we want that?? Suddenly, I knew he was right. We were in Turkey after all. Besides, I was still hoping to spend a few more years working at this university. Fashion and Design was far away from my department. Why make trouble? But letting them off completely still seemed dishonest, so I said weakly,

"What shall we do, then?"

"Just talk to the class teacher. She will take it into account when she marks the papers."

That I did. She listened politely, but looked surprised. There was a why-are-you-telling-me-this look on her face, and I knew then that she would ignore it all. She had dreadful students, unsuited to academic study of any kind. But she had a job and a salary, and she wanted to keep them.

Drama in the Department

I used to teach the one-year preliminary English course (Prep English) in the university department of *Turizm*, which might be rendered Hospitality Management Studies in English. Usually we just called it Tourism. This subject was not high up on the ladder of academic status. The course lasted only two years, getting a place was comparatively easy, and our students were far from brilliant. However, in contrast to some departments where English was regarded as a waste of time, our students all had a vague idea that it might be useful. On this fertile ground energetic teachers could create much.

It was Halime who first suggested getting students to write plays. It had nothing to do with the curriculum, but our bosses were on the main university campus, about eighty kilometres away, so it was unlikely to bother them. We were a group of ten teachers who worked in an unfinished concrete building close to a popular seaside resort. The university had chosen it, presumably, because there were plenty of hotels and restaurants to provide summer jobs in *Turizm* nearby. Our coordinator, Latife, was efficient at collecting attendance lists and ferrying exam papers, but it was not her inclination to ask what page of the grammar book you were on this week or whether you had yet got the students to write the paragraph entitled My Most Exciting Day. In short, we all taught English, but we did it any way we liked; we were as free as the sea winds that blew in across the Aegean from Greece. Halime and I made use of that freedom, and we got everyone to learn and use English, somehow, even the people who thought they hated it and couldn't do anything.

The first plays were awful. At least they were in awful English. Much of the content was so poor that we could not understand it at all. Accordingly we returned these works to their authors, saying, "You've got great ideas, but there are a lot of mistakes. Please find a student who is good at English to help you. Discuss everything in Turkish. Then rewrite the English and bring it back."

This strategy produced miracles. Ideas behind the jumbled language suddenly emerged, though there were still many mistakes. So then I sat down with a pencil to edit seriously, fascinated with what they had done. The plays were social and political satire, making fun of traditional gender roles, the cultural divide between village and city, and the frustrations of ordinary people who felt exploited by public authorities. We received the beginnings of five plays in bad handwriting, and we ended up with three complete ones, roughly typed up on typewriters somewhere by volunteer students who had barely the necessary skills. Halime then charmed the accounting office into photocopying for us. (Mere English teachers were not supposed to need a facility like that. Handouts for students were sent out ready from headquarters from time to time, and nobody could imagine us ever needing anything else.)

Initially planning some kind of classroom performance, we auditioned for roles and started rehearsing. There was much correction of pronunciation, and a lot of training in giving expression to the words, a skill most students didn't possess at all. However, they all got better, and better still. Their enthusiasm grew, till one day somebody said, why can't we do it in the conference hall?

I had been there for occasional staff meetings, so I knew there was a stage, but I had no idea who might have the key, much less how one might get permission to use it. But Halime was up to all this. In her free time she went patiently from office to office, explaining, smiling and cajoling. Eventually she was successful, and a date for the performance was fixed.

After that, it was full speed ahead. Memorize those lines by tomorrow! Speak slower and don't mumble! That word is *here*, not *hair*! Halime made friends with a small local hotel and borrowed hand-woven cushions and rugs for the village house scenes. We made lists of props and costumes and decided who was to bring what. For one scene, someone had a large tray and I supplied half a kilo of green beans. In the story the village woman who was stringing the beans jerked the tray in surprise when a lady journalist entered, scattering green vegetables all over the stage. This play was about the cultural contrast between village and city. As we worked, students came up with many good ideas, and the productions grew more interesting with each rehearsal.

Another play had an old woman in it. As I was at least twice as old as anyone else in the department, I volunteered for the part. I dressed up in a long black skirt with a big headscarf and hobbled along, bent over a walking stick. "They stole our pensions!", I screeched at a bemused sergeant of police, banging my stick in protest against inadequate government provisions for the elderly.

The last week we worked very hard to bring the performance up to a satisfactory standard. We had rehearsals every lunch break and even on the weekend. Another teacher, the helpful Mesut, managed to get hold of an office computer and created invitations with the logo of the university on them. Translated into English, the message read: "With the request that you honour us (with your presence) on Preparation English Class Drama Day". Copies were sent to various people in authority, including our head of department and his assistants back in Izmir. None came, but they thanked us for the invitation. The head of *Tourizm* was less gracious, he wanted to know why we had used the university logo without his permission. However, the tactful Mesut managed to soothe his ruffled pride.

When the afternoon of the performance came, the hall was full. We put our best energy into it, and were rewarded with much enthusiastic applause. Said one boy after acting the lead role in his own play, "Now I know why I came to university."

Academic Anomaly

Zeynep B, postgraduate student at the Department of Fine Arts in the Faculty of Education at a large and long-established Turkish state university, had a problem. It was to do with an assignment in a subject called *Philosophy of Art*. The assignment was to summarize, in a few pages, the content of two chapters of the book *Arguing about Art: Contemporary Philosophical Debates*, edited by Neill and Ridley. The problem was that the assignment had to be in English, and the book also existed only in English.

Zeynep actually knew English quite well; she had comfortably passed the proficiency exam required for every student in Turkey who embarks of any kind of postgraduate study. But summarizing academic philosophical writing requires more than merely good English on the part of a non-native speaker. To complicate matters further, the relevant course, based on *Arguing about Art*, had actually been taught in Turkish. Since none of the staff in the art department knew enough English to read the book, the task of teaching that particular course was given to a gentlemen from the Department of Religious Studies, who, it was said, had been to America. That gentleman was strict and believed that rules should be obeyed. He had set the deadline for the assignment at noon on Friday, February 9.

The baffled student began to look for a helper, but this proved extremely difficult. She asked more and more people if they knew anyone who might be able to help, and finally through a friend who knew my daughter's music teacher, she reached us, the Cabas. On Thursday afternoon, the day before the deadline, my son Ozan, bilingual speaker and art school graduate, met up with Zeynep and her massive illegal photocopy of "Arguing about Art". She emphasized the importance of the deadline, but said the quality of the work did not matter: "Just get it done somehow!" Together they selected the two shortest chapters from the list of contents and made a deal for twenty-five pounds.

Ozan arrived home quite late; at once I fetched a pencil and paper sat down with the huge book. In an hour I struggled through a couple of pages on the subject of Sentimentality, underlining key sentences and phrases. Then I scribbled down the summary, padding it out with short quotations marked and numbered in the text. After that I gave the book to Ozan. Ten minutes sufficed for him to announce, "I can't understand this stuff."

We had made a deal; not only did we wish the charming Zeynep might pass her course, but we both felt our professional integrity was at stake. There was no way to say "can't". So we discussed strategies. Then we took the spiral back out of the photocopy book, thus creating 450 loose pages. Ozan took the pages of text I had already worked on, so he could copy the quotes, together with my scribbles, and headed for the computer. I placed the rest of the pile of paper on the kitchen table, with the second selected chapter, Public Art, at the top. Then I went to bed, setting my alarm clock for dawn next morning.

The birds were singing outside the windows and the morning sky was pink with the promise of a fine sunrise. I switched on the kitchen heater and sat down. It felt rather like working for an exam when I was a student, more than forty years ago. Filled with glorious determination, I began to read and paraphrase the more comprehensible sentences, adding quotes as before.

After an hour, I made coffee. Later, I had breakfast with the family, then moved to the sitting room to be away from the chat. By the time I had finished Public Art and went back to Sentimentality, I was tired. My brain was fast acquiring that fuzzy sensation that melts easily into complete confusion. However, I scribbled down something. Then I joined Ozan at the computer and dictated the rest of my notes for him to type. We each had one eye on the clock, matching our combined progress against the passing minutes.

This story has a happy ending. At 11.30 Ozan clicked on the SEND button, and a few minutes later Zeynep phoned his mobile to say she had got it. She also said, "It's great; I can understand it."

Moonlighting

My extra-curricular teaching began almost from day one – well, certainly from week one. When I arrived in Turkey I had not yet signed my contract but merely filled in several forms which had been posted to me nearly a year before. The questions had mainly concerned my father's name, mother's name (it was unclear as to whether this meant maiden name or first name), my date of birth and nationality. The form itself was poor quality recycled paper of a dingy grey/brownish colour with print from what must have been some kind of ancient typewriter. However, this was 1986-87 and the age of the word processor was not quite upon us yet, but I had expected better quality paper, headed and stamped with the university's insignia or some such distinctive logo and format.

Feeling a little uncertain, I had filled in these forms and returned them, since they were obviously not legally binding but just the first tentative steps towards my possibly accepting this strange job offer and the chance to leave the UK for a country I knew nothing about.

The interview itself had taken place on a freezing cold day in London when I'd been forced to leave my warm sick bed – suffering with a heavy cold – to go and meet my future boss in Covent Garden. We'd both wandered around the tube station's two exits, eyeing each other up and down and deciding that 'it couldn't be *her'* until one of us finally dared to ask. We'd repaired hastily to the warmth of the nearest café – a 'Cranks' wholefood restaurant. What an appropriate venue for us, I'd thought, as the other interviewee teacher and I sat and discussed our futures with the petite ex-ballerina and boss-to-be. My co-interviewee was to become the first contemporary modern dance teacher at the Conservatoire, and was fresh out of training, gushing her enthusiasm. I, however, grunted and croaked out more cynical questions about accommodation, language and culture/lifestyle, as well as salary of course!

After sending the forms I'd heard nothing until a phone call out of the blue towards the end of the autumn term. Boss-to-be greeted me on a crackly line and immediately asked me when I would be arriving. Nothing about contracts or formalities at all. The modern dance teacher had already started and was "loving every minute of it, and here, speak to her now". My colleague-to-be was still gushing – I wickedly imagined a gun to her head at the other end of the line – and told me how marvellous it was and how lovely the students were. On questioning her about her contract she was evasive and I was quickly passed back to the boss.

We agreed I would come in their semester break, which almost coincided with my spring half term break in February, giving me enough time to offer half a term's notice at my many various teaching establishments – I was a peripatetic jack of all trades in those days, and welcomed the idea of one decent salary under one roof, albeit in Turkey. Boss-to-be assured me that all my contract formalities could be swiftly sorted on arrival in Turkey. I must have been mad to believe this.

On arrival in Ankara I did not even know if I was to start teaching the next day, and as nobody said anything I assumed that I would start forthwith. I was used to being paid by the hour for work carried out, rather than just for being there. This meant that I slept fitfully, sure that I would be summoned to start teaching at 9am on my first real day there. In fact my boss did not arrive until around 10am and when I asked about starting work she then explained that we would have to prepare a curriculum which would then be translated into Turkish. Lessons would start the following week as they were still on their semester break. It would have been nice to have been given definite dates for these semester breaks before I arrived, but I was to learn that academic years had flexible start and finish dates, according to circumstances. These circumstances included weather and political events as well as religious holidays and transport problems.

So, there was no rush and I could relax and write my programme and explain its contents to the poor overworked History of Dance teacher who was to translate it in her spare time. Ef was also an ex-ballerina and was responsible for the first years' ballet class every morning, 9am till 10.30, plus her History of Dance lectures, and now me. She was to become my greatest ally and counsellor, as well as a lifelong friend.

Thus the problem of cash to survive was now uppermost in my mind. No lessons meant no money, I thought, and assumed they would not start paying me until after I started teaching. I was still thinking like a peripatetic teacher. I also had no contract. Again I'd assumed it would be there to sign on day one.

Moreover I had a lot of free time with no lessons, and nowhere to escape to as my temporary accommodation was a room in the middle of the ballet department next to the tea room and the costumes room, and diagonally opposite my director's office. The floors of these rooms had cheap worn carpet on them and the walls were concrete. Corridors had marble floors and all the doors were grey plywood, most of them with handles which had come off and cracks in the wood and frames. This meant that there was a lot of noise and echo as soon as the department door was unlocked in the mornings. I was given a key to this door so that I could reach the 'facilities' during non-working hours – a girls' toilet way down along the corridor.

To help me get by, Ef quickly found me a ballerina from the State company who wanted to learn more 'Dance Notation'/Benesh Choreology – the subject I had been hired to teach and build a department in. I was to take the bus downtown on Saturday mornings and teach her for an hour a week for the princely sum of 10,000 Turkish lira. This was about £10 in those days, and I could easily survive on that while I lived in the department, as lunch and dinner were about 25p each in the school canteen, and food generally was cheap, as was transport – even taxis. I didn't seem to need to spend money on anything else as yet.

On the day of my first lesson with Nur, I boarded the long 'concertina' bus outside the building and arrived in Kizilay (the centre of town) about ten minutes later. It was a short walk along to Nur's street and her apartment building was clearly named and numbered, with her own name neatly written in the space by her bell. This is not usually the case in Turkey. Street names can be hard to discern and are often changed after political 'events'. This makes people reluctant to give addresses and they usually arrange to meet one at an obvious landmark such as a supermarket or big hotel. They then lead one to their home and one has to hastily note the name and number of the apartment and even the street if one wants to find it again on one's own. One is unlikely to be given this information by one's host. Ever. Letters are not expected, except for bills. I used to find this seeming lack of organisation infuriating, but I am now quite used to it and even find it more hospitable to be 'met and led' the first time I visit someone at home, rather than struggling to find the place on my own.

Nur's house had been easy to locate and she led me into her living room where we sat down for the introductory chat before the lesson. However, Nur was soon on her feet offering tea and then planning to cook for me too. I had come expecting a European style of private lesson, with a quick introduction and chat followed by an hour's work and off home sharp.

I was probably there for three hours or so, and left well fed and watered. This was to be the pattern for most of our lessons.

Indeed this is not uncommon in most private lessons throughout the country, especially for the first session when the student and perhaps their entire family may be present to welcome one and also weigh up one's teaching abilities, persona, dress sense, and a whole range of other details they may find important during the course of a kind of 'high tea'.

Another time when I arrived at Nur's she looked exhausted and told me she had been up all night waiting 'for the water to come on'. Water cuts are common throughout Turkey, and I experienced the lack of hot water most of the week in my 'room' in the ballet department, as did all the students who boarded there. However, the fact that one had no idea when it would come back on again really surprised me. Nur had lain on the sofa all night listening for the sound of gurgling in the pipes that heralded the rush of water coming out of taps which may have been left ON! People often forgot to turn their taps back off when they discovered there was no water in them. Or they left them like that so they would quickly hear when the water came on. It was also easy to get confused about which way was 'off' and which way 'on', especially when one was an inexperienced foreigner. This could, and did, have disastrous consequences even in the most meticulous of households.

Nur had risen at 3am to the sound of the gurgling pipes and then done all of her housework – dishes, washing, cleaning, showering – as she did not know if it would be cut off again soon.

I am afraid I didn't take this too seriously during those early lessons, but soon learned that this was a real problem and a common one. Imagine being without running water for three days or a week, and maybe being unprepared with no large buckets of water sitting ready for such an event.

That day Nur also offered me 'kitchen' and 'Spanish'. After a few minutes of floundering around in the conversation we resorted to the dictionary: of course she had meant 'chicken' and 'spinach', and duly prepared a wonderful meal, as usual.

Another time she told me how tired *I* looked when I arrived, and immediately offered breakfast, cooking me Turkish 'bacon' and eggs. The bacon was spicy 'sucuk' and left a lovely garlicky taste in the mouth which I am sure my friends did not appreciate later that day. I soon cottoned on to Nur's ruses and delaying tactics as she had rarely done her homework, claiming rehearsals and too many performances, along with the tiresome water problem.

Nur's lessons didn't continue for too long, and after I got my first pay packet in May the State ballet closed up for the summer and Nur quietly slipped away from Benesh Movement Notation.

I often wondered whether *she* had actually been roped in to help *me* in those first three wageless months. It would not surprise me to learn that Ef had organised this all behind the scenes for my benefit, such was the nature of her support and goodwill towards everyone she worked with.

My next private student also came from the State Ballet Company and also wanted the Benesh. However, she was more serious and quite ambitious.

Sedef had been with the company a good few years now and was looking for a career change for her pre-retirement years. She was already working as a repetiteur (someone who rehearses the ballets and often teaches the steps before the director or choreographer adds the finishing touches). She felt the choreology would be useful for her as she could then read the dance scores and prepare better for rehearsals. What is more, our new university conservatoire programme in Benesh Movement Notation meant she would have a university degree and thus qualify for a higher salary and position in future.

She planned to learn enough in these private lessons so that she could take a kind of exemption exam and start my 4-year course fulltime in year two. Since she would continue to work for the State ballet she would be able to continue privately with me and take another exemption exam the following year to enter year four, thus graduating in two years. This also suited my finances perfectly, and I can honestly say I would not have survived those early months without Nur and Sedef. Indeed, my salary in Turkish Lira was worth about half its value in sterling 6 months after my arrival.

Sedef was a dream student; always on time, well-prepared, homework done or at least attempted, and eager to learn more. She found the notation hard to learn sometimes, and the theory of the signs was sometimes puzzling and perplexing to her, but she never gave up. We had a long standing joke as she would always say at the start of each lesson as she walked slowly and ponderously down the corridor to my office "I am coming slowly slowly Rosalynd" (the Turkish for slowly is the same word repeated twice: *yavaş yavaş*), but at the end of the lesson she would skip out of the door with a wide grin saying "now I am leaving quickly quickly!" relieved that her mental torture was over for the day.

These first private lessons were hardly an effort for me. I was teaching my own main subject to people who wanted to learn and who gave me my first insights into life in Turkey, the language and the people. They struggled to make themselves understood in English, rather than me struggling to speak in their language.

A year later, as my salary plummeted ever southwards with the rate of inflation, I was forced to go out and look for extra work, and thus began my forays into the world of English Language teaching.

Pomegranate

At New Year some people believe that smashing a pomegranate on their doorstep can bring good fortune for the coming year. We use it to symbolise the prosperity that may follow for teacher and student alike through private lessons.

10 - Private Lessons

Travelling Saleswoman

Recently I received a phone call from a former student of mine, a businessman, wanting to know if I was still available for private lessons – for a colleague of his.

How nice, I thought, that they still remember me and recommend me to their friends. When lessons suddenly dry up and one is not informed as to the reason, one can imagine all sorts of silly things – such as 'I said the wrong thing in the last lesson and upset them', or 'they found someone else', meaning 'someone better'. Insecurity is not restricted to students!

So Şerif (pronounced 'Sher-eef') said he would give my number to Sevil and I forgot all about it for at least a day. Sevil rang the following day and chatted in Turkish on the phone. She sounded very young and outgoing, and told me she was finishing her course in English at a reputable language school in the centre of town, after which she wanted to start private lessons with me for conversation.

We discussed the fees, which meant I got beaten down to my bare minimum price for lessons at my house – which was miles away from hers – or sessions at her home, which would entail more time and petrol costs for me.

I thought we had more or less agreed by the end of the conversation, and she told me she had another friend who needed to start now as she was going to the USA for the summer.

Next day Sevil rang again. She had talked to her friend and wanted to reduce the price still further as she was a student – the friend, that is. More bargaining ensued and I thought I agreed to a lump sum in advance for four lessons.

After this, Suna finally got in touch and we arranged (in Turkish) to meet at the Quayside near my home – a journey of about two hours for Suna coming by bus from the other side of the gulf of Izmir. I often do the initial arrangements in my poor Turkish as they are so nervous and panicky at the other end of the phone, and it makes it easier as I certainly remember what I said and they can communicate fluently. Hesitant pidgin English arrangements are a recipe for misunderstandings which can lead to people waiting in the wrong place on the wrong day at the wrong time.

Suna's first session went well and she chatted quite fluently in English and told me of her plans to spend three months in the States on a work placement holiday. I assumed it was related to her university studies, but on closer questioning got the impression she would be helping out as a cashier or something at an amusement park/funfair type of place. It is always interesting how one's own conclusions about what someone is telling one can be so far from the truth, simply due to the difference in cultures and life experience.

At the beginning of the session Suna had told me she couldn't pay in advance for four lessons, so would I accept the payment lesson by lesson? Well, what could I say by this stage? I made a mental note not to meet her anywhere other than where I was already going to be, to avoid further expenses for myself!

As it turned out, she came again the next day and then had university exams so was busy up till the time she left for

America. By the time I realised that we wouldn't have another session I had already photocopied lots of useful materials for her and found cassettes she could listen to on her Walkman, as we had planned. I made another mental note not to be so well prepared, knowing I would never heed it.

A few weeks later Sevil rang me again. I was driving at the time and thought the call might be from the person I was going to meet, so I answered it. A name was on the cell phone screen but I couldn't read it, and it was very hot. A strange conversation ensued, as I couldn't hear the other person either, and ended up telling them in Turkish that they had the wrong number. A few miles further on I realised that this was impossible since my cell phone had recognised the caller enough to show the name on the screen. I stopped the car and checked. Yes, it was from Sevil's company. I immediately phoned back and as soon as they answered I started to gush in Turkish about how silly I had been not to recognise her on the phone. Then I realised I was talking to a recorded message, and as I didn't know her extension number or surname it was probably a waste of time trying to locate her via the operator.

We talked the next day – still in Turkish – and arranged a meeting at a place near to where she lived which coincided with my trip to the airport to drop off a friend returning to the UK.

Parking the car in the Tansaş supermarket car park I noticed two very pretty young ladies seated outside chatting. Might be one of them, I thought, but they didn't seem to notice me or even be looking, so I dialled Sevil's cell phone. "I am here," I said, "outside Tansaş now."

"So am I," she replied and we realised we were by now face to face with our mobile phones to our ears, and burst out laughing.

She jumped up and came to greet me with a spontaneous kiss on each cheek – a normal Turkish greeting but not one I usually encounter from students. There is usually a nervous politeness about them, and a fumbling hand shake, or very rarely a peck on the cheek. Sevil's greeting was quite natural.

That first session was lively and enjoyable, as Sevil seemed to be an extrovert and bubbly girl, and she sounded clear about her needs in English. We sat in a café and had coffee while I found out about her life and her English. At the end of the hour she insisted on paying for the coffees and we walked back towards my car and her *dolmuş* (minibus) stop, shook hands and parted. Empty handed.

We had agreed to meet the following Tuesday, so although I was surprised and a bit put out by the lack of lesson payment, I was sure she had simply forgotten and would pay up next lesson. It is strange how one's sense of politeness prevents one from simply asking the student for the money, and it is embarrassing to try to remind them by fidgeting or coughing or general nervous delaying tactics, usually performed at the front door.

Arriving home after the hour long drive I checked my mobile and found a message from Sevil in good English, saying how sorry she was that she had forgotten to pay, and she would give me all the money on the Tuesday. So that was alright then!

Tuesday duly came and I arrived in Gaziemir at the meeting point. This time she was to meet me at Otokent and take me to her house near there. I had understood that she lived in Gaziemir, which is a fairly new town now with nice apartment blocks, not too high, set in lovely rolling landscaped gardens. Some of the old village remains in the central square area, but the village has been developed and developed over the past ten years or so and has ballooned in size, with these modern flats covering the old tobacco fields of the farming community. It's a clean and tidy town. I imagined Sevil living in one of the apartments there.

However, she had told me that really they were nearer to the Karabağlar area.

This immediately changed my mental image of Sevil and her mother's living space. Karabağlar is quite a mixed area, with an industrial estate behind it and the railway line following the main road up towards Izmir city centre. Houses look quite run-down and flats are small and simple, with a rather dirty and almost seedy feel to it. However, this is just the main road side where all the huge and luxurious furniture shops are located, with the smaller carpenters and furniture *ateliers* behind them. One never ceases to be surprised in Turkey by suddenly coming across superb luxury flats tucked away behind a really unsavoury district. So I was prepared for any kind of dwelling really.

Arriving at Otokent, the huge car sales 'city', there were many people waiting for a *dolmuş* or a bus to get home after work. It was 6.30pm and the roads were quite busy and noisy. It was a dry dusty area, with lots of building sites in various stages of development and not many trees for shade, or plants or grassy areas. I picked Sevil up easily at the main gate and she practised her directions in English as we drove "straight on, turned back" (do a U turn) and "turned right", then stopped "here where you see the garden and the black door". I couldn't see any kind of garden, since I am programmed to expect grass and flowers when I hear that word. The Turkish for garden also means school playground, yard and perhaps any earthy area belonging to someone. Anyway, I stopped and pulled onto a piece of waste ground in front of a few bungalow-type shacks with children playing hopscotch barefoot outside in the dust.

"Over there", she said, pointing to the other side of the road where I could now see the black iron gate and a small garden behind it.

We crossed the road and went inside where Sevil's tiny mother was waiting at the bottom of the front steps. Like Sevil, she immediately came to kiss me and welcomed me to her home. She must have just washed the steps as they were spotless and dust free, so I felt embarrassed following Sevil up them in my shoes, seeing the marks from her shoes on the clean steps and wondering what manner of dirt I was leaving behind my feet. We took off our shoes outside the door and I stepped into a cool hallway covered in pieces of carpet and rugs – again, all spotlessly clean. There was hardly any furniture in sight, just the floor carpets as we went along the corridor to the kitchen. This was a huge square room with another surprise: the back door looked out onto another larger garden and across land and 'fields' towards a distant Karabağlar main road area. There were leafy trees and plants in the statutory huge tin oil cans, a light breeze and complete peace and quiet. It was almost like stepping back in time into one of those Anatolian houses in the musical film *Fiddler on the Roof*.

I went to wash my hands and found a simple bathroom with several large plastic storage jars full of water – one with the rim cut off so water could easily be poured out, as I discovered: there was no water in the taps or cistern. This is quite a common experience in Turkey, as the local water board will regularly cut the water off to maintain supplies in long hot dry summers. Or to make repairs on the ageing pipelines, sometimes even renewing them or putting in larger ones to meet the rising needs of expanding villages and towns.

Sitting in the kitchen with a glass of water, Sevil's mother explained they had lived there for 29 years, and another flat was built on top of theirs for her brother who had married, giving the appearance of a two storey house while they lived just on the ground floor. Sevil's father had died six years earlier after a car ran him over and he'd stayed in a coma for a month. I felt sad for them and began to understand that Sevil was perhaps the main bread-winner for her mother now.

They asked if I was hungry and I said "No," but Sevil looked disappointed, so I asked if she was. "Yes," she said, "very hungry!" So I suggested she ate something quickly before the lesson, as I really didn't want to spend longer than the hour there since I was leaving for the UK next day and needed to pack and get ready.

They murmured something about *sarma* and asked if I liked them. "Oh yes!" I replied, "but not with yogurt!" I hastily added.

Expecting Sevil to quickly rustle up a plate of *sarma* (stuffed vine leaves) from the pot on the stove, I followed her into her room, which comprised a table, telephone and very old music set on a shelf, as well as the requisite floor covering of carpet. No bed.

"Where do you sleep?" I asked her.

"Oh," she said, "I just moved in here. This was my brother's room, but now they have a new baby they have moved upstairs."

"I see." But I didn't really – where was the bed? Did she lie on the carpet at night? Or sleep in the single-bed-sofa we had been sitting on in the kitchen? I didn't ask. It was also a tiny room, barely large enough for a single bed even.

The lesson continued more or less according to plan and I realised that food was not going to appear, even for her, until after the session.

This time the holes in her English appeared more often, but I kindly put that down to the heat and her hunger.

As I packed up to leave she asked me where I wanted to have the *sarma* so I gave a polite non-committal reply and she suggested the garden. I headed for the kitchen, thinking we'd sit outside the back door, but she was heading for the front door, with the tray of vine leaves and a couple of drinks. I assumed she was going to sit us under a tree outside in her front garden. Wrong again. We got outside the front door and with her mother nowhere in sight she handed me the tray and began to unfold a thick green carpet on the top step or landing area in front of the door. Outside.

I caught on quickly and sat down cross-legged on the carpet where we ate our *sarma* in the cool evening breeze. It was delicious, and the first time I had ever had such an experience in a student's home. Students will often press food and other refreshments on one, but I had never done a lesson in such a delightful village-style house nor eaten on the floor with students.

Sevil for her part said that she didn't like her home, even though I thought it was really charming. She told me that none of her neighbours' daughters worked or even finished school. She was unusual in that she had been to university and now had a good job with a European company.

"Just luck," she said, smiling. I looked into her beautiful eyes and thought to myself "No, not luck. You are a special girl."

As I left, finally, she pressed some money into my hands saying, "This is for the two. Next time I will do bank transfer."

"Fine," I said, and took the money, checking it briefly and noticing it was rather less than I had expected…

When I got home I checked again, and sure enough she had only given me the rate which I had agreed for her friend, and only for the two lessons, not four in advance. How could I complain though? These misunderstandings are common in Turkey, and one has to weigh up the rewards against the pitfalls.

I made another mental note that we would discuss the price next lesson, and I would only do the cheap rate if it meant no extra travelling for me. At least, that is what I planned to say next time.

Home Visits

Turkey is developing very fast. Great emphasis is placed on formal education. The proliferation of private schools is a symptom of the growth of the new and wealthy middle class. Mastery of English, the world's lingua franca, is seen as a passport to riches and happiness in the form of a university education and a well-paid professional job. So the race is on: people from all sorts of backgrounds want to learn the language or give their children a better chance to learn. Most come with some existing knowledge but are keen to hone their skills.

Giving private lessons has become an industry in itself. Students come in all shapes and sizes, starting with pre-school tots and extending to the adult businessman. You may be expected to perform as a motivator, a translator or an expert in the technical language of law or medicine, not to mention advanced engineering. Above all you will have to do your magic tricks, waving your wand to produce fluency and accuracy at the drop of a hat. This will be especially necessary if the student in question is trying to pass an exam, possibly within a week of you starting your teaching.

If you are already a teacher in an institution of some kind or have good contact with other teachers, you will probably not need to formally advertise your services. The grapevine spreads far and wide. As teachers are not allowed to give extra paid lessons to students from their own school, there is a regular swapshop, with anxious parents asking you to recommend a good teacher.

Once contact has been established, the issues of venue and payment arise. There is much discussion among teachers of who is charging what and the current going rate. English is not the only subject involved. The mathematicians seem to top the fees table, closely followed by the scientists. We are not the only branch to be engaged in this industry.

Do you go to the student's house or do you invite them to your place?

Some teachers do one or the other as a point of principle, where others decide ad hoc. As travelling will involve time and expense a higher fee may be paid in recompense. Agreeing a price can be tricky as the Turks are consummate bargainers and practise their skills with vigour. That is not the end of the story: actually getting your fee in your hand can prove more problematic. Some teachers demand a month's money up front as a way of preventing last minute cancellations. Others ask for cash in hand at the end of each lesson, which means that should the student decide to cancel, sometimes when you are actually on the doorstep, you lose your fee for the day. Either way it is good idea to set the ground rules in order to avoid the prolonged exchange of pleasantries, on the brink of departure, which leave you wondering whether it would be impolite to remind your host that you haven't actually been paid yet!

You will indeed be treated like an honoured guest, however humble the household, which makes you feel that mentioning money is somewhat rude. Most do pay without demur and I have even been offered money for lessons not given.

The family involved was inordinately wealthy. They had arranged a Sunday morning lesson but were not in when I arrived at their palatial house, the only sign of life being the gorgeous Max, their golden retriever. Once they realised their mistake, they apologised profusely, came to pick me up, whisked me off to a smart country club and offered me breakfast while my student finished his game of football. When I politely declined as I could see that I would have to spend the whole day with them, they insisted on paying for a full lesson and driving me more than half way home.

Turkish people are uniformly hospitable and the 'rules' dictate that every visitor must be offered food and drink. On arrival at the student's house, you may be delayed by the consuming of tea and cake, or these 'essentials' may arrive during the lesson. If you have come after a hard day in the classroom, all you want to do is finish and go home. The student may also have similar thoughts, but the niceties have to be observed. It can be a chance to see how the family dynamic works, which in turn can give you a clue as to the reason for a less than sparkling performance in English. If parental ambition is the only driving force, motivation can be lacking.

This I discovered with my 'footballer'. Already bilingual in German and Turkish, his father was pushing him, at the grand old age of ten, to add English to his list. Once they asked me to teach his younger sister as well, every lesson started with a battle as to who should go first.

I had a very different experience with another German-Turkish family who were so interesting and charming that I was the one reluctant to take their son away and get down to some hard work. When it came to bargaining about lesson fees, however, a steely note entered the conversation. Nevertheless, I missed them when they decided to emigrate to Austria.

Sometimes it is obvious that the desire for the beloved child to learn English is not matched by an ability to pay the going rate. This will be more common among families with children at state rather than private schools but not exclusively so. You may wrestle with your conscience or suggest small groups, making it cheaper for individual families.

Neighbours may expect lessons for free or in return for some small service. To my shame I got quite resentful when asked to give up my Sunday afternoon on a regular basis in return for an occasional cake. It is a common misconception that giving lessons requires little or no effort and certainly no planning because you are a native speaker. Worst of all is the neighbour who pleads abject poverty. As you are about to give in, you notice the father driving up in his smart new car and you harden your heart.

There have been times when I wanted very much to help. Very new to Turkey, with little teaching experience behind me and very little language, I was taken aback one day to see a small girl on my doorstep. She had come to ask me to explain all the tenses in English! She had been given this project by her teacher. I did my best but realise now that I should have taken it all much more slowly. Clearly I frightened her off and unfortunately was never able to repair my relationship with her family.

Small groups can be easier to teach. Slightly less intensive for the student, it gives the teacher a chance to do pair and group work and provide more natural practice but there can be tensions among the participants. In one mid-year break I taught four eleven-year-olds from a state school. I was happy to try and help and for a modest fee we had an intensive fortnight of lessons. All seemed pleased with the arrangement but in the summer holiday, I got a call from one of the girls who wanted lessons just for herself and her best friend because she didn't want to be held back by the weaker boys.

Demand for private lessons often peaks in the mid-year break when parents begin to panic because of poor grades in the school report. Then you become a hothouse gardener, forcing the 'plants' into unnatural growth spurts. My faith in miracles is not strong. However hard you and your protégé work, it is sometimes difficult to overcome years of underachievement or bad teaching. Restoring confidence in a few weeks or even months can be an uphill struggle. Happily there are exceptions that prove the rule. Bright children who have perhaps transferred from a state to a private school or who are suddenly fired with a desire to learn or who have just found the right rapport with you as a teacher, can give you real pleasure along with financial reward.

More often than not you have been employed for a very specific purpose – to get the student through the next exam. The fact that he needs two years of remedial work is neither here nor there to the anxious or demanding parent, who only wants a quick fix. Should the beloved offspring continue to fail, you may be ousted without much notice. Conversely the achievement of a single but narrow pass may equally spell the end of your tenure, as that may be enough to secure a sufficient average to pass this year. Next year's problems seem too far away to worry about!

Then there are the parents with no (or a little – even worse!) knowledge of English, who insist on interfering with your lesson plan or strategy.

"Don't worry, I'll make him memorise that," was supposed to be a measure of support for me from the mother of an uninspired fourteen-year-old student. In fact I had just spent an hour telling him not to rely on such techniques.

More miracle work is required for the child aspiring to make the leap from state to private education. Many fee-paying schools take such children after a written or oral test. So you watch as the ten-year-old in question has to do three years of learning in as many months, when they would far rather be playing on the beach with their friends. I have to confess that the teacher's thoughts can also stray in a similar direction. Once again if they fail to make the grade you may expect to be instantly ostracised for your 'failure' to produce the required miracle. Even success does not guarantee gratitude.

Having helped a colleague's son to pass the Cambridge First Certificate, albeit with a C, the lowest passing grade, I was greeted with the response, "Oh, didn't he get a B?" I have to admit that I was hurt. We may do it for the money but we are not totally emotionally detached.

Then there are those rare and perfect beings who have a good grasp of the language and ask intelligent questions. You are spurred to help them linguistically so you can pursue more esoteric subjects in your lessons. Two sets of husband and wife doctors definitely fell into this category and the hour flew past for all concerned. Even these did not go without a hitch as one pair decided they wanted more than I was prepared to offer for the fee agreed. In the second case the husband was noticeably more advanced than his wife but I had to sympathise when she was doing her best with advanced reading after night duty. When such students come through their advanced exams with flying colours, you bask in reflected glory.

That is not to say that only advanced students are rewarding. Seeing any learner make progress is always satisfying but the world of private lessons is uncertain and insecure. If you want to know where next month's rent is coming from, don't give up the day job.

There are, however, advantages! You do not have to write exam questions, mark papers, or attend departmental meetings. No more long hours of sitting over exam papers with a red pen. You can teach what you like, how you like, when you like and as much as you like. You can lose a student, but not your job, and new ones pop up to fill the gaps. You meet a huge variety of characters, from starry-eyed little children to ambitious business people and middle-aged university professors.

I would like to add the following anecdote as a footnote. I had been teaching a sweet but shy twelve-year-old boy, who lived within walking distance. Our allotted slot was Tuesday at five. Once used to my ways, he confessed to enjoying our lessons: definitely not 'cool' for a budding teenager but safe enough to admit within the confines of our 'classroom.'

At the end of one lesson, I told him that I would not be able to come the following Tuesday.

"Why not?" he asked.

"Because I have a meeting," I truthfully replied.

"Where?" was the riposte, accompanied by a distinctly puzzled look.

"At school," was my response.

After a brief pause, during which he seemed to be digesting this information, he ventured,

"Are you a teacher?"

I wondered then if he thought I was just some eccentric foreigner who happened to live down the road.

Students I Have Known

Since 2005 I have been one of those retired teachers who give private lessons. All sorts of people want to learn English, which is my subject. Let me tell you about some of my students.

I'll begin with the oldest, who was also one of the first. Frau Reizend was a Swiss lady in her eighties who came to live with her daughter and family nearby. Her own language was German, but her grandchildren were being educated in English and her Turkish son-in-law knew English, not German. She thought at first that Turkish would be too difficult for her, so she took English lessons.

It was summertime and we sat in my garden, at the marble table, with a thick canopy of green creepers overhead. Now and then a leaf or a spider would drift down onto our papers. She made notes carefully and repeated patiently sentences like *I am a grandmother. Tina is a teacher.* We used colourful little children's books: *This is Jane. Has she got a pink dress? No, she hasn't. It's blue.* Frau Reizend forgot words easily and needed lots of repetition, but never seemed to lose patience and I enjoyed teaching her.

Later her grandchildren took trips to Switzerland and got better at German. Also Frau Reizend, to her own surprise, picked up quite a lot of Turkish. Our lessons came to an end, but our friendship continued. We met often and she would chat about her life in Switzerland in the old days. She lived to the splendid age of 97.

Ayşegül had acquired my phone number from somebody somewhere, and asked me, as I understood it, to go and see her. Her house was a long way from my home, in a district called Villalar in the street behind the big garage. There I discovered a palatial establishment with well-watered lawns, a swimming pool and lots of exotic trees. The front door was suitably huge and imposing. Well, well! What would the lady of the house be like? The woman who answered the door seemed pleasant, but more homely than I expected. She made coffee and we talked, more about my personal history than about learning English, but I didn't mind that, if she was interested. Then she made a phone call. It was a cordless telephone with a loudspeaker that was turned on so that I could hear both sides of the conversation clearly. This revealed that I was being entertained, or rather interviewed, by the househelp. The lady herself was at the other end of the telephone, asking questions. "What's the teacher like? Is she moderately acceptable?" At this point the woman with the phone had the grace to move out of earshot into another room, but the loudspeaker continued: "OK then. I'll talk to her." We talked, and arranged a time for an English lesson, so evidently I was acceptable.

A week later I was back at the huge front door, armed with my best smile and plenty of colourful English material. Ayşegül proved to be as glamorous as her surroundings, with expensive clothes and perfect hair. It transpired that she owned a beauty salon. Her somewhat older husband seemed an ordinary business type; he was polite and friendly. The couple did their lesson together, the househelp served coffee and pastry, and everything went really well. They wanted to learn English, they said, in order to travel. Already they had a textbook, a good one, and they asked what other materials would be useful. I recommended the CD for listening practice, and suggested they try to study on their own each week between lessons. Their enthusiasm was delightful. After we had finished the hour, Ayşegül drove me home in her car and we had some English conversation practice on the way. *Do you have children? Yes, I have a daughter.* That kind of thing. We parted most amicably.

Happily I prepared the second lesson. Two days before it was to take place, I got a phone call saying Ayşegül's husband was on a business trip for a few days, and could we postpone the lesson till he got back? She would phone again. No problem. Except that she never did phone again. The file entitled Ayşegül and Mehmet gathered dust on my shelf for three months, after which I put away the materials and erased the name.

I have often wondered what happened. A quarrel? Financial crisis? Accident, illness, fire or murder? Or did they suddenly decide to learn French instead? The mystery remains.

Next I will tell the story of Nurcan, pronounced Noorjan, which means Light-life. She studied first with my son, and when he went off to Britain she became my student. Since we lived far away from each other we did the lessons at a place in between, which was my mother-in-law's house. That dear lady liked having people around and was always happy to brew up a pot of tea and supply biscuits. Nurcan's English was advanced so we had wonderful conversations. I made notes as we went along, and each week we revised the vocabulary from the week before; she seldom forgot a new word. When we covered grammar topics, she was the fastest learner I ever met. At her request we also did literature, in short extracts because she had little time for reading. We dipped into *Alice in Wonderland* and the limericks of Edward Lear, we read Shelley's sonnet *Ozymandias* and a bit of the novel *Frankenstein*. When this last proved too difficult, we relaxed with a session on Beatrix Potter and *Peter Rabbit.*

Much of the time we just talked. Nurcan was warm, kind, knowledgeable, and interested in many things. We talked about travel and holidays; she had been to Iran with her tour guide husband, and later visited him in Spain when he went there to learn Spanish. We discussed the health-care system in Turkey, education, social conditions, politics and environmental problems. Also we discussed the conflicts women have between careers and children. Nurcan wanted children – "I should like to have a son like yours, he's perfect," – but she also wanted to do medical research in Public Health. Doctors who wanted research positions competed for places by taking a special exam that took place every autumn.

Nurcan took this exam but her marks were not high enough to get into public health. She was offered a place in Embryology, which she took, but she became very unhappy because of unfair behaviour by fellow students. This posed a further dilemma. Should she drop out or keep going? Return to general practice? Or take the exam again the following year? Meanwhile her husband, she told me, really wanted them to have a baby. "The years are passing! If I wait too long, it may be too late." Then she looked at me thoughtfully and said, "What would you advise me to do?"

I was touched that she should ask me. I said cautiously, "You should decide what is most important in your life, and go for that. Very few people can have everything they want." Later she said that she really wanted, more than anything, to do research. She would take the exam again and try to get better marks, so as to pursue the subject that interested her most. Of course, this would require a great deal of study, and so, reluctantly, she would have to give up English. I was sorry, but I had every confidence that our friendship would continue. We had long planned to visit one another at home. The only problem was that her husband was so often away with tours on the weekends. But it was only a matter of time and organization. After her exam, if not before, we would certainly meet up again; they would come to dinner.

It was April then. There was much excitement in my family because our son was getting married. Since his return I had asked him to come to a lesson one day and see Nurcan, but he never found the time. I could only pass on his greetings, and hers in the other direction. The wedding was in May, and we had visitors from Britain. Our happy couple departed on their way, the visitors left, and then we went away on holiday. After that the hot weather settled in with a vengeance, bringing a state of dreamlike inactivity. When it cooled off in September I e-mailed Nurcan, but got no answer. After three tries, I phoned her house, but the phone was either out of order, or the number had changed. Her mobile number didn't work either.

Thoroughly puzzled, I e-mailed the only friend of hers I knew, another doctor called Müzeyen who had also taken some English lessons. The answer came next day. "Nurcan committed suicide in May. That's why you couldn't contact her." As I read the message, an enormous stone seemed to grow in my stomach. I read it again. Then the letters went all blurry and I could no longer read, because I was crying.

There is one more student that I'm going to write about, and that's a young woman called Makbule. She was visiting my neighbour regularly to study the doctrine of the Jehovah's Witnesses, and I met her by accident over there. My hospitable neighbour insisted I should have a coffee with them, and then Makbule said that she would like to take English lessons.

She drove a 4x4 and owned a restaurant, but worked as an artist. I saw only a few photographs of her work; I thought it skilful and chaotically decorative. Mostly, she told me, she sold small pictures to Belgian tourists.

Makbule was a beginner at English, but a good student. When well supplied with cups of strong black coffee, she concentrated well and learned steadily. In between, of course, we chatted a bit in Turkish. I learned that she was divorced, and had a teenage son with problems at school. About her future as a Jehovah's Witness she remained non-committal.

For a few months we got on really well. Her payments were always late, but she did bring some money so I didn't worry much. Then, one day, she appeared really distracted. "Oh, I'm in such trouble! I don't know what to do!" (All this in Turkish, naturally.) When I invited her to explain, she said, "I shot a cow! It died, and the owner is furious. He is taking me to court."

I enquired why she had shot the cow, and she explained. "It was around midnight, very dark, and I heard this noise in the garden. I thought it was my ex-husband coming after me and I was terrified. So I took the shotgun and fired. It turned out to be a cow, and the owner is really angry."

Interestingly, my husband read the story in a local newspaper. According to that version, the unlucky cow was not in her garden at all, but simply straying along the public road. No wonder the owner was furious! However, I had no chance to ask Makbule any more questions, because she disappeared. She sent no word, and for two successive weeks I waited at home for her, with the sitting room tidy and the lesson prepared. Then I asked my neighbour, who said the religious instruction was now finished, and she thought Makbule had financial problems. So that was that; I did not expect to see her again.

There are so many interesting students. I haven't told you about the capricious teenage boy who taught me a lot about cars and shared his chocolate. Nor have I mentioned the sparkly-eyed seven-year-old who can do a perfect

English accent. Then there were the amateur artists who wanted to read English newspapers because they didn't trust the Turkish ones, and the neighbour from the farm who brought milk or yogurt as payment. But this is all I'm going to write about now.

Stepping Out In Ankara

Another salary supplement came about when Christine asked me to start an evening class in tap dance for herself and a few friends from the BWGA (British Women's Group in Ankara). They were looking for an enjoyable activity that might also help to keep them fit. I agreed to ask my boss if this might be acceptable under State Conservatoire rules and regulations. I emphasised that it was a small group, six or seven ladies whose husbands held posts in the British Embassy in Ankara, and that they would be paying me privately so the Conservatoire Directory need not concern themselves with any special arrangements at all. We just needed the studio, on Monday nights, from around 7pm to 8pm please.

Amazingly my boss agreed! In retrospect I am doubly amazed, as the formalities involved in organising any event at a Government institution are a minefield of red tape and delaying tactics.

My group of ladies duly arrived the following Monday in tracksuits and outdoor shoes to try out the tap first. We would sort out the tap shoes if they decided to continue after that night.

Well, Christine herself is a lively lady full of fun, so she made sure that they all enjoyed it. She was larking about and making jokes all through the session, so they really had a ball and yes, they all wanted tap shoes; how could they get some please?

Here I must digress to explain about the shoemakers' room in the basement of the ballet department. I had not realised this tiny room existed under the studios until my ex-ballerina boss had asked me to start teaching tap to the younger students, aged eleven to fifteen. She thought it was a good opportunity while I was there and I needed a new project to get involved in (suffering from broken heart syndrome at the time).

We had investigated the possibility of finding tap shoes and 'taps' (the special metal pieces attached to soles and heels) in Ankara. Turkey is the country of 'genuine fakes', so you can buy copies of fashion designer accessories everywhere. Copying a pair of UK tap shoes did not seem to pose a problem. My trusty assistant and I trailed around the Ankara industrial estate to find the right kind of metal to copy my 'taps' and make the right sound on the floors – and at the right price for mass production.

The shoes themselves were similar to 'character shoes' which the students already used for character dance classes – the kind of stylised national dances found in full length classical ballets such as Swan Lake and The Nutcracker. The shoes were a plain black court shoe, with a small heel and one strap across the arch fastened with a button. It was now that I found out that these shoes were made right there in the ballet department in the basement. We needed about 120 pairs for our young students.

With hindsight I now understand why the two shoemakers were always so pleased to see me. Of course they were earning extra tax-free money from making all these extra shoes which the students' parents had to pay for. I was naïve in thinking they were only charging cost price since they worked for the Conservatoire on a salary basis anyway – though it was probably a pittance they earned.

So, to get back to the BWGA ladies' shoes, they all drew around their left and right feet on a piece of blank paper, labelled them with their names and handed them to me. I took the drawings to the cobblers and they duly produced the goods, new leather tap shoes, within the week. All at a fraction of the price they would have been if bought in the UK or Europe. Everyone was happy.

That class survived two terms of a Turkish academic year, and two of the group even agreed to perform a short tap number for a fund raiser – a Victorian Music Hall night the BWGA was producing downtown. It was so much fun to teach these 'mature students' who were more interested in enjoying themselves while keeping fit than staying on the beat and getting the technique right! My younger students were in serious training for the stage, so although they enjoyed the classes they were a bit too straight-laced for real musical theatre tap dance.

After a few weeks, a couple of young Turkish students from another university got to hear about that class and came along to join it. They wanted to add a routine to their evening cabaret act in a bar somewhere downtown in Ankara. Through this couple I was then asked to start another group for students from the big new university just outside Ankara. These students were looking for evening activities too, as they were far out of town and had very little to do on campus at night since their university had only recently opened.

I checked with my boss again, and she agreed. On the night of Group 2's first class I waited in the dark and silent department, wondering if anyone would turn up. Imagine my surprise when about 25 young men of assorted shapes and sizes arrived for their first tap class. I had expected girls, but there were only two or three of them in this group of young men.

Again, the first class was hugely enjoyable as they learnt how to do straight taps, and 'flaps,' and 'tap springs,' and 'toe beats,' with turning steps from the corner, stop time and double time sequences. What a racket we made! Everyone drew around their feet after class and agreed to pay the 30TL (about £12) for their shoes the following week.

Once again the shoemakers were delighted, but this time it took them about three weeks to fill their order.

Sadly these classes were terminated a couple of months later, all good things coming to an end. The 'directory' had apparently got wind of the influx of outsiders and decided to clamp down. Extra-curricular tap was now forbidden and my boss sadly informed me that I would have to cancel all further classes.

This was perhaps the first warning of the dire changes which were to affect my life within the following year.

Supplementary Benefits

Clarinet and Dance Classes in Ankara

"Hello, my name's Julie!" a fresh-faced young woman bounced up to me at the Hilton Hotel's coffee morning for the British Women's Group in Ankara (BWGA). "I saw your notice on the board about clarinet lessons and I've always wanted to learn! Somebody pointed you out to me. I've got a clarinet," she added, brightly.

So began my eighteen-year friendship with Julie and her husband, and eventually their growing family.

We started with clarinet lessons and I was soon roped in to babysit William when he appeared a year later.

By this time the clarinet lessons had been abandoned and we were good friends sharing experiences of good and bad times in Turkey and swapping advice on where to find good hairdressers, supermarkets and other issues of daily life.

In fact most of my private music and dance lessons came about through the BWGA. I had met Christine, a well-connected English lady at the Turkish language classes, who had invited me to come to a coffee morning at the Hilton Hotel as her guest. I have to say I was rather wary of being thrown into a huge group of ex-pats, since my work and life style had immersed me in a sea of Turkish colleagues and a totally different way of thinking and being. The last thing I wanted was to meet a group of bored housewives whose husbands, I imagined, had good jobs through embassies or NATO and suchlike, and who would complain about the numerous difficulties of life in Turkey as they saw it.

I couldn't have been more wrong. The women were nothing like that.

I entered the suite reserved for the coffee morning and found about 100 ladies busily setting up book-swap stalls, notice boards, a raffle (of course), and the table arrangements for that day's speaker. The notice board was a resource for everyone – buying and selling furniture and baby goods, advertising lessons and services, recommending plumbers who spoke English, hairdressers, sports salons, bridge club, painting classes, and so on. It was a hive of activity, and I quickly signed up and added my own list of the services I was able to offer.

I was soon propositioned by another young woman, Tina, who had two lovely daughters. She wanted me to teach them piano. I was very unsure about this as I hadn't taught piano before, and my teaching qualification was in clarinet. However, Tina reassured me that as my Final Grade piano exam was higher than her grade 6, I would be better than she was. She herself could not teach them any more. 'Why?' I asked in surprise.

'Because they are mine', she replied. 'They can't handle the teacher-pupil relationship along with the mummy-child one'.

Tina was a professional double bass player with a teaching qualification in that instrument and piano as her second subject. The daughters were only six and three years old, so I was worried about how much they could actually manage. Again, Tina had it all worked out and showed me the book they'd been using and set me up for lesson one.

Little Anna, the three-year-old, was first. An absolute poppet, she sat alert and bright eyed on the piano stool and answered all my exploratory questions:

R: 'What note is that?'

A: 'C'

R: 'Which hand is to play?'

A: 'This one'

R: 'Which finger starts?'

A: 'This one'

R: 'How many counts in a bar?'

A: 'Four'

I couldn't believe her maturity, and was to see more of this elsewhere when they persuaded me to start the dance classes....

Anna's big sister Jasmine was no less well-trained, politely answering my questions and asking intelligent ones about various markings on the music; and playing with care.

That is not to say we didn't have fun in the lessons! Lesson one is usually the most serious, as both sides are weighing each other up and deciding where the lines are drawn – lines which may not be crossed. Anna and Jasmine were to become lively and impish little piano students, then imaginative and creative young dancers later.

Dancing class was already run by another BWGA wife at the British Embassy School. Rae had started it as a hobby for herself and an outside school hours activity for the children. She was leaving Turkey as her husband's job was locating them elsewhere, so she wanted me to take it over and suggested I come and watch a session. I was again rather wary of teaching a mixed group of boys and girls; after school; doing both ballet and tap dance. I had painful memories of my first dance classes teaching four-year-olds when I was training, and didn't feel I was the right person for such little ones!

Rae was a radiologist by profession but had trained in dance and also ran a keep fit class in her front room for the BWGA ladies.

She persuaded me to give it a go, and I decided to try out a session, rather with the attitude that 'if she can do it, so can I', I must confess.

However, Rae had also shown me how to split the session into three parts and do tap, ballet and improvisation/creative dance. This way the 45 minutes would fly by.

Despite the sinking feeling in my stomach, and the gradual arrival of a motley class of children aged three to ten, the session went well! I had a ten-year-old boy, two American girls, a young German girl who had done a lot of ballet, a small and restless boy, an English girl, and a

Japanese/American girl. The two American sisters were totally different, one being blonde and fair skinned while the other was of Afro-Caribbean origin; I was to learn that the latter had been adopted and was much more mischievous than her more rational sister. A week later the children were already standing in a circle when Anna and Jasmine arrived late for their first class. I have already stated that Anna was a poppet, but the whole class went 'Oooh!' in wonder, as these two elegant children (immaculately turned out in pink ballet tights, pink ballet shoes and leotards, hair neatly tied back and held in place with pink hairbands) trotted gracefully to join the circle and stand in perfect 'first positions' with the feet pointing outwards and heels together. They just had 'it'! I speculated that the combination of tall-elegant-blue-eyed-musical-blonde mother and tall-handsome-Pakistani father had produced the perfect physique for ballet.

The school asked us to do a 'morning assembly' as part of their open day policy for parents to see what their offspring got up to in the after school activities. The class really did a good job and were so professional that I only had to cue them with the music. One of them even asked to be the MC and introduce each of their pieces herself.

That class was such a success it was a joy to teach them, if I can even call it teaching, as I was more like a guide than an instructor. The three sections meant they had little time to get out of hand and there was something for everyone to enjoy. Their creativity and ideas were inspiring, and I usually left at the end of the session feeling that *they* had actually taught *me*, rather than the other way round.

The improvisation section seemed the most popular, and they loved doing mimes and getting the group to guess their occupation or their story. I clearly remember the ten-year-old boy, Adam, using amazing footwork to express his 'bird' dance, rather than the expected flapping of wings/arms that most children would tend to demonstrate.

They also loved making up their own dances to classical music. One time I put on a tape of Saint Saëns 'The Carnival of the Animals' and a small boy remarked "Ah! Proper music!" They appreciated 'the real thing' as opposed to the tinny sound of the classroom piano music tapes I used for the ballet and tap exercises.

Anna and Jasmine wanted to do more ballet at home so we added that to the repertoire of private lessons. They were planning to leave Turkey at the end of that year and wanted to resume their classes in the UK at the appropriate level. It was my task to teach them the syllabus for their grade exam so that they would be ready. These two were always self-disciplined, yet imaginative and lively, so we had a lot of fun in their attic playroom which was big enough for the dancing lessons. I can recall in particular one 'lesson' which had continued into the evening's babysitting. They had been trying to make letters of the alphabet with their bodies, separately and together, so they decided to test their skills by spelling 'words' letter by letter for me to guess – a kind of 'dance charades'.

One might assume I was making an absolute fortune in private lessons by now, but this was never the case! By the time I started the BWGA classes I had left my prestigious job at the Conservatoire and was roughing it as an English Language teacher paid poorly by the hour at a busy language school. The more hours I could take on, the more I earned, but it was really only enough to cover my rent and utility bills; I still needed money for food, clothing, fares, and getting to the UK once a year; as well as all the other joys of life.

My last little batch of music lessons in Ankara were all boys, and not the easiest to teach, nor especially motivated. Yet another BWGA member asked me to take on her two lively Dutch boys for piano, as their last teacher had left or given up on them. She wanted them to reach a certain level of proficiency and discipline although she suspected they would probably give up when allowed to do so, as they were not particularly interested. Their father loved the piano and played well himself, and they wanted to pass this love of music on to their children. These lessons were challenging as the boys were mischievously intelligent and knew all the tricks in the book to wind me up and get them out of playing. Their kind and patient mother had to put in the odd sharp word from the kitchen to keep the sessions on track. However, I learned a lot from them and am eternally grateful to this amazing mum for helping me learn how to handle them.

Being from Holland they celebrated St. Nicholas' Day on 6th December every year, and therefore I was invited to help them with the musical part of the ceremony. "Purely informal fun," their father hastened to assure me. Their mother made us each a special seventeenth century noblemen's stylish cap to wear, which she rustled up the night before from some scraps of material. Their father wrote the musical parts for us all, conducting a motley band of trumpet, recorder, saxophone, clarinet, violin and keyboards as we waded through the appropriate Dutch carols and traditional songs, including Santa Klaus is coming. Santa Claus did indeed arrive and distributed gifts to all the children from the Netherlanders' community in Ankara. It was all performed impromptu without any rehearsal – a nerve-wracking nightmare for me, the outsider.

My last music pupil from those Ankara years was a young Dutch saxophonist, and was the least successful from my point of view as he was unwilling to put in any minutes, let alone hours, of practice – even though he really wanted to play the instrument. A product of the 'get-famous-and-musical-quick' brigade of children, he failed to understand that a certain amount of effort and consistency on his part was required.

Nevertheless I have to remember that these children taught me more about 'enabling them to learn' than all my years of teacher-training courses – especially those for teaching young children. The old adage 'an ounce of experience is worth a pound of theory' could not have been more true.

Fair Exchange in an Unfair World

Barter, they say, is the oldest form of trade, and it is still alive and well in Turkey today. The particular commodity I have to sell is English language lessons, and while most of my students do come up with cash, there are those who, for various reasons, do not.

The first one I encountered was the daughter of a neighbour. Her father was a fisherman, her uncle kept a few cows, and her mother was an illiterate housewife. Hatice was eager to get a secondary school diploma, but she could not manage the required level of English. Accordingly, her father asked my husband if I would be willing to help her. My husband decided that I would, and told me about it. He also warned me not to ask for money, as the family were poor. Just say *komşuluk*, he told me, neighbourliness. But Hatice, or her family, had their own ideas on the subject. For the first lesson she arrived with a great pot of yogurt. They had made it themselves, and it was delicious. The following week there was a pat of butter, and after that a can of milk. So it continued. We enjoyed their produce, and Hatice's English improved steadily. In the end she passed her exams and duly got her diploma.

My next experience of this type was with family. My husband had about twenty aunts and uncles in the good days when they were all still alive, and they had numerous children between them. One of the children had been ill and missed a lot of school, would I help her with English? As before, it was my husband who received the request, and immediately agreed to my services being provided. "You mustn't accept any money, though," he said. "They're relatives."

The girl was extremely bright. She is now an administrator in the Fine Arts Faculty of a local university. Anyway, she caught up with her lost English lessons quickly. I rather regretted turning down their offer of payment, as her dad was a successful psychiatrist, but I did what I was told. My husband is the supreme authority on family duties and cultural affairs. (Not on other things, though.) Well, we did perhaps half a dozen lessons together, and then she had had enough, so that was fine. I had enjoyed teaching her but the hour-long bus journey each way was a bore, so I was glad it was over. I didn't think much more about it, until about a month later when I was visiting my mother-in-law one day. She presented me with a large parcel. It's from *Yenge,* she said. *Yenge* means Aunt. After further enquiries I was able to work out which aunt. It turned out to be the sister of the mother of my recent English language student. She had knitted me a beautiful woolly jacket as a reward for my efforts.

More recently I met an ambitious young girl called Meryem who worked as a cleaner in a local nursery school. Her hope was to get a job in a good hotel, and to do that she had to learn some English. She had already acquired quite a lot of words from here and there, but hadn't much idea how to put them together into sentences. Well, I had joined a yoga group who met in the nursery school one evening a week, and it was the yoga teacher's bright idea that I should barter English lessons for domestic assistance. She knew my house, and how untidy it usually was, but it was her wish to help Meryem that really prompted the suggestion.

My family were initially sceptical, but agreed to a trial. As I write this, more than a month has passed and our partnership seems well established. Our kitchen tiles shine, the shelves of books have all been dusted, and her strong hands chopped up a whole basket of hard quinces which are now nicely processed inside a row of jam pots. Meanwhile Meryem has learned the difference between have and has, and knows when to use please and thank you. Her English is progressing in fair exchange.

A Glimpse of Government Education

I have brought up two children in Izmir, but it is now more than ten years since they left the state education system. In that time, there has been much talk of reform and improvement, and probably good things are happening in many places. However, there are still problems. Here are some stories of recent encounters I've had with people in the system, all of them from the first decade of this century.

The bell at the gate rings softly, modestly, and I see a little figure in pink standing there. It is Selin, daughter of the woman across the road who sometimes cleans for us.

Selin is nine, and attends the local school. In her pink tracksuit, with a pink bow in her hair, she looks pretty enough to advertise chocolates, but her big brown eyes are worried. She carries a large book.

The problem, it turns out, is maths homework. My daughter, bilingual in Turkish and English, turns her attention to the subject. She is thirty years old, a qualified and experienced English teacher, but maths is not her strong point. After a few minutes I hear her call, "Mum? Can you help?"

Slowly I translate the problem. (Turkish is not my strong point.) The sum of the ages of Defne and her parents is 87. Her mother is 25 years older than Defne and her father is 4 years older than her mother. How old is Defne?

OK, I say, easy enough. You just write an equation. Defne's age is X. Then the mother's is X+25 and the father's must be X+25+4. Add them all up and solve it. I am on the last line before I realise that this is not, in fact, at all useful. Selin had not learned algebra and she has no idea how to manipulate symbols.

We will have to find another method. Pure reasoning is possible, of course, but would challenge many adults. Imagine trying to explain in Turkish. Definitely not a good idea.

Then I think of drawing. I draw a tower and write Defne beside it. Then, next to it, I repeat the tower, draw a box on top, and label the box 25. Beside it I write *annesi,* the word for her mother. A third tower alongside has two boxes on it, one above the other, labelled 25 and 4. That one is *babası,* her father. Finally I drew all the towers and boxes again, straight up and one on top of the other. The height of this giant tower is 87. Now Selin can see what to do. First subtract 25 from 87, and cross out the 25 box. Then take away another 25, and then the 4. Cross them out. Selin does all this quickly and efficiently. Now what's left of our giant tower is three lots of Defne's age, and that equals 33. She divides by 3, and, bingo, we have the answer. Defne is 11.

Next problem. A gardener grows tomatoes, peppers and cucumbers. The number of pepper plants is three quarters of the number of tomato plants and one and a half times the number of cucumber plants. If 42 of these plants are cucumbers, how many plants are there altogether?

Again we draw towers, but this time they must be subdivided. There must be three boxes in the tower for peppers, four in the tomatoes and two in the cucumbers. One box represents half the cucumbers, and that's 21. Then we can count up all the boxes for all the plants and multiply by 21 to get the total.

Then this one. A wholesale baker sells to a big shop and a small shop in the same village. The big shop orders six more than three times the number of loaves the small shop orders. If the small shop orders 15 loaves, how many are ordered altogether? Again we draw, and find the answer. (66, if readers are interested.)

By this time, we are all feeling quite cheerful and confident. There is a small snag, though: the space in the book where Selin is supposed to show her calculation is too small to draw towers of any kind. She has to make sticks instead, lying sideways, and so tiny that even with my reading glasses I can't see them. Fortunately, Selin's eyesight is good. Then there is a worse snag; we discover that she has 40 of these problems to do. Of course she has tried by herself, before coming to us, but most of her attempts are wrong. We redo about five of them, and then stop for biscuits and juice. My daughter and I have a cup of tea. A couple more problems, and then that must do. Perhaps she can also manage some by herself, later on?

As I start cooking our evening meal, I ponder this experience. Forty maths problems in one homework. Certainly she has also got Turkish to do (who knows how much?) and probably Social Studies as well. There is a deeper question that bothers me, too. Why are these children learning stuff which has no conceivable relation to practical life? Surely there is enough useful mathematics to keep nine-year-olds busy at school? Wouldn't these fantasy questions be more suitable for, say, a maths club, where those who wished could do them for fun?

We used to have a neighbour called Hatice. In the days when I had a baby who cried endlessly, Hatice was a dreamy-eyed teenager with immense patience. She loved to carry my daughter around and play with her, and in this way she gave me some extremely valuable free time. Thirty years later, her son Selçuk is a lanky lad of 14 who is in danger of failing English at school. For this family, paying for private lessons is out of the question. Because Hatice and I are old friends, I agree to help, and I assure them that no money is expected.

Selçuk presents his homework: three pages to study, no writing required. It is all about a listening passage. I ask if they did the listening in class. Apparently not. Didn't the teacher read the passage? No, he just gave them the answers to the true/false questions. Does the teacher ever use a cassette recorder or a CD player? The answer is no, he doesn't. I sigh inwardly. Is there a script for the listening, so we can read it? No. Oh, well. We look at the introduction. It begins: Do you have difficulties learning a second language? Which of these areas do you have difficulty with? Tick the appropriate boxes. There follows a list: vocabulary, reading, writing, listening, grammar.

I ask Selçuk to read this. He does. Then I ask if he understands it, which he does not. His first problem is the first word, *do.* He does not recognise the auxiliary verb, but thinks it means some kind of action, as in do homework, or do the dishes. I write the sentence Do you play basketball? on a piece of paper, emphasising the question mark. He manages to recognise that, so after a few more examples we return to the text in the book. He knows the word language, but does not know what difficult or second means, let alone area or appropriate. Word by word, we plod through this. When we get to actually making ticks, he agrees vocabulary is difficult, but he says writing is easy.

Some weeks earlier I had helped him with his Term Homework, an essay entitled "How the environment can be protected?" (Readers may note the error in the word order.) Selçuk did not know the meaning of either environment or protect. After I explained in his own language, though, he had lots of ideas. He wanted to write about global warming, recycling rubbish, solar and wind energy, hydropower, public transport, and low-energy light bulbs. I was really impressed. However, he had no idea how to make a plan or organise paragraphs, and he needed a lot of help with every English sentence. So I was surprised when he said writing was easy, but I didn't argue.

Selçuk has had English at school for four years. In that time his brain has collected some vocabulary, but it is like wire netting, full of holes. He knows mountain, but not sea, table but not sofa. He is not sure how to write a sentence; he thinks there is usually a *the* and an *is* and an *ing*, but their arrangements are still mysterious. Readers may feel this is a hopeless case, as I did, when we started. With just one hour of private tuition each week, how would this student ever pass a test? But one day Hatice came by with hugs and kisses; Selçuk had got 60 percent in his exam! Sometime after that she produced an exquisite hand-crocheted curtain as a present. Its creation must have taken many more hours than I had spent with her son.

Meryem is a neighbour's daughter who attends the *Yüksek Spor Okulu,* the university department for Sports Studies. Unfortunately, like other university students, she also has to learn English. The English teacher has given her a project: the translation from English into Turkish of six pages of text on basketball strategies. There is no way she can understand the English; it is completely beyond her. Protest, she says, is useless. The teacher just says she has to do it and that's that. Well, I do not do translations, because my Turkish isn't good enough. Besides, I know nothing about basketball. But Meryem has no one else to ask, and she cannot possibly pay a professional. Her Turkish is perfect, and she knows a lot about basketball. Somehow we have to work together. So I make some strong coffee and we sit down. Phrase by phrase, I try and put the English into Turkish. We use a dictionary frequently. Meryem listens, and reprocesses what I say into some acceptable form of written language.

In two afternoons, we manage to get a version of the text written down. My husband, when I tell him about it, says that the English teacher probably does not understand the text either, and won't think of checking its accuracy. She is simply using the students for a free translation service. Somehow they will produce something, if they are ordered to. The teacher can then use the texts in her lessons, or even publish the translation as her own work. He may be right.

We have many friends in Britain. One of them, eighteen-year-old Judy, decides on a gap year between school and university, and asks if she can spend a few months with us in Turkey. She will volunteer to help with English teaching somewhere.

It sounds like a good idea. First of all, my daughter and I take Judy to several of our private lessons. She provides the students with excellent conversation practice and charms them as well; she is a great success. Next I take her to an English teachers' meeting organised by the British Council. There are about twenty teachers present, all from different institutions in the city. I present Judy, and explain that she will be pleased to visit schools and meet students, anywhere and anytime. A real live native-speaker: young, attractive, well-spoken and for free! But not one single teacher gets in touch. What a wasted opportunity! We think of two possible reasons. First of all, teachers might be afraid of a native-speaker noticing their mistakes. Second, there could be problems getting permission to bring an outsider into a school.

After that, I take Judy to our local primary school. First we talk to the headmaster, who is friendly and says he will ask the English teacher. To her great credit, she greets us warmly and agrees to have Judy come to some lessons. I am surprised that our conversation is all in Turkish. However, I translate for Judy. A time is arranged and she goes along.

She reports later. The children went wild with enthusiasm and all wanted to hug her. The teacher taught what was in the book: *This is a ruler. That is a pencil.* That kind of thing. Judy read sentences to the class. She found her experience a bit daunting because the English teacher couldn't actually speak English. They had a lot of trouble understanding each other.

That's the last of my anecdotes about state education in Izmir. Of course it is a vast and complex world; these stories are only a glimpse through a crack in the door. But still, I think they say something interesting.